DATE DUE FOR RETURN

27

EARLY TUDOR ENGLAND
PROCEEDINGS OF THE 1987 HARLAXTON SYMPOSIUM

EARLY TUDOR ENGLAND

PROCEEDINGS OF THE 1987 HARLAXTON SYMPOSIUM

Edited by
Daniel Williams

THE BOYDELL PRESS

© Harlaxton College and individual authors 1989

First published 1989 by The Boydell Press, Woodbridge

The Boydell Press is an imprint of Boydell & Brewer Ltd
PO Box 9, Woodbridge, Suffolk IP12 3DF
and of Boydell & Brewer Inc.
Wolfeboro, New Hampshire 03894–2069, USA

ISBN 0 85115 511 1

British Library Cataloguing in Publication Data available
Early Tudor England: proceedings of the 1987 Harlaxton symposium.
  I. Williams, D. T. (Daniel Thomas), *1937–*
  942-05
  ISBN 0–85115–511–1

Library of Congress Cataloging-in-Publication Data
Early Tudor England : proceedings of the 1987 Harlaxton symposium /
  edited by Daniel Williams.
      p.   cm.
    Proceedings of the Symposium upon Early Tudor England, held at
  Harlaxton College, Lincolnshire, July 1987.
    ISBN 0–85115–511–1 (alk. paper)
    1. Great Britain – History – Tudors, 1485–1603 – Congresses.
  2. England – Civilization – 16th century – Congresses. I. Williams,
  Daniel, 1939– . II. Symposium upon Early Tudor England (1987 :
  Harlaxton College)
  DA325.E2   1989
  942.05 – dc19   88–7934
                                                                  CIP

∞ The paper used in this publication meets the minimum
requirements of American National Standard for Information
Sciences – Permanence of Paper for Printed Library Materials,
ANSI Z39.48–1984.

Printed in Great Britain by
St Edmundsbury Press, Bury St Edmunds, Suffolk

Contents

Contributors

Janet Backhouse	The British Library
Peter Fleming	Bristol Polytechnic
J. M. Fletcher & C. A. Upton	University of Aston
John Glenn	Harlaxton College
Christa Grossinger	Manchester University
S. J. Gunn	Merton College, Oxford
Andrew Martindale	University of East Anglia
Richard Morris	Warwick University
Elizabeth Porges Watson	Nottingham University
John Scattergood	Trinity College, Dublin
Pamela Sheingorn	Baruch College, City University of New York
Pamela Tudor-Craig	Harlaxton College
Daniel Williams	Leicester University
Janet Wilson	Trinity College, Dublin

Illustrations

All plates appear in the plate section at the back of the book; figures appear in the text and their page numbers are given below

ILLUSTRATIONS

Andrew Martindale: The Ashwellthorpe Triptych

Acknowledgements. Plates 1–5 are reproduced by courtesy of the Norfolk
Museums Service (Norwich Castle Museum). Plates 6–9, 11 and 12 are
from negatives in possession of the University of East Anglia, Norwich.

ILLUSTRATIONS

Richard Morris: Windows in early Tudor Courtier Houses

All plates copyright of the author.

E. A. F. Porges Watson: The Denzill Holles Commonplace Book

Pamela Sheingorn: The Te Deum Altarpiece and the Iconography of Praise

ILLUSTRATIONS

Preface

The papers published in this volume represent the lectures delivered at the Symposium upon Early Tudor England held at Harlaxton Manor, Lincolnshire in July 1987. The fourth of its kind organised by a steering committee of scholars under the patronage of Harlaxton College, the British Campus of the University of Evansville, Indiana, USA, it followed the now well established pattern of interdisciplinary research papers covering the fields of the history, art, architecture and intellectual ideas of the period under focus.

The early Tudor period was something of a departure from the more usual 'century' format. This was because the early Tudor context followed spontaneously from the discussions and ideas formulated in the previous 1986 Symposium upon the Fifteenth Century. The subjects of these papers also reflect the sense of continuity between the first half of the sixteenth century and the preceding hundred years. There are hints, even indications, of change but these are evolutionary perhaps culminating in the radical breaks with the past brought about by the events of the period 1530 to 1558.

The artistic and intellectual dominance of continental influences and fashions, discernible in the previous century, is still there. In a criticism of his fellow countrymen written as late as 1531, Sir James Elyot commented 'if we wyll have any thinge well paynted, kerved or embrawdred... (we) abandone our own countraymen and resort unto straugners'.

This essential truth is supported by the contents of this volume. The portrait miniature is a continental off-shoot of manuscript illumination introduced into England by Lucas Horenbout and developed under the patronage of Henry VIII. The more sophisticated carved Misericords are copies from German and Dutch prints. The Ashwellthorpe Triptych 'fits into the pattern of the Netherlandish domination of English patronage'. Even the windows of early Tudor courtier houses get their Renaissance influence second-hand from French sources.

Even so, the pattern of artistic patronage was changing as a consequence of changing patterns within the social and political structure of the period. The crown dominates more than ever under the grand and awesome power of the not larger than life Henry VIII. We also get glimpses of his allies, the 'new' Tudor gentry. Their importance as patrons and as key figures in royal government pervades. Men like Sir Richard Weston, Sir William Sharington and to a lesser extent Christopher Knyvett were the 'in set', the favoured gentlemen of the court of Henry VIII who were to benefit from the 1515 Act of Resumption. The consequences of being outside this favoured circle are illustrated by the predicament of the Catesby family. The medieval knight has become a courtier requiring culture and education, though, as the case of Denzill Holles shows, sometimes with bizarre results.

A common theme in these papers is of course the influence of that most radical king, in effect rather than by design, Henry VIII, the English King David priest and king. Yet behind him and within these papers is the moderating influence in both church and state of Cardinal Wolsey.

Change is in the air nevertheless, the winds of religious change that confuse poets, conservative churchmen, even would-be King Davids. Some bend with the wind, some snap, those powerful enough even change its direction. It is all here.

This volume like the three others stands as a permanent record to the success of the Harlaxton venture and to the enthusiasm and hard work of those who have brought it about.

Daniel Williams

Illuminated Manuscripts and the
Early Development of the Portrait Miniature

JANET BACKHOUSE

The art of portrait painting in miniature reached a pinnacle of achievement in the work of Nicholas Hilliard, a goldsmith by profession, who rose to prominence during the second and third decades of the reign of Elizabeth I. To him we are also indebted for one of the first written records of the trade secrets of the miniature painter's art.[1] This distinctive art form, as a type of portrait painting in its own individual right, was a speciality of the sixteenth century and was particularly favoured in England though it was of course practised elsewhere, notably in France. In the summer of 1983 Hilliard's work provided the nucleus of a dazzling exhibition at the Victoria and Albert Museum, which also focussed on the work of his chief forerunners, Horenbout and Holbein, and attempted a demonstration of the roots from which the English portrait miniature had developed.[2] The role of the illuminated manuscript was very properly stressed, as it had been by Torben Colding some thirty years earlier.[3] However, examples were selected from the point of view of the historian of portrait miniatures looking backwards rather than from that of the historian of illuminated manuscripts looking forwards, and they were restricted to Flemish and Flemish-related material. The circumstances under which members of the Horenbout family settled in England in the 1520s were somewhat fancifully interpreted in the light of recent misguided attempts to credit Henry VII with a large and flourishing Flemish-orientated manuscript workshop at Richmond in the years around 1500.[4] This paper therefore seeks to re-examine the background

1 R. K. R. Thornton and T. G. S. Cain (ed.), Nicholas Hilliard, *A Treatise Concerning the Arte of Limning*, (1981).
2 *Artists of the Tudor Court: the Portrait Miniature Rediscovered, 1520–1620*. Exhibition catalogue by R. Strong, with contributions by V. J. Murrell. Victoria and Albert Museum, (1983).
3 T. H. Colding, *Aspects of Miniature Painting*, (1953).
4 See G. Kipling, *The Triumph of Honour: Burgundian Origins of the Elizabethan Renaissance*, (1977), esp. ch. 2, and *idem*, 'Henry VII and the Origins of Tudor Patronage', *Patronage in the Renaissance*, ed. G. F. Lytle and S. Orgel, (1981). For a re-examination of Henry's claims as a patron of illuminators see my own article, 'Founders of the Royal Library: Edward IV and Henry VII as

1

against which the first individual portrait miniatures appeared in England, apparently about the middle of the 1520s, and to re-assess some of the documentary evidence relating to them.

The small and usually circular portrait miniatures of early Tudor England are painted on vellum laid down on card, and the techniques employed are in all basic respects those developed over the centuries by the painters of illuminated manuscripts, though special methods for representation of such details as lace or gold jewellery were refined by the new practitioners. The development of these little circular portraits on vellum should occasion no surprise in anyone familiar with the illuminated books of the fifteenth century. In the first place, circular picture spaces on a scale comparable to that of the first individual portrait miniatures are a commonplace of manuscript decoration throughout Europe. They are particularly associated with calendar miniatures but are also frequently to be found as a feature of the marginal decoration of text pages in such lavishly ornamented books as the Bedford Hours, produced about 1423.[5] Then too realistic portraits from the life were increasingly favoured in manuscript contexts from the late fourteenth century onwards, in parallel with the development of the true portrait on a larger scale.[6] Illuminators in England at the beginning of the fifteenth century seem to have been very much attracted by the challenge of representing the human features, and lifelike but anonymous faces appear in the initials and margins of several of the finest manuscripts of the period, including the Bedford Psalter and Hours,[7] the Hours of Elizabeth the Queen,[8] and the Sherborne Missal.[9]

Increased demand for *de luxe* illuminated books during the fifteenth century, and increasing specialisation among those who produced them, probably encouraged the employment of specialists in portrait

---

Collectors of Illuminated Manuscripts', *England in the Fifteenth Century*, ed. D. Williams, Proceedings of the Harlaxton Symposium for 1986, (1987), pp. 23–41.

5 Some typical examples of the use of circular picture spaces in manuscripts are available in J. Backhouse, *Books of Hours*, (1985), pls. 6, 18, 23 (Italian), 10, 30, 43 (French) and 27, 28 (Flemish).

6 For one specific early group see C. R. Sherman, *The Portraits of Charles V of France (1338–1380)*, (1969).

7 D. H. Turner, 'The Bedford Hours and Psalter', *Apollo*, lxxvi (June, 1962), pp. 265–70, esp. figs. 2–9.

8 *Ibid.*, fig. 12; R. Marks and N. Morgan, *The Golden Age of English Manuscript Painting, 1200–1500*, (1981), pl. 36.

9 *Ibid.*, pls. 29–30.

painting to add the often very fine likenesses found on the owner/ donor pages of some of the most expensive examples. The portrait of John, Duke of Bedford in the Bedford Hours is a fine example from the leading Parisian workshop of his day.[10] The head of the Duke, complete with 'five o'clock shadow', double chin and prominent nose, is no idealisation but surely reflects the accurately-observed living man. Similarly the head of Pierre Louis de Valtan, presenting his poem on the Apostles' Creed to Charles VIII of France shortly before 1498, bears every sign of reality, though the surrounding courtiers and even the king himself are vague and ill-defined of feature.[11] It is seldom possible to demonstrate beyond doubt that a portrait face has been added by a separate hand. There is however one excellent example in another French manuscript of about 1500, the so-called *Emblesmes et Devises d'Amour* which royal servant Pierre Sala offered to his lady love, Marguerite Bullioud.[12] The little volume contains the lovely and often-reproduced portrait of Pierre attributed to his friend, the painter Jean Perréal (pl. 1). It also contains a miniature of the author symbolically placing his heart in the care of a marguerite.[13] This miniature is the work of the lesser talent responsible for the general illustration of the book. The face is however left unpainted and we can reasonably assume that Perréal should have provided there a tiny version of the larger portrait. Also worthy of mention in this connection is the allegorical frontispiece to *Le Fort Chandio* by François du Moulin, the Franciscan mentor of Louise of Savoy, which was probably painted about 1522 (pl. 2).[14] The head of the figure of Louis de Chandio can reasonably be attributed to Jean Clouet, though it has escaped discussion in recent published literature. Of great interest is the inscription below the figure, written in the hand of du Moulin himself, who excuses the shortcomings of the 'effigie' because the artist had not the leisure to do it better and was obliged to work on paper 'which good painting cannot tolerate'.[15]

10 Backhouse, *op cit.*, pl. 1.
11 Reproduced in A. Blum and P. Lauer, *La Miniature française aux xve et xvie Siècles*, (1930), pl. 83.
12 J. Backhouse, 'Pierre Sala, *Emblesmes et devises d'amour*', *Renaissance Painting in Manuscripts: Treasures from the British Library*, ed. T. Kren, (1983), pp. 169–74. A small reproduction of the miniature of Pierre Louis de Valtan is given as fig. 22g.
13 *Ibid.*, fig. 22b. The larger portrait is given in colour in this publication as pl. xxvii.
14 C. Couderc, *Album de Portraits*, [1909], no. clv.
15 I am very grateful to Myra Orth for her views on this miniature and for providing me with a copy of the relevant extracts from her unpublished thesis, *Progressive Tendencies in French Manuscript Illumination 1515–1530: Godefroy le Batave and the 1520s Hours Workshop* (Institute of Fine Arts, New York, 1976), pp. 117–19, 222–3. The dating given here is hers. A preference for the

By the late fifteenth century the circular picture space and the true-to-life portrait had already come together in the manuscripts of northern Italy.[16] Of particular interest are such examples as the roundels of Ludovico 'Il Moro' Sforza and his wife, Beatrice d'Este on the Sforza marriage deed of 1494, the decoration of which is attributable to Giovan Pietro Birago and his assistants. Mark Evans has recently shown that this type of portrait of the Duke is dependent upon a medal cast for him sometime between 1488 and 1494 to commemorate his acquisition of Genoa.[17] It is by no means a unique instance of such copying[18] and introduces a timely reminder of that other flourishing form of portable portrait, the renaissance medal, which developed so swiftly south of the Alps during the fifteenth century and was to become increasingly fashionable in northern Europe during the early years of the sixteenth century.[19] Classical coins and medals quite frequently appear in their own right in the marginal decoration of Italian renaissance manuscripts,[20] but in the Sforza image modern metal is translated into naturally coloured portraiture.

Italian manuscripts were widely admired and it was not uncommon

---

period 1512–15 is shown in another unpublished thesis, that of B. Walbe, *Studien zür Entwicklung des allegorischen Porträts in Frankreich*, Frankfurt, (1974). For this reference too I am indebted to Mrs Orth.

16 Although it is not strictly a miniature, as it is carried out in enamels, mention should perhaps also be made of Fouquet's self-portrait now in the Louvre (see *Jean Fouquet*. Exhibition catalogue by N. Reynaud, 1981, no. 6). It does exemplify a French illuminator producing a circular (self)-portrait with identifying inscription and was apparently intended as part of the decoration of a picture frame (= border).

17 M. Evans, 'Giovanni Simonetta, *Sforziada*', *Renaissance Painting in Manuscripts: Treasures from the British Library*, ed. T. Kren, (1983), pp. 107–112, with relevant reproductions.

18 For example, see O. Pächt and J. J. G. Alexander, *Illuminated Manuscripts in the Bodleian Library, Oxford: 2 Italian Schools*, (1970), no. 418.

19 For an outline of the development of the portrait medal in Italy and its spread north of the Alps, which has much in common with the history of the portrait miniature, see the opening chapters of M. Jones, *The Art of the Medal*, (1979). See also H. Maué, 'The development of Renaissance Portrait Medals in Germany', *Gothic and Renaissance Art in Nuremberg 1300–1550*, the catalogue of an exhibition in New York and Nuremberg, (1986).

20 Fine examples are reproduced in J. J. G. Alexander, *Italian Renaissance Illuminations*, (1977), pl. 14 (from Paris, Bibliothèque nationale, MS lat. 5814) in M. Salmi, *Italian Miniatures*, (1957), fig. 86 (from Rome, Biblioteca nazionale, MS Vittorio Emanuele 1004), and in I. Berkovits, *Illuminated Manuscripts from the Library of Matthias Corvinus*, (1964), pl. xxiv (from Budapest, National Széchényi Library, clmae. 413).

for their characteristics to be imitated elsewhere in Europe. Their elegant and spacious appearance was to a greater or lesser degree recreated in a group of attractive little books associated with François du Moulin, author of *Le Fort Chandio*, and produced for Louise of Savoy and her two children, King Francis I of France and Marguerite, Duchess of Alençon. Du Moulin worked in conjunction with a Flemish illuminator named Godefroy le Batave, whose drawing style suggests an Antwerp Mannerist background and who was very fond of producing circular illustrations.[21] Godefroy's finest work is contained in a three-volume sequence of manuscripts made at Louise's request in 1519 and 1520, intended originally to flatter her son's imperial ambitions by equating him with Julius Caesar.[22] The text makes very amusing reading as the two rulers encounter each other in parks and shrubberies and chat away about their respective military triumphs! At the beginning of the first volume Francis and Caesar are both depicted, the latter by means of a stylised profile resembling a coin or medal and the French King by a three-quarter face bust painted in grey and gold, each set against a solid circular bright blue ground (pl. 3). This colour scheme is dictated by the overall scheme of the manuscript, which is carried out almost entirely in greys, blues, browns and golds, with occasional touches of other colours. The image of Francis is somewhere between a medal and a naturally coloured portrait. It was probably painted, like the other miniatures in the book, by Godefroy himself, following the image of the French king current at the time.

The second of the three volumes, dated 1520, includes seven circular miniatures of Francis's military leaders which have inspired vigorous and often bitter controversy since they were first noticed in the mid-nineteenth century.[23] The identity of the painter has been hotly disputed and the significance of the images within the overall framework of the development of the individual portrait miniature has

21 For an outline of Godefroy's work see M.D. Orth, 'Godefroy le Batave, illuminator to the French Royal Family, 1516–1526', *Manuscripts in the Fifty Years after the Invention of Printing*, ed. J.B. Trapp, (1983), pp. 50–61.

22 The three volumes are now in three different collections, viz: vol. I = British Library, Harley MS 6205, vol. II = Bibliothèque nationale, MS fr. 13429, vol. III = Chantilly, Musée Condé, MS 764. See M. D. Orth, 'François du Moulin and Albert Pigghe, *Les Commentaires de la guerre gallique*', *Renaissance Painting in Manuscripts: Treasures from the British Library*, ed. T. Kren, (1983), pp. 181–6.

23 All seven miniatures are reproduced in P. Mellen, *Jean Clouet*, (1971), pls. 3, 5, 7, 9, 11, 16 and 56, together with the related drawings. One example, that of Guillaume Gouffier, is additionally included among the colour plates, no. IV. In each case the entire manuscript page is seen. Earlier opinions are discussed by Mellen *passim*. See also J. Adhémar, *De François I à Henri IV: Les Clouets et la Cour des Rois de France*, (1970), pp. 14–15.

been variously interpreted. Rational assessment has not been assisted by the tendency to reproduce these roundels in isolation, ignoring the manuscript pages of which they are an integral part.[24] The relationship of these seven portraits to the Clouet drawings at Chantilly is beyond dispute and attribution of the miniatures themselves to Clouet, called in to make a specialist contribution to the project, seems entirely reasonable. The use of naturalistic colouring for flesh tones and for such details as hair and eyes sets them somewhat apart from the other illustrations in the volume. The bright blue backgrounds, already noted in the portraits of Francis I and Caesar in volume I of the work, underline the resemblance to the slightly later independent portrait miniatures with which our eyes are familiar. However, as we have seen, this blue is also consistent with the general range of colours used in the manuscript as a whole and it should not go unnoticed that the tones chosen for the garments of the seven subjects, although they are painted very positively, are confined to the blacks, browns, whites and golds of the underlying colour scheme.

The placing of these miniatures on their respective manuscript pages is perfectly consistent with a studied attempt to emulate Italian work. Each one occurs between passages of simply-written text, set against plain vellum and supplied with spacious margins. A very similar effect is achieved on the dedication page of the treatise which Antonio Cornazzano presented to Eleanor of Aragon at the time of her marriage to Ercole I d'Este in 1473, now in the Pierpont Morgan Library.[25] There too the portrait and the dedicatory text – in this case a small rectangular picture and five lines of calligraphic capitals – are placed against plain vellum amid spacious margins. It is interesting to note that the bust of Eleanor is also set off by a bright blue ground and that she is shown attired in white and tones of golden brown. This is not to deny that Clouet could have painted independent circular portrait miniatures in or before 1520, the year to which the Godefroy manuscript is dated. It merely indicates that the manuscript cannot be seen as evidence that he did so. The miniatures of the French military leaders would be equally at home in their host manuscript had they been conceived as picture spaces within elaborate marginal decoration, like

---

24 See for example, Couderc, *op cit.*, pl. cxxxvii and Blum and Lauer, *op cit.*, pl. 89.

25 Pierpont Morgan Library, M. 731. The miniature is reproduced in colour, but isolated from the text, in M. Harrsen and G. K. Boyce, *Italian Manuscripts in the Pierpont Morgan Library*, (1953), pl. 2 and on the cover of the Morgan Library exhibition catalogue *Italian Manuscript Painting 1300–1550*, (1984). The entire page may be seen in *The First Quarter Century*, Pierpont Morgan Library, (1949), pl. 29.

the portrait miniatures in the various copies of the *Sforziada*.[26]

Some five or six years after Godefroy and his colleagues produced their miniature masterpiece, the first of the sequence of independent portrait miniatures connected with the court of Henry VIII made its appearance. It is generally accepted that the three-quarter face image of the king in the Fitzwilliam Museum in Cambridge (pl. 5) is the earliest of several closely related examples.[27] Inscriptions flanking the image identify the sitter and record his age, and the whole is enclosed in a square border in Flemish style in which angels support tasselled cords entwined with the initials of Henry and his first wife, Katharine of Aragon. The age is ambiguous. It can be read either as 'in his 35th year' (28 June 1525–28 June 1526) or as 'aged 35' (28 June 1526–28 June 1527). Three other versions of the same image are known, two of them inscribed with the same age.[28] One of the three shows the king wearing a well-grown beard, but this does not apparently offer any certain dating evidence.[29]

In 1953 the Fitzwilliam image was attributed to the immigrant Flemish painter, Lucas Horenbout.[30] Lucas was the son of Gerard Horenbout, one of the leading Flemish book painters of the period. He came to England, in circumstances unrecorded, about the middle of the 1520s

26 See above, n. 17. Many examples of the use of portraits in Italian books may be seen among the coloured illustrations in the books cited in n. 20 and in C. Csapodi and K. Csapodi-Gárdonyi, *Bibliotheca Corviniana*, (1969). The choice of blue as a background colour is very common.

27 R. Bayne-Powell, *Catalogue of Portrait Miniatures in the Fitzwilliam Museum, Cambridge*, (1985), pp. 129–30, reproduced in colour, pl. 1. Also reproduced in colour, greatly enlarged, in R. Strong, *The English Renaissance Miniature*, (1983), pl. I. No. 5 in *Artists of the Tudor Court*.

28 One, showing the king cleanshaven, is in the collection of the Duke of Buccleuch and Queensberry and was no. 7 in *Artists of the Tudor Court*. The other two are in the Royal collection, see the exhibition catalogue *Holbein and the Court of Henry VIII*, (Queen's Gallery, 1978–9), nos. 89 and 90. The second of these portrays Henry with a beard.

29 An accurate history of Henry's beard would be of interest. Both he and Francis I swore in 1519 not to shave before their meeting at the Field of the Cloth of Gold in 1520 though in the event Henry did not keep his promise, see J. G. Russell, *The Field of the Cloth of Gold*, (1969), p. 16. Depictions of the king on legal documents show him variously bearded and unbearded during the 1520s, see pls. 10–13 in E. Auerbach, *Tudor Artists*, (1954). As certain images are clearly repeated somewhat uncritically, no reliance can be placed on these as a whole. However, the unique bearded image on the Plea roll for 1527–8 (Auerbach, pl. 11) and the figure in the superb drawing on the patent for Cardinal College, Oxford, dated 5 May 1526 (Auerbach, pl. 12a) may reflect reality. This would support the earlier date for the Horenbout image. The Oxford drawing has been associated with Gerard Horenbout; Auerbach, p. 42 ff.

30 Colding, *op cit.*, pp. 63–5.

and the first known reference to him occurs in Henry VIII's Chamber Accounts for September 1525.[31] The series of Chamber Account Books is however far from complete and so this entry does not necessarily reflect the true time of his arrival in England. It is reasonable to assume that he had been trained up in the workshop of his father, who was employed by Margaret of Austria, Regent of the Netherlands and who had been commissioned to supply to her (among other things) a series of miniatures to complete one of her most important manuscripts, the Hours of Bona Sforza.[32] This she had inherited through her husband, Philibert of Savoy, who was Bona's nephew, and she brought it with her when she took up residence in the Low Countries. The Hours of Bona Sforza was produced in Milan about 1490 by Giovan Pietro Birago, also responsible for the decoration of the Sforza marriage deed of 1494 and the frontispiece illuminations to the *Sforziada*.[33] Its extremely rich decoration thus offered Margaret's Flemish book painters direct experience of a luxury Milanese manuscript of the last decade of the fifteenth century, with its repertoire of portrait roundels, jewels, medallions and all the ingredients potentially influential in the development of a painter of portrait miniatures (pls. 7 and 8). To this manuscript Gerard Horenbout was required to add substitutes for sixteen missing miniatures and several elements of decoration.[34] Documentary evidence dates his work to 1519–20.[35] Subjects include a very beautiful rendering of the Visitation[36] in which the face of Margaret herself is recognisable, representing the virgin's cousin, St Elizabeth (pl. 6). This image strongly resembles the Fitzwilliam image of King Henry. There is also a small marginal portrait of Margaret's nephew, Charles V, elected Emperor in 1519, in the form of a medal dated 1520 (pl. 4). A real medal close in type to the painted one does actually exist, cast by Hans Schwarz of Augsburg in 1519,[37] so it seems

31 The known documents relating to the Horenbout family have been brought together in L. Campbell and S. Foister, 'Gerard, Lucas and Susanna Horenbout', *Burlington Magazine*, (1986), pp. 719–27. The Chamber Accounts for 1525 are now British Library, Egerton MS 2604 and the reference to Horenbout appears on fol. 1b.

32 M. Evans and T. Kren, 'Hours of Bona Sforza', *Renaissance Painting in Manuscripts: Treasures from the British Library*, ed. T. Kren, (1983), pp. 113–22.

33 See above, n. 17.

34 Listed by G. F. Warner, *Miniatures and Borders from the Book of Hours of Bona Sforza*, (1894), pp. xi–xii.

35 R. Flower, 'Margaret of Austria and the Sforza Book', *British Museum Quarterly*, x (1935–6), pp. 100–2.

36 Evans and Kren, *op cit.*, fig. 15g.

37 Reproduced in the catalogue of *Early German Art*, (Burlington Fine Arts Club, 1906), pl. liii, no. 11.

possible that the Horenbout workshop was following the practice already noted above in the case of the Sforza marriage deed. It is probable that more than one hand contributed to these additions. It is also quite obvious that the Flemish artist (or artists) studied the Hours of Bona Sforza with close attention in order to ensure that their additions were stylistically as compatible as possible with the earlier north Italian work.

Lucas Horenbout thus most probably arrived in England with direct experience of providing the types of portraiture currently fashionable within the context of a top-class illuminated book and having almost certainly studied in detail one of the finest of the many magnificent manuscripts commissioned at the ducal court of the Sforzas in the previous generation. The coincidence in date between the first recorded mention of his presence in England and the earlier of the possible dates for the miniature portrait of Henry VIII encourages the assumption that he was responsible for the introduction into his adopted country of the new, not to say revolutionary, concept of the independent portrait miniature, in or about 1525. The lack of any earlier surviving dated examples elsewhere in Europe implies that his self-sufficient miniatures were in fact the first anywhere. A number of other subjects can be grouped around the images of the king, forming a corpus which prefigures the work of Holbein and of Hilliard.[38]

The situation cannot however be defined solely in terms of surviving examples of Horenbout's work. In the first place it is necessary to consider the implications of an exchange of gifts between Henry VIII and Francis I during the preliminaries to the Treaty of Amiens in 1526–27. According to the correspondence of Gasparo Spinelli, a Venetian diplomat in London, in the late autumn of 1526 Henry received at the hands of the secretary of the French king's sister, the Duchess of Alençon, portraits of Francis and his two sons.[39] Early in the year the two little princes had been exchanged as hostages for their father, who had been the Emperor's prisoner in Spain after his defeat at the Battle of Pavia. The gift was a first move in the chain of events leading to an alliance with England which it was hoped might help to free the children. Spinelli's description of the gift, although somewhat ambiguous in detail, leaves little doubt that it took the form of portrait miniatures enclosed in lockets which were embellished in colour with heavy emblematic symbols.[40] The miniature of the young Dauphin now

38 Listed by R. Strong, *The English Renaissance Miniature*, (1983), pp. 34–8.
39 *Calendar of State Papers, Venetian*, iii (1869), no. 1451. The letter is dated 2 December 1526.
40 G. Lebel, 'British-French Artistic Relations', *Gazette des Beaux-Arts*, i (1948), pp. 272–3.

in the Royal collection at Windsor may be a version of one of the portraits.[41] Henry was very much pleased with his present and duly reciprocated with similar portraits of himself and his daughter Mary, whose possible marriage either to the widowed French king himself or to the younger prince was an integral part of the treaty negotiations. Princess Mary was, of course, not merely the only legitimate child of the king of England but also, through her mother, Katharine of Aragon, first cousin to Francis's adversary, the Emperor Charles V. It is possible that Horenbout's miniature of her, in which she is shown wearing a large onament inscribed 'EmPour', reflects the one provided for the occasion.[42] The English miniatures were delivered to Francis by Henry's envoys at the beginning of the following June, his emissary 'declaring and unciphering to [Francis] the devices of your Highness on both sides thereof'.[43]

Negotiations ended in the Treaty of Amiens, concluded in August 1527, which was given concrete form in a sequence of illuminated documents, those received by the English ambassadors still preserved in the Public Record Office.[44] Most of their decoration, though itself heavily symbolic, is the pedestrian work of not very inspired professional book painters. However, the ratification of the main treaty destined for Henry VIII himself, written in book form, sealed with a golden bull and delivered to him in October 1527 by an embassy also charged to present him with the insignia of the Order of St Michael, is adorned with a rectangular portrait miniature of Francis I enclosed within a decorative border in the style of the leading French manuscript workshop of the day.[45] It is entirely different from the other treaty documents and must have been dictated by Francis's own personal taste. The image, although not painted by the best of hands, follows the standard Clouet pattern of the period.[46] The whole sequence of events suggests that portrait miniatures were very much in the minds of both kings as novel diplomatic offerings. If the later of the two possible dates is assigned to Horenbout's image of Henry, it is feasible to view the whole early development

---

41 *Artists of the Tudor Court*, no. 4, reproduced in Mellen, *op cit.*, pl. 34 and in R. Strong, *The English Renaissance Miniature*, (1983), pl. 11.
42 *Artists of the Tudor Court*, no. 9.
43 *Letters and Papers Foreign and Domestic of the Reign of Henry VIII*, hereafter L and P, iv, pt. ii (1872), no. 3169, dated 10 June 1527. It is transcribed from the badly damaged and partially incomplete original in British Library, Cotton MS Caligula D. x, fol. 121.
44 Listed *ibid.*, no. 3356.
45 Reproduced in colour in N. Williams, *Henry VIII and his Court*, (1971), p. 73. See M. D. Orth, 'A French Illuminated Treaty of 1527', *Burlington Magazine*, cxxii (1980), pp. 125–6.
46 Mellen, *op cit.*, p. 237.

of the portrait miniature in England as a consequence of the French gift of 1526, to which Henry found himself obliged to respond in kind. However, both Spinelli and the author of the English envoy's report from Paris lay most stress on the symbolic content of the settings in which the miniatures were presented. It may be that it was not the portrait itself but rather its container that provided the novelty. In similar vein is a reference in one of Henry's love letters to Anne Boleyn, apparently also dating from 1527, in which he mentions his gift to her of 'my picture set in a bracelet, with the whole device which you already know'.[47]

A further complication has been added by a discovery made in 1983. In July, during the run of the exhibition at the Victoria and Albert Museum, Messrs Sotheby's offered for sale an illuminated charter, previously completely unknown, dated 28 April 1524 and including within a decorated initial a small circular portrait of Henry VIII (pl. 9).[48] This image, although badly rubbed, is in all essential details identical to the bearded version of the Horenbout image now in the Royal collection at Windsor.[49] The charter records a grant of property in the city of London to Thomas Foster, who can be identified as Comptroller of the King's Works and who, as a royal servant, would certainly have been in a position to commission Horenbout to decorate his letters patent for him. At first sight the date of the charter suggests that the date of Horenbout's arrival in England and the date of his first image of the king should both be advanced by something like eighteen months. However, April 1524 does seem extraordinarily early for the first appearance of the image used on the charter. The miniature at Windsor is one of those inscribed 'anno etatis xxxv°', which indicates a period not earlier than June 1525, the bearded version of the portrait has generally been regarded as later than the clean-shaven one, and the example on the charter is not likely to be an original *ad vivum* but rather a copy of an existing type. It is not in fact necessary to assume that the date of the charter and the date of its decoration are coincidental. According to standard practice the text of a document is supposed to be complete at the time of the application to it of the seal, but finer detail may be added at any time thereafter. The only firm terminal date is therefore that provided by Foster's death at the beginning of February 1528.[50]

None of the miniatures ascribed to Horenbout retains any trace of its original setting. All have been mounted and framed in accordance with the taste of much later periods. Discussions of sixteenth century

---

47 L and P, iv, pt. ii (1872), no. 3321. See also E. W. Ives, *Anne Boleyn*, (1986), p. 107.
48 Sotheby's sale-cat., (11 July 1983), lot 25, reproduced in colour.
49 Above, n. 28.
50 Discussed by Campbell and Foister, *op cit.*, n. 41.

presentation rely on later examples and records.[51] The earliest known concrete example is the turned ivory box of Holbein's Anne of Cleves, which Colding has quite rightly compared with the containers provided for small scale German portraiture and, more universally, for the protection of seals.[52] It is interesting to note that the miniature, which presumably dates from the time of the marriage negotiations in 1539, lacks the gold edge which is a standard feature of the majority of early miniatures and seems to have been cut down to fit the container.[53] The use of a circular likeness as an embellishment for a charter, where it is set (albeit not very happily) within a larger area of decoration, serves as a reminder of the original function of the portrait roundel as an element of manuscript illumination and prompts further consideration of the possible uses of the Fitzwilliam miniature, with its squared-off border of red and gold (pl. 5). It is in effect a small rectangular decorated page, with a circular image surrounded by a fairly standard form of book decoration, and this arrangement bears comparison with the miniature of a deathbed scene in the Grimani Breviary, where a circular picture space is superimposed upon a landscape with the Three Living and the Three Dead.[54] The Grimani miniature is one of those attributed to Lucas Horenbout's father, Gerard, whose connection with the manuscript is long-established. The Fitzwilliam miniature, although only a fraction of the size of the Breviary, could readily take its place in a tiny book, and there is indeed a special class of manuscript within which such a page could belong, though this has not previously been discussed in the context of the development of the portrait miniature.

Mention has already been made in this paper of the manuscript *Emblesmes et Devises d'Amour* which Pierre Sala presented to his lady love in France at the beginning of the sixteenth century.[55] It was a very personal

---

51 See R. Strong in *Artists of the Tudor Court*, p. 9.

52 Colding, *op cit.*, pp. 70–2.

53 *Artists of the Tudor Court*, no. 30. Reproduced in colour in R. Strong, *The English Miniature*, (1981), pl. 2. There are a number of other examples of miniatures which have apparently been cut down after completion. R. Strong, *Gloriana: the Portraits of Queen Elizabeth I*, (1987), fig. 105, notes a 1580s Hilliard of the queen herself, once rectangular and now oval. We do not know what form the miniatures took while they were being painted. It would certainly be extremely hard to handle an independent circle only about 1½ inches in diameter which had to be painted right up to the edge. It should also be noted that small circular miniatures can very readily be divorced from a larger area; for example see J. J. G. Alexander, *The Wallace Collection: Catalogue of Illuminated Cuttings*, (1980), no. 19, which certainly originated in an Italian humanist manuscript.

54 G. E. Ferrari, M. Salmi and G. L. Mellini, *The Grimani Breviary*, (1972), pl. 57.

55 See n. 12 above.

offering and the little velvet-covered book was accompanied by a gilded leather carrying case, adorned with the initials of the lovers and provided with rings by which it could be suspended at Marguerite's girdle.[56] The Perréal portrait of Sala which it contains (pl. 1) is thus not a formal depiction of owner or donor, or of someone to be commemorated, but a realistic portrait of a living person, presented in such a form that the recipient could carry it about with her as a permanent remembrance of his appearance. The mirror writing on the opposite leaf reads, in effect: 'Remember me when this you see'.[57] The whole concept reflects the humanism of the age. Because the Sala manuscript is not bound in precious metals, it has survived intact. A more extravagant adornment, like any other piece of personal jewellery, would have been very vulnerable once its original owner died or fashion changed. It is not however unique of its kind and a number of other 'girdle books' which are bound in gold and gems have come down to us. They must once have been far more common than now appears and there is reason to suppose that they were particularly fashionable in England. Several examples can be seen in portraits of the 1550s and 1560s.[58] Designs for girdle book covers in black enamel on gold are among the Holbein sketches in the British Musem[59] and two pairs of real covers, decorated with Old Testament scenes and coloured with enamels, may be seen in the Museum's department of Medieval and Later Antiquities.[60] One is dated to the 1520s, the other to the 1540s.

The English girdle books display a fair consistency of dimension, being generally slightly over two inches high and slightly under two inches wide.[61]

---

56 *Ibid.*, fig. 22a.

57 The inscription actually reads: 'Reguardez en pyte/ votre loyal amy/ qui na Jour ne demy/ Bien pour votre amytye'.

58 R. Strong, *The English Icon: Elizabethan and Jacobean Portraiture*, (1969), nos. 46 (Anne, Lady Penruddocke, 1551); 51 (called Mary I, *circa* 1550–5); 79 (Anne Browne, Lady Petre, 1567).

59 Inventory numbers 5308–8 and 5308–10.

60 See H. Tait, 'Historiated Tudor Jewellery', *The Antiquaries Journal*, xlii (1962), pp. 232–7, idem., *7000 Years of Jewellery*, (1986), pp. 151–4. The Holbein designs are reproduced as pl. 347, the enamelled covers as pls. 348 and 349. Pl. 352 shows Lady Philippa Speke wearing an old-fashioned girdle-book, possibly no. 349, in 1592.

61 The complete enamelled girdle book (inventory no. 94, 7–29, 1) measures 2½ x 1¹⁵⁄₁₆ in. (65 x 47 mm) externally. The book which it now contains is 2⅜ x 1¾ in. (61 x 44 mm). The separate covers are much the same size, as are the Holbein drawings. Queen Elizabeth's prayerbook (below n. 64) is 2⅝ x 1¹⁵⁄₁₆ in. (68 x 47 mm). The Fitzwilliam image of Henry VIII is 2⅛ x 1⅞ in. (54 x 48 mm); Katharine of Aragon (below, n. 62) 2⅛ x 1⅞ in. (54 x 48 mm); the Hilliard diptych (below, n. 63) 2⅜ x 1⅞ in. (56 x 48 mm) and 2⅛ x 1¹³⁄₁₆ in. (54 x 47 mm) respectively.

Of exactly similar size is the Fitzwilliam miniature of Henry VIII (pl. 1) and the unusual rectangular image of Katharine of Aragon with her pet marmoset, now in the Buccleuch collection (pl. 11).[62] So too are Hilliard's rectangular portraits of an unnamed man (pl. 10) and woman dated 1572 (of which the Victoria and Albert Museum exhibition catalogue remarked 'the format must have been dictated by the client, presumably to create some form of diptych').[63] I strongly suspect that all these were originally intended to be set inside the covers of girdle books. The probable arrangement may be seen in the facsimile of the lost prayerbook of Elizabeth I (pl. 13), where miniatures by Hilliard of Elizabeth herself and her suitor the Duke of Anjou, squared up with suitable marginal decoration, are set inside the back and front covers respectively.[64]

Confirmatory evidence of the use of portraits in portable books comes from continental sources. Probably (like the Sala) by Perréal are the portraits of a man and woman secreted within the inner faces of the covers to a small selection of prayers and gospel extracts in the Bibliothèthque nationale.[65] The subjects are popularly but not entirely convincingly identified as Charles VIII and his queen, Anne of Brittany. The most ambitious example is also French, put together in the 1570s for Catherine de' Medici, widow of Henry II of France. It occurs in a small Book of Hours, also in the Bibliothèque nationale, to which have been added twenty-two miniature portraits of thirty-seven members of the French royal family.[66] The scope of this collection would not disgrace a Victorian family album. Most of the miniatures painted for Catherine are rectangular and are derived from earlier drawings and portraits. Later owners of the manuscript made their own additions to it. The manuscript is very small and was clearly intended to be portable.

A Flemish example has also come to light in the collection of the

---

62 *Artists of the Tudor Court*, no. 6, with colour reproduction.

63 *Ibid.*, nos. 58 and 59. The male sitter reproduced in colour in R. Strong, *The English Miniature*, (1981), pl. 3.

64 A facsimile of this manuscript is in the British Library, Facs. 218. Another version of the image of Anjou, to whose household Hilliard was attached during his sojourn in France between 1576 and 1579, is in the Kunsthistoriches Museum in Vienna, see *Artists of the Tudor Court*, no. 72. This second miniature is today attached to a small square leaf measuring approximately $2\frac{1}{4} \times 2$ in.

65 See V. Leroquais, *Les Livres d'Heures manuscrits de la Bibliothèque nationale*, (1927), i, pp. 137–9, pls. xcix, xcx. The female portrait is reproduced in colour in J. Porcher, *French Miniatures from Illuminated Manuscripts*, (1960), pl. lxxxviii.

66 Leroquais, *op cit.*, ii, pp. 230–4, pl. cxxiii. Further miniatures from this book may be seen in D. Seward, *Prince of the Renaissance: the Life of Francis I*, (1974), p. 229 and in *The Queen's Image: a Celebration of Mary, Queen of Scots*. An exhibition catalogue by H. Smailes and D. Thomson, (1987), fig. 2.

Huntington Library in California.[67] It is a single portrait of a lady (pl. 12) probably dating from the 1520s and it is inserted into a volume containing vernacular psalms, biblical extracts and prayers which, given an apparently deliberate stress on the qualities that go to make up a good wife, could well have been a marriage gift. The portrait is rather rubbed, but of excellent quality. It measures approximately two by two and threequarter inches, much like the English girdle books, and in general appearance is very like Horenbout's rectangular image of Katharine of Aragon (pl. 11).

There is one further extant example of an English girdle book, much smaller in size than those already mentioned (pl. 14). It is bound in gold, with openwork panels and traces of black enamel decoration, and contains an English translation of the Penitential Psalms by Master John Croke, one of the six clerks in Chancery during the greater part of the reign of Henry VIII.[68] According to another copy of the same translation, it was undertaken at the request of Croke's wife, Prudentia.[69] Both copies are apparently in Croke's own hand. The gold-bound version contains a postage stamp size portrait of Henry VIII, following the image made current by Holbein in the late 1530s.[70] This is not well painted and it is tempting to dismiss it as a later addition. However, the image is of exactly the right date for the manuscript in which it appears and is appropriate to a place in a girdle book, so it probably is indeed contemporary.[71]

67 I am grateful to James Marrow for drawing this example to my attention and to Mary Robertson for sending me a copy of the draft description of the manuscript, which will appear in the forthcoming catalogue of the illuminated books in the Huntington Library.

68 Stowe MS 956 in the British Library. The book is discussed by Tait, 'Historiated Tudor Jewellery', p. 235, and he reproduces its covers as pl. xli c.

69 The second copy is also in the British Library Add. MS 30981. It measures 3½ x 2¾ in., as against the 1½ x 1¼ in. of Stowe MS 956. For the text see *Thirteen Psalms and the First Chapter of Ecclesiastes, translated into English verse by John Croke ... with other documents relating to the Croke family*, ed. A. Croke (Percy Society; Early English Poetry etc., vol. 11, no. 40, 1844). In the 1520s Croke worked closely with Cromwell in establishing Wolsey's colleges at Oxford and Ipswich (L and P, iv, pt. ii (1872), no. 5117). About 1529 he acquired estates in Buckinghamshire, which he consolidated at the Dissolution (L and P, xiv, pt. ii (1895), no. 790). He was a member of the embassy that concluded the Treaty of Amiens in 1527 (L and P, iv, pt. ii (1872), no. 33–69). He held various lucrative posts in the Chancery throughout his career but has been wrongly identified as the MP for Chippenham in 1547, see S. T. Bindoff, *The House of Commons 1509–1558*, i (1982), pp. 726–7. A great many further references to him may be found in L and P.

70 A very similar but circular image was offered in Sotheby's sale-catalogue, (11 July 1983), lot 9. Both conform to Type V (1537), 'The Holbein Frontal Pattern', in R. Strong, *Tudor and Jacobean Portraits*, i (1969), pp. 158–9.

71 Philippa Glanville has kindly pointed out to me documentary evidence for a

A persistent but clearly inaccurate tradition associates the Croke manuscript with Anne Boleyn.[72] While it is most unlikely that this particular book can be connected with Henry's second queen, it is not at all out of the question that her ladies were supplied with miniature devotional books of this general kind. Brought up in France, under the protection of Queen Claude who most certainly did own several tiny prayer books,[73] Anne may well have encouraged this particular fashion. Whether or not she offered such books to her attendants on the scaffold we cannot now establish, but it is recorded that Lady Jane Grey carried a small book of prayers to her execution. Slightly larger that the manuscripts discussed above but consistent in character, it survives as Harley MS 2342 in the British Library.[74]

There is also at least one piece of documentary evidence which seems to connect a girdle book with a pair of portraits, presumably miniatures. An inventory of Princess Mary's jewels taken in 1542 lists what are almost certainly two of these little books. The first is described as 'a Boke of golde garneshed w^t little Rubies and Clasped w^t oon litle Diamond'. The second is a 'Boke of golde w^t the Kings face and hir graces mothers [Katharine of Aragon]'.[75]

All in all there seems little doubt that Lucas Horenbout can indeed take credit for the introduction into England of the circular miniature on vellum as a form of portraiture in its own right. This was not, however, a sudden revolutionary new development peculiar to England. What Lucas was in fact doing was refining upon a well-established manuscript tradition which had been particularly strong in northern Italy at the end of the preceding century, as he probably knew from first-hand experience of Italian manuscripts. A very similar development was taking place in France at much the same time. In both countries the moving spirits seem to have been immigrant Flemish

---

girdle book supplied in June 1564 to the wife of another lawyer, John Bowyer of Lincoln's Inn; see her article 'The Plate Purchases of a Tudor Lawyer', *Collectanea Londiniensia: Studies Presented to Ralph Merrifield*, London and Middlesex Archaeological Society, Special Paper no. 2, (1978), pp. 290 and 298.

72 Ives, *op cit.*, p. 315, note 50.
73 See C. Sterling, *The Master of Claude of France*, (1975).
74 Like the larger of the two Croke manuscripts, Lady Jane's prayerbook measures approximately 3½ x 2¾ in.
75 F. Madden, *The Privy Purse Expenses of the Princess Mary*, (1831), p. 178. He wrongly suggests (p. 213) that the references may be to ornaments or brooches merely in the shape of a book. However, the reference in the Bowyer inventory, above n. 71, also specifies 'a Book of gold'.

craftsmen – Horenbout on one side of the Channel, Godefroy and Clouet on the other. At least two of the early Horenbout images of Henry VIII were painted in the context of traditional Flemish manuscript border decoration, one to embellish a charter, the other quite probably for insertion into a special but already established type of book. We do not in fact know how any of the other images was intended to be used, but the documents recording the exchange between Henry VIII and Francis I in 1526–7 lay so much stress upon the rich and emblematic nature of the settings in which the portraits appeared as to suggest that a whole new prospect was even then opening up. The mention of Anne Boleyn's bracelet in the same year points in a similar direction.

Lucas Horenbout was almost certainly a professional book painter before his move to England. New outlets must have been eagerly sought for what, in the face of the expansion of the printing trade, was rapidly becoming a somewhat esoteric skill. Much has been made of the fact that Horenbout seems to have taught Holbein to be a miniature painter.[76] What the record actually says is that he taught him how to illuminate – in other words, the technique of painting on vellum. Holbein was already a versatile and innovative portrait painter whose output embraced the small-scale circular portrait, but he was not by trade a book painter.[77] We can probably reasonably assume that his main interest in Lucas's professional skills was to enable him to produce for himself the tiny images which were in popular demand in his circle. By the time these skills had descended through yet another generation to Hilliard they were, in England at least, no longer primarily associated with book decoration. The portrait miniature painter, like the printer before him, had emancipated himself from his roots and his craft was ready to move forwards as an art form in its own right.

76 The original reference may be found in Carel van Mander, *Het Schilder-Boeck*, (Harlaam, 1604), fol. 222b.
77 For small-scale circular portraits by Holbein and his circle see J. K. Rowlands, *Holbein*, (1987), pp. 77–9, 94–6.

Household Servants of the Yorkist and Early Tudor Gentry

P. W. FLEMING

The early modern 'family' was not only a kin group, but comprised all those who regularly shared the same roof as the head of the house-hold.[1] And yet, among all that has been written on this subject, it is the modern, anachronistic concept of family that seems to dominate. In particular, servants have been neglected, even though contemporaries regarded them as fully part of the *familia*. Without servants, the family at all but the lowest levels of society would have been unable to function.

Admittedly, servants do not make easy subjects for study. Generally speaking, the majority of them did not marry, did not own substantial amounts of property, and nor did they often die in service; thus, they tend to slip through the prosopographical net cast by historians. Definitions are also a problem. During the early-modern period 'servant' could mean anyone employed for a wage, from the day labourer hired to gather the harvest home to the family retainer grown old in loyal service.[2] This article concentrates on those servants of the gentry who were hired for a period of months or years to perform duties within their master's household and in receipt of some combination of board and lodging, wages, fees, or livery. Such a distinction was employed by contemporaries, but it was a characteristic of gentry establishments of this period that their personnel were called upon to perform a wide variety of duties, some of which took them far from the household. This lack of specialisation can of course be seen as a characteristic of society as a whole at a certain stage of development.

Standing in their masters' shadows, servants are easily obscured from our view. One shaft of light may be cast by courtesy books. These manuals of household management and polite behaviour enjoyed

1 M. Girouard, *Life in the English Country House: a Social and Architectural History* (New Haven and London, 1978), p. 16; P. Laslett, *The World We Have Lost* (2nd edn., London, 1971), pp. 2, 20–1, 181; L. Stone, *Family, Sex and Marriage in England, 1500–1800* (London, 1977), pp. 21, 27.
2 For the problems associated with identifying and defining early-modern servants, see P. J. P. Goldberg, 'Female labour, service and marriage in the late medieval urban north', *Northern History*, XXII (1986), 18–38; and A. Kussmaul, *Servants in Husbandry in Early Modern England* (Cambridge, 1981), *passim*.

considerable popularity during the fifteenth and sixteenth centuries.[3] Before the Reformation, works such as Caxton's *Book of Curtesye*, John Russell's *Boke of Nurture*, and *How the Good Wijfe taughte Hir Dougtir*, stressed the importance of deference, honesty, diligence and obedience among servants.[4] This list of serviceable qualities was shot through with puritan rigour in later works. From Hugh Rhodes' *Book of Nurture*, published in 1577 but written at some point in mid century, to *A Godly Form of Household Governement*, which appeared in 1598, the tone is much more one of repression:[5] servants must do everything asked of them, provided it is not sinful, and they must do so in dread of their masters; the master should not be too trusting, and should delegate as little as possible; and servants should rarely be left unsupervised, lest their bestial and corrupt natures get the better of them.[6] And the master must not spare the rod, for to do so is of course a great cruelty to the servant:

> If any stryfe or debate bee among them of thy house, at nighte charytably call them togyther, and wyth wordes or strypes make them all agree in one. Take heede, if thy servaunt or chyld murmure or grudge agaynst thee, breake it betyme. And when thou hearest them sweare or curse, lye & fyght, thou shalte reprove them sharpelye.[7]

But some degree of moderation was also counselled: 'And therefore the lawe of God did charge the master, that hee should not inflict above fortie stripes upon his servant'.[8] In 1563 Laurence Humphrey recommended the recital of all twenty-four letters of the Greek alphabet before striking, so that punishment would be administered in cold blood.[9] Coming to the subject from a reading of this literature, it would be easy to imagine that early-modern household servants spent their rare off-duty moments cowering below stairs, smarting from the stripes inflicted by their tyrannical masters.

The majority of these courtesy books were ostensibly written to

---

3 For a general discussion of this literature, see C.L.Powell, *English Domestic Relations, 1487–1653* (New York, 1917), especially pp. 101–46.

4 F.J.Furnivall (ed.), *Caxton's Book of Curtesye* (Early English Text Society, Extra Series III, London, 1868); for *Boke of Nurture* and *Good Wife* see *idem* (ed.), *Manners and Meals in Olden Time* (Early English Text Society, Original Series, XXXII, London, 1868).

5 For Rhodes' *Book of Nurture* see *ibid.*; 'R.C.', *A Godly Form of Householde Gouернement: for the Ordering of Private Families, according to the Direction of God's Word* (London, 1598), henceforth referred to as *Godly Form*.

6 *Godly Form*, pp. 20, 375, 377, 385–9.

7 From Rhodes, *op. cit.*, p.65; see also *Godly Form*, pp. 4–5, and L.Humphrey, *The Nobles, or of Nobilitye* (London, 1563), no pagination, Book III.

8 *Godly Form*, p.381.

9 Humphrey, *loc. cit.*

instruct princes, and the servants of princes, although doubtless they inspired many lesser mortals as well.[10] Comparison of these works with the documentary sources should enable some estimate to be made of how accurately literature reflected reality, and of the extent to which courtesy books provided ideal models of behaviour and household organisation. To attempt this comparison across all levels of servant-retaining society would be a task beyond the scope of one article, and so this study will be restricted to gentry households between 1460 and 1530, and, among other sources, it will employ letters, wills, and such gentry household accounts as have survived. Most of these sources were written by or for the gentry, and so, inevitably, we see servants nearly always through the eyes of of their masters, a fact which must be borne in mind throughout.

The gentry inhabited a wide range of social and economic levels, and their households reflected this. Those of the more substantial would not have disgraced a minor member of the peerage. During the reign of Edward IV Sir John Scott's household at Nettlestead in Kent reputedly numbered around sixty servants, while in 1523 there were three chaplains and about ninety servants on the pay-roll of the courtier Sir Thomas Lovell.[11] At the other end of the scale came the establishment of William Brent, a Kentish gentleman who died in 1496. His household probably consisted of himself, his wife and four children, and only six servants, of whom one was his valet and another his wife's maid.[12] Such an establishment is unlikely to have attracted any share of the criticism habitually levelled at the bloated, vice-ridden entourages of the ostentatious magnates.[13]

The gentry made a clear distinction between the upper servants – the household officers – and the lower servants, or meinie.[14] The officers

10 Furnivall, *Manners and Meals*, p. 1; *idem, Caxton's Book of Curtesye*, p. 13.
11 J. R. Scott, *Memorials of the Family of Scott, of Scott's Hall, in the County of Kent* (London, 1876), p. 159; Historical Manuscripts Commission, *Rutland Papers*, IV (London, 1905), pp. 260–2.
12 This is based on the evidence of an inventory of Brent's household drawn up soon after his death: Kent Archives Office, U47/49/T73. For a further discussion of Brent and this inventory, see P. W. Fleming, 'The character and private concerns of the gentry of Kent, 1422–1509' (unpublished University of Wales (Swansea) Ph.D thesis, 1985), pp. 181–92.
13 Humphrey, *loc. cit.*; J. M. Cowper (ed.) *England in the Reign of King Henry VIII: a Dialogue between Cardinal Pole and Thomas Lupset, Lecturer in Rhetoric at Oxford, by Thomas Starkey, Chaplain to the King* (Early English Text Society, Extra Series, XII, London, 1871), pp. 78–9, 150.
14 For example, Sir Thomas Lovell's pay-roll account of 1522–3 was divided under the headings 'chapleyns', 'Gentylmen wayters', 'Offycers', 'Servantes exerciseing ther faculteis' and 'Women servauntes': *Rutland Papers, loc. cit.* A mid-fifteenth century *Boke of Curtasye* divided its discussion of the various

included chamberlains, valets, receivers, porters, cooks (sometimes with an undercook and baker), and superior maidservants; among the meinie were various grooms, boys, 'hynds' and labourers performing domestic chores.[15] The more substantial gentry households would also have had a small staff to manage the horses: in her will of 1493 Katherine Haute of Kent left 6s 8d to 'Joky my horse kepar', in addition to his wages.[16]

The lower servants may often have been recruited at hiring fairs, but many of the upper servants were probably already known to their masters before they were hired, or were employed on the strength of recommendations from family or friends.[17] In 1489–90 Edward Plumpton recommended one of his servants to Sir Robert Plumpton in the following terms:

> Sir, Robart, my servant, is a true servant to me, neverthelesse he is large to ryde afore my male, and over weyghty for my horse; wherfore he hartely desireth me to wryte to your mastership for him. He is a true man of tongue and hands, and a kind and a good man. If yt please your mastership to take him to your service, I besech you to be his good master, and the better at the instaunce of my especyall prayer. Sir, I have given to him the blacke horse that bar him from the feild.[18]

Another glowing reference is to be found in a letter which Margaret Paston wrote to her husband in 1461:

---

duties of servants between officers and the 'smaller mené': Furnivall, *Manners and Meals*, p. 309 f.

15 For various titles applied to positions in gentry establishments, see the wills of Reginald Peckham, 1523 (PRO, PCC 31 Bodfelde); Sir Piers Legh, 1522, in W. F. Irvine (ed.), *A Collection of Lancashire and Cheshire Wills* (Lancashire and Cheshire Record Society, XXX, 1896), pp. 33–6; Sir Edmund Rede, 1487, in J. R. H. Weaver and A. Beardwood (eds.), *Some Oxfordshire Wills, 1393–1510* (Oxfordshire Records Society, 1958), pp. 42–6; Elizabeth, the widow of Sir John Speke, 1518, and Sir George Speke, 1528, in F. W. Weaver (ed.), *Somerset Medieval Wills, 1501–1530* (Somerset Records Society, XIX, 1903), pp. 195–6, 275–8.

16 PRO, PCC 4 Vox. The earliest recorded usage of 'Jockey' as a diminutive of John or James is given by the *Oxford English Dictionary* as occurring in 1529; the earliest recorded usage of the word to denote one who manages horses is given as 1638.

17 Goldberg, *op. cit.*, pp. 21–2.

18 T. Stapleton (ed.), *Plumpton Correspondence* (Camden Society, Old Series, IV, London, 1839), p. 89. The 'feild' in question was probably Stoke: Edward Plumpton was secretary to Lord Strange, who was present at this battle (*ibid.*).

And if it like you to have with you my cosyn William ... I trow ye shulde fynde hym a necessary man to take hede to yowr howshold, and to bye all maner of stuffe nedefull therto, and to se to the rewle and gode gidyn therof. It hath be told me be for that he can gode skill of such thyngs;[19]

Some gentry employed what appear to be family groups of servants. In their wills of 1516 and 1518 respectively Sir John Speke and his wife Elizabeth mentioned their servants John and Thurstone Harop and William and Elizabeth Marshal.[20] Among the Stonors' servants were six members of the Blakehall family.[21]

Servants were generally indentured to serve for one year, although those termed 'labourers' would have been employed on a more casual basis.[22] While the upper servants may often have continued in service with the same family for many years – among the Stonor servants, Thomas Mathew remained in that family's service for eight years, Henry Chowne for thirteen, John Mathew for twenty-four and Henry Dogett for thirty-nine years – the lower servants were usually more transient.[23] In the 1430s the author of *How the Good Wijfe taughte Hir Dougtir* advised the mistress to

... geve thi meyne ther hire A^t ther terme day whether that thei dwelle stille or thei wende awey,[24]

Wages were due quarterly – Michaelmas, Christmas, Easter or Lady Day and Midsummer or the feast of St John the Baptist – half-yearly or yearly, although, as P.V.B.Jones has pointed out, many servants may have had to wait for payment until their masters had sufficient ready cash.[25] Wage rates are difficult to determine. In 1468 Thomas Pratt

19 N.Davis (ed.), *Paston Letters and Papers of the Fifteenth Century* (Oxford, 1971), no. 166.
20 F.W.Weaver, *op. cit.*, pp. 189–96.
21 C.L.Kingsford (ed.), *The Stonor Letters and Papers, 1290–1483* (2 vols., Camden Society, 3rd series XXIX, XXX, London, 1919), nos. 147, 234; henceforth referred to as *SL*.
22 Goldberg, *op cit.*, p. 23; Kussmaul, *op. cit.*, p. 135. For servants' indentures or covenants, see P.V.B.Jones, *The Household of a Tudor Nobleman* (University of Illinois Studies in the Social Sciences, VI, Urbana, 1917), pp. 48–9. See also the will of Agnes Burton, 1503: 'I will that every of my servants have their couvenants' (F.W.Weaver, *op. cit.*, pp. 52–7). In 1468 the Stonor servant Thomas Pratt was indentured to serve for one year from Michaelmas to Michaelmas: *SL*, I, p. 99.
23 Thomas Mathew: *SL*, nos. 126, 282, 285, 298. Chowne: *SL*, no. 234, II, p. 182. John Mathew: *SL*, no. 60, II, p. 169. Dogett: *SL*, I, xxii–xxiii, no. 305. For transient lower servants, see Goldberg, *op. cit..*, p. 23.
24 Furnivall, *Manners and Meals*, pp. 11–3.
25 Jones, *op. cit.*, pp. 49–51. For quarterly payments see the wills of Sir John

agreed to serve for one mark and a set of clothes *per annum*.[26] Five servants of John Hudleston esquire of Millom received annual wages of between eight shillings and one mark in 1513–14.[27] Wage differentials between various servant ranks are likely to have been considerable. In 1469 the pay-roll of the duke of Clarence's household recorded payments *per diem* of 7d for esquires, 4d for yeoman and 2d for grooms.[28] Some idea of the wage differentials in gentry households can be gained by the level of money bequests given by testators to their servants. In his will of 1487 Sir Edmund Rede of Buckinghamshire left 20s to each of his gentlemen or gentlewomen servants, 13s 4d to each *famulus*, and 6s 8d to each *garcio*.[29] By his will of 1522 Sir Piers Legh of Lancashire left to each gentleman of his household 13s 4d, 6s 8d to each yeoman, and 3s 4d to each 'laborer'.[30]

In addition to their wages, many gentry servants would have received gowns of livery, and other clothing. In 1472 Cecily Kyriel of Kent bequeathed two and a half yards of livery cloth to one of her servants, while six years later a clothier supplied to Sir William Stonor 'ij yerdes and quarter of bran medly for your meyny'.[31] The same year Sir Henry Ferrers of East Peckham in Kent was summoned before the court of King's Bench to answer the charge that on Christmas Day 1477 he gave a gown of livery to John Belsot of Ightham, whom he had not retained as his servant, *famulus*, or official, nor as his legal counsel. Sir Henry did not appear, and a writ of *venire facias* was issued. Belsot, meanwhile, had secured a pardon for all offences he had committed.[32] From the accounts of Millom Castle it is possible to reconstruct the suits given to three household servants by their master, John Hudleston, in 1513–14: they were provided with white woollen hosen, smocks and shirts of linen, frieze jackets, and doublets and harvest gloves of sheepskin.[33]

Darell, 1509 (PRO, PCC 24 Bennett), and Hamnet Harrington esquire, 1527: G.J. Piccope, *Lancashire and Cheshire Wills and Inventories Part One* (Chetham Society, XXXIII, 1857), pp. 29–32. For payment at Easter and Midsummer, see *SL*, no. 146. For half-yearly payments, see A.J.L. Winchester, 'The castle household and demesne farm at Millom in 1513–1514', *Transactions of the Cumberland and Westmoreland Antiquarian and Archaeological Society*, LXXXIII (1983), 85–99, p. 85.

26 *SL*, I, p. 99.
27 Winchester, *loc. cit.*
28 Jones, *op. cit.*, p. 50.
29 Weaver and Beardwood, *op. cit.*, pp. 42–6.
30 Irvine, *op cit.*., pp. 33–6.
31 For Cecily Kyriel's will, see PRO, PCC 9 Wattys. For Stonor, see *SL*, no. 235.
32 PRO, KB 27/901 Rex m. 2 *d*.
33 Winchester, *op. cit.*, p. 88. Sir William Stonor also provided shoes for his

The servants of the gentry were mostly male. On average, the wills of gentry testators mention twice as many male as female servants, while in the household of Sir Thomas Lovell in 1522–3 there were only five female servants in a total establishment of ninety.[34] Many servants would have been children or in their teens and early twenties. The writers of courtesy books assumed that those seeking their advice on how to serve a prince would be under age, and the household accounts of Tudor noblemen make frequent mention of children and *garciones*.[35] Sir William Stonor was served by a child of the buttery, a child of the chamber, and at least one other child.[36] In her will of 1493 Katherine Haute bequeathed 6s 8d to Richard, whom she described as 'childe of my chambre'.[37]

Children often entered service at around the age of twelve, and might have continued as servants until their mid to late twenties.[38] By the time they left household service most of the lower servants would probably have hoped to marry, having amassed sufficient savings during their period of employment. Few, if any, of the lower servants would have married while in service. Some masters actually forbade their servants to marry, but in most cases it is likely that economic constraints were as effective as any prohibition.[39] The wills of several gentry testators contain provisions for dowries to be paid to maidservants, ranging in value from one pound to ten marks, in much the same way as other testators provided dowries for poor girls in order to save them from sin and destitution.[40] Cardinal Pole – as portrayed by Thomas Starkey – believed that poverty prevented many servants from ever rising above their stations, and he complained of:

---

household: *SL*, no. 234. In 1522–3 Sir Thomas Lovell provided livery for his servants: *Rutland Papers*, p. 262.

34 *Ibid.*, pp. 260–2; and see also, Girouard, *op. cit.*, p. 27, and Laslett, *op. cit.*, p. 2. 'R.C.' believed that a maidservant had to be neat, clean and handsome, and was to 'have skill in washing, baking, brewing, sowing & spinning, but chiefely in holding her peace': *Godly Form*, p. 389.

35 Furnivall, *Caxton's Book of Curtesye*, p. 23; *idem, Manners and Meals*, p. 18; Jones, *op. cit., passim.*

36 *SL*, nos. 234–5.

37 PRO, PCC 4 Vox. In this period, 'child' could also refer to an adolescent or young adult: H. Kurath and S. M. Kuhn, *Middle English Dictionary*, II, 245, 5b.

38 Goldberg, *op. cit.*, pp. 22–3.

39 Laslett, *op. cit.*, pp. 3, 21.

40 For example, see the wills of John Alfegh, 1488 (PRO, PCC 18 Milles), Sir John Darell, 1509 (PCC 24 Bennett), Joan Mareys, 1464 (PCC 9 Godyn), John Roberts, 1460 (PCC 22 Stokton), Thomas Roper, 1492 (Kent Archives Office, PRC 32/3/359), and Stephen Slegge, 1460 (PCC 21 Stokton). See also Goldberg, *op. cit.*, pp. 37–8.

The grete multytude of servyng men, wych in servyce spend theyr lyfe, never fyndyng mean to marry convenyently, but [who]lyve alway as commyn corruptarys of chastyte.[41]

Whatever their age, as unmarried dependants, most of the lower servants would have enjoyed a status little different from that of their masters' children, and so they were often treated. The position of the head of the household as both master and parent is clearly expressed in *A Godly Form of Householde Gouernement*, published in 1598:

The householder is called *pater familias*: that is, a father of a familie, because hee should have a fatherly care over his servants, as if they were his children.[42]

This near equivalence in status between servants and children made it easier to control what might otherwise have been an unruly household and, by extension, an even more unruly society.[43] The identification of servants with children was facilitated by their shared functions. Like Chaucer's 'Squyer', who 'carf biforn his fader at the table', gentle children performed household duties whose function was partly symbolic – emphasising the child's subordination to the head of the household – and partly educational, since by waiting at table the child learnt etiquette and the basics of household management.[44] In many gentry households, the master's servants and children would have been joined by heirs held in wardship and by the offspring of other gentle families sent for training, thereby further confusing the roles of servants and children.[45] One consequence of such practices was that gentle-born children were made to rub shoulders with their lower-ranking contemporaries. Indeed, surrounded by nurses and servants from birth, gentle children's formative years would have been spent largely in the company of their social inferiors. Everyone may have known their place, but there is unlikely to have been an unbridgeable gulf between master and servant.

For the most part, there seems little that can be discovered about the lower servants, and so the bulk of this article must be confined to their

41 Cowper, *op. cit.*, p. 150.
42 *Godly Form* p. 307; this is a late expression of this belief, but it puts in a concise form views which had been prevalent for several generations. See also, Furnivall, *Manners and Meals*, pp. 64–5.
43 Laslett, *op. cit.*, p. 191.
44 *General Prologue*, 1. 100. See also, N. Orme, 'The education of the courtier', in V. J. Scattergood and J. W. Sherborne (eds.), *English Court Culture in the later Middle Ages* (London, 1983), pp. 63–85; and Jones, *op. cit.*, pp. 26–7.
45 Girouard, *op. cit.*, pp. 17–18; Furnivall, *Manners and Meals*, pp. vi–xi; I. Pinchbeck and M. Hewitt, *Children in English Society*, I (London, 1969), p. 26.

superiors. Traditionally, the yeomanry provided most of the upper servants.[46] The very word 'yeoman' may derive from 'yongeman', in the sense of young serving-man, and its Latin equivalent, *valettus*, further points to its servile associations.[47] Yeomen are indeed to be found serving in gentry households, but also in evidence are servants of gentle rank.[48] Clearly, gentlemen did not find service as household officers demeaning, even in the establishments of their fellow gentry.[49] Sir John Scott, Controller of the Household under Edward IV, retained at least three gentleman servants at various stages in his life.[50] A shoemaker's bill addressed to Sir William Stonor in 1478–9 records money owing for a pair of shoes made for 'my ladys gentlywoman'.[51] In 1473 Sir John Paston wrote to his elder brother with the news that 'Janore Loveday [Paston's cousin] shall be weddyd to on Denyse, a fuattyd [*sic*] gentylman wyth Syr G[eorge] Brown, nowther to weell ner to ylle'.[52] This 'Denyse' was probably of the Kentish family of Denys, perhaps the grandson of John Denys of Well Hall, variously described as esquire and gentleman, who died between 1434 and 1441.[53] Gentle servants were not the prerogative of knights and noblemen: John Alfegh, a gentleman of Chiddingstone in Kent, and the Kentish esquire John Pympe, were both attended by gentlewomen.[54]

Sometimes the bond between master and servant was strengthened by

46 Girouard, *op. cit.*, p. 16; Cowper, *op. cit.*, pp. 78–9.

47 M. Campbell, *The English Yeoman under Elizabeth and the Early Stuarts* (London, 1942), pp. 7–9.

48 For gentry testators mentioning yeoman servants, see the wills of Sir Piers Legh, 1522 (Irvine, *op. cit.*, pp. 33–6), Isabel Newton, 1498, Sir John Wadham, 1501, and Sir George Speke, 1528 (F. W. Weaver, *op. cit.*, *1383–1500*, pp. 375–5, *ibid.*, *1501–1530*, pp. 28–30, 275–8), Katharine Haute, 1493: PRO, PCC 4 Vox. Among the Stonors' servants, Thomas Pratt and John Mathew were both yeomen: *SL*, no. 214; *Calendar of Fine Rolls, 1461–1471*, p. 158.

49 Girouard, *op. cit.*, p. 16; D. Marshall, *The English Domestic Servant in History* (Historical Association, General Series, XIII, London, 1949), p. 4. Servants in royal and magnate households to whom courtesy books were addressed were assumed to be of gentle rank: Furnivall, *Manners and Meals*, pp. ii–iii, 82–105; Jones, *op. cit.*, p. 26; R. W. Chambers and W. W. Seton (eds.), *A Fifteenth-Century Courtesy Book and Two Fifteenth-Century Franciscan Rules* (Early English Text Society, Original Series, CXLVIII, 2nd edn., 1937), p. 6.

50 Fleming, *op. cit.*, pp. 198–9.

51 *SL*, no. 234.

52 *PL*, I, 458. The meaning of 'fuattyd' is obscure; it could equate to 'snattid' meaning 'snub-nosed', which was current in the fifteenth century (H. Bradley, *A Middle English Dictionary* (Oxford, 1891), p. 559); if so, it would seem that Sir John's opinion of Janore's fiance was not wholly complimentary.

53 Fleming, *op. cit.*, p. 196.

54 *Ibid.*, pp. 196–7. Also, see the wills of Sir Edmund Rede and Sir Piers Legh: above, p. 24.

ties of kinship.[55] By his will of 1527 Hamnet Harrington, a Lancashire esquire, left bequests to James Harrington, a gentleman whom he described as 'my cosyn and se[r]vant' and who also witnessed his will.[56] Sir William Stonor's steward and receiver was his cousin, Walter Elmes.[57] William Brockhill, a Kentish gentleman who died in 1519, numbered among his household servants his grandson, William Cobbes, the younger son of Robert Cobbes, a gentleman of Newchurch.[58] Some of these gentle-born servants may have been youths in training, but others were definitely adults. Margaret Norton, John Pympe's gentlewoman, had also served his parents.[59]

The upper servants – gentle and non-gentle – could be prominent local figures in their own right. In 1478 Thomas Pratt, a yeoman in the service of the Stonors, held property in Henley valued at 40s a year, and his father mortgaged a croft in the same place for £20.[60] Henry Dogett, a Stonor receiver from about 1443 until at least the early 1480s, held property in Berkshire which his inquisition *post mortem* valued at £9 3s 4d per annum.[61] While a Stonor servant, Dogett was of sufficient substance to merit having his own servants: a clerk called Gervase, another man, Richard Pygot, who was probably related to Dogett's son-in-law, Robert Pygot, and possibly also one John Wagge.[62] In 1463 John Mathew, another Stonor receiver, took on a twelve-year farm of the royal manor of Benham Lovell in Berkshire at an annual rent of £11 10s 0d.[63] Thomas Mathew, presumably his kinsman and on the Stonor pay-roll in the 1470s, was among those commissioned to collect the fifteenth and tenth in Oxfordshire in 1468.[64]

It is difficult to believe that these particular serving men and women were treated in the haughty and authoritarian manner prescribed by the courtesy books. Rather, we may imagine them as providing not only the household officers, but also the gentleman's gentlemen and lady's companions of their day. Many of the gentry may have even shared the opinion of the ninth earl of Northumberland when he said:

55 Girouard, *op. cit.*, p. 16.
56 Piccope, *op. cit.*, pp. 29–32.
57 *SL*, I, p. xxiii.
58 Fleming, *op. cit.*, pp. 197–8.
59 In his will of 1496 Pympe referred to Margaret 'which some tyme was servaunte to my fader and moder': PRO, PCC 2 Horne.
60 *SL*, no. 214.
61 *Ibid.*, I, pp. xxii–xxiii; *Calendar of Inquisitions Post Mortem, Henry VII*, I, no. 801.
62 *Ibid.*, and *SL*, nos. 143, 231, 265, 305, 256. Gentle servants often had their own servants in noble households: Jones, *op. cit.*, p. 28.
63 For his receivership, see *SL*, no. 146; for his farm, see *Calendar of Fine Rolls, 1461–1471*, pp. 138–9, *Calendar of Patent Rolls, 1461–1467*, p. 435.
64 *Calendar of Fine Rolls, 1461–1471*, p. 230.

And in this I must truely testify for servants out of experience, that in all my fortunes good and badde, I have found them more reasonable than either wyfe, brothers or friends.[65]

The relationship between Sir William Stonor and his long-serving receiver, Henry Dogett, was especially close: to Sir William Henry was 'my old frynd' or 'my trusty frynd', while in 1479 Henry began a letter to Sir William with 'My good and feythfull maister, I recomaund me to yow with all my service'.[66] It is interesting that faithfulness was an attribute valued in both servant and master.

Friendship has its burdens, and some of the gentry did not think it unreasonable to make use of their servants' property. In his will of 1496 John Pympe bequeathed £3 in gold to his servant, Margaret Norton, 'in recompense of money to me at dyverse times lente both in my childe-hode and pryme and for many other kindenes to me shewde'. He also left her two silver salts and a silver cup and spoons, 'which all I borowed of her and have occupied hit be long space. And I will that this bequesth by the Forst thing that be paid next after my severall expenses'.[67] Despite Pympe's insistence on the urgency of his bequest, Margaret died before she could be fully recompensed; in 1500 John Botiller and his wife Anne, who was Margaret's cousin and executrix, acknowledged receipt of £4 and a standing cup from Elizabeth, John Pympe's widow and executrix, in satisfaction of his bequest.[68]

Joan Sydenham of Somerset did not restrict herself to tableware. In her will of 1498 she left considerable bequests to her servant, William Trowbridge, as well she might, for she 'hadde long tyme the use and pleasure of his house, gardyn and orchard, with the frutes and profites without paying of any rent'.[69] The writers of courtesy books counselled:

What man thou servest, evermore him drede,
And hise goodis as thine owne evere thou spare;[70]

---

65 Jones, *op. cit.*, p. 68.
66 *SL*, nos. 256, 296. The following testators rewarded their servants for 'good and trewe' service: Sir Thomas Danvers, 1501, Sir Edmund Rede, 1487, and Thomas Pomerey, 1508 (Weaver and Beardwood, *op. cit.*, pp. 42–6, 75, 97–8), Alexander Tuse, 1490, and Joan Sydenham, 1498 (F. W. Weaver, *op. cit.*, pp. 288–9, 363–6), and Sir Richard Haute, 1492: PRO, PCC 21 Dogett.
67 PRO, PCC 2 Horne.
68 J. R. Scott, *op. cit.*, p. lxiii. See also, Fleming, *op. cit.*, p. 197.
69 F. W. Weaver, *op. cit.*, pp. 363–6. In 1521 Sir Edward Poynings left two beds and bedclothes, together with numerous pieces of silverware, to his servant Rose Whettell, 'in recompence of certeyn money and plate that I have had of the said Rose at diverse tymes here Tofore': PRO, PCC 21 Maynwaryng. For the possibility that Rose was the mother of at least one of Sir Edward's illegitimate children see Fleming, *op. cit.*, p. 225.
70 Furnivall, *Manners and Meals*, p. 34.

Evidently, this could sometimes work both ways.

Mutual trust lay at the heart of these relationships. Apart from their formal duties within the household, servants also appear as witnesses to their masters' wills, while Henry Dogett regularly acted as a Stonor feoffee.[71] Edmund Thwaytes was given even greater responsibility by his master, Sir Edward Poynings. In 1521 Sir Edward appointed him as the sole executor of his will, and he instructed the foeffees of his manor of Ostenhanger and of his purchased lands in Kent to allow Thwaytes to take the profits of these properties for twelve years, during which time he was to apply them to the upbringing and maintenance of Sir Edward's three illegitimate sons, and to the provision of prayers for his late master's soul. The twelve-year period was to end with the coming-of-age of Thomas, the eldest son, at which time Thwaytes was to account for his administration to the overseers of Sir Edward's will. He was guaranteed his costs for business connected with his executorship, and he was also provided with a life annuity of twenty marks.[72] Four years into his executorship, Thwaytes concluded a marriage settlement with Humphrey Lewkenore esquire of Legh, on behalf of Mary, Sir Edward Poynings' daughter, who was to marry Humphrey's son Robert.[73]

The upper servants of the gentry were called upon to fulfil a wide range of duties. On the Stonor estates, Henry Dogett held manorial courts, while Thomas Mathew and Alexander Blakehall acted as, respectively, bailiff and rent collector.[74] Walter Elmes took his duties as receiver very seriously; around 1480 he wrote to his cousin Sir William Stonor that he had been unable to collect all the money due from certain Stonor properties for which he was responsible, and that because of this, 'By my trouth I kowde not slepe for sorowe this nygth'.[75] Stonor servants travelled widely on their masters' business, delivering letters, money and, among other commodities, clothes, venison and rabbits.[76] Servants also took part in family ceremonies; present at a christening,

71 For servant witnesses, see the wills of Hamnet Harrington, 1527 (Piccope, *op. cit.*, pp. 29–32), William Chamberlayn, 1470, and Thomas Pomerey, 1508 (Weaver and Beardwood, *op. cit.*, pp. 29, 97–8), Agnes Cheyne, 1487 (PRO, PCC 6 Wattys), and Sir Richard Haute, 1492: PCC 21 Dogett. For Dogett, see *SL*, nos. 254, 283, II, p. 174; *Descriptive Catalogue of Ancient Deeds*, I, C124, 145, 158, 945, 1639, II, C2391, III, C3132, 3407; *Calendar of Close Rolls, 1468–1476*, no. 1583.

72 PRO, PCC 21 Maynwaryng.

73 Oxford, Bodleian Library, Charter 191.

74 *SL*, nos. 126, 171, II, p. 167.

75 C. L. Kingsford (ed.), 'Supplementary Stonor Letters and Papers, 1314–1482', *Camden Miscellany*, XIII (Camden Society, 3rd Series, XXXIV, London, 1924), no. 354.

76 *SL*, nos. 156, 172–3, 222, 262, 283, 285, 327.

possibly of Sir William Stonor's son in 1482, were the servants John Doyly, Maurice Estcourt and Christopher Holland.[77]

Advice, on legal and other matters, was freely given by servants and, presumably, gratefully received by their masters. In 1478 Richard Page urged Sir William Stonor to pursue legal action – which Page had already initiated on his master's behalf but apparently not at his prompting – against William Est of Wycomb, who had felled some of the Stonors' timber.[78] Four years earlier, Henry Dogett had also been involved in legal proceedings for the Stonors.[79]

Occasionally, the master needed a good talking to. In 1462, during John Paston's long, and not entirely voluntary sojourn in London, his servant, John Russe, wrote to him in the following terms:

Sir, I prey God brynge you onys to regne amongs youre cuntre men in love, and to be dred. The lenger ye contynwe there the more hurt growyth to you. Men sey ye will neyther folwe the avyse of youre owyn kynred, nor of youre counsell, but contynwe your owyn wylfullnesse, whiche, but grace be, shal be youre distrucion. It is my part to enfourme youre maistirshyp as the comown voyse is, God betir it, and graunt yow onys herts ease; for it is half a det̃1 to me to here the generall voyse of the pepyll, whiche dayli encreassyth.[80]

In return for their diligence, servants expected their masters' support. Again in 1462, John Russe wrote to John Paston asking him to use his influence with the earl of Worcester, who was shortly to be appointed Treasurer of England, in order to secure for Russe the office of controller or searcher of Yarmouth.[81] Servants also sought their masters' backing in their quarrels. In 1472 Edward Langford, a Berkshire gentleman, wrote to Thomas Stonor to complain that one of his servants was owed twenty quarters of barley by two Stonor tenants. Langford went on to claim that his servant had not dared to take legal action against them, for fear of Stonor's wrath.[82] Four years later Elizabeth Stonor intervened in a dispute between her servant John Mathew and her cousin, Thomas Rokes, and prayed Rokes, 'To be good master unto hym'.[83] William Est, whom Richard Page had accused of felling timber belonging to the Stonors, was the servant of Edmund Hampden, and following Page's accusation Hampden wrote to Sir William Stonor:

77 'Supplementary Stonor Letters', no. 358.
78 *SL*, nos. 220–1.
79 *Ibid.*, no. 144.
80 *PL*, II, no. 666.
81 *Ibid*, no. 671
82 *SL*, no. 119.
83 *Ibid.*, no. 172

Syr, I have hard say that ye schold be infformyd to take dysplessuyr with a servant off myne in Whecombe. Syr, and he hathe offendyd yow in eny point I scall put him under no manys correccion but yowris: but for the infformacion off hym that I here say scholde infforme yow, I pray yow, Syr, to be hys good master.[84]

Masters sometimes had to suffer the consequences of their servants' actions. The following comes from a letter received by Sir Robert Plumpton from William Wittcars, in which the writer requested that he:

be good master unto this poore woman, the bearer hereof. Sir, it is so that a servant of yours hath gotten a child with hir, the which is lost for lacke of keeping, as God knowes. She hath kept it as long as she may, whils she hath not a cloth to her backe but which I have given hir, since she came to my service. And if it wold please you to heare this poore woman speake, I trust to God ye wilbe good master to hir, and rather the better for my sake. And if I had not bene, she wold have rune hir way; and all this wile I keep the child of my own proper cost, and will doe, till I here some word from you.[85]

'Good mastership' did not need to end on the deathbed. Testamentary bequests to servants were many and various. Gifts of money were the most common form of bequest, and could range from as little as one shilling – given to every maidservant in the house of Henry Pauncefoot, a gentleman of Wiltshire (the manservants each received 20d) – to the sum of £10 bequeathed by Richard Sydenham of Somerset to his servant John Weneman, 'for his good service rendered to me, and hereafter to be rendered to my heirs and executors'.[86] Money gifts were sometimes accompanied by the payment of outstanding wages – in addition to their many other necessary qualities, servants often had to be patient.[87]

A lucky – but no doubt deserving – few were rewarded with annuities. In 1525 Sir John Fyneaux provided a life annuity for one of his servants of £1 6s 8d, while four of Sir Edward Poynings' servants were to receive life annuities ranging from £1 6s 8d to forty marks by the terms of his will of 1521, and each servant was to be enabled to bring an action of distraint in the event of non-payment. Fyneaux's servant was to receive his annuity at the hands of his late master's widow, as were three

---

84 *Ibid.*, no. 219.
85 T. Stapleton, *op. cit.*, no. 83.
86 For Pauncefoot's will, 1522, see F. W. Weaver, *op. cit.*, *1501–1530*, pp. 217–19; for Sydenham's, 1499, see *ibid.*, *1383–1500*, pp. 387–8.
87 For examples, see the wills of Laurence Dutton, 1527 (Piccope, *op. cit.*, pp. 22–9), Elizabeth Chocke, 1493 (F. W. Weaver, *op. cit.*, *1383–1500*, pp. 305–7), and Agnes Burton, 1503: *ibid.*, *1501–1530*, pp. 52–7.

servants of Sir John Scott, one of whom was to retire from work immediately after Sir John's death, while the other two would receive their annuities when they were also too old to work.[88]

A gift of land or rent was another way of providing for the continued welfare of old servants. Sir Edmund Rede willed that, 'William Gaynesford, for his good & trewe service to me before this tyme and hereafter to me during my lif to be done, have for terme of his life my chief place in Walingford', while in 1524 Sir Richard Sutton left his beerhouse to one of his servants to hold in tail male.[89]

Clothes, household goods and livestock formed the substance of many other bequests. In 1473 John Thornbury of Kent willed that all of his 'aray' was to be distributed between three of his servants.[90] By her will of 1525 Katherine Chiche, also of Kent, provided for a kirtle of strong cloth to be given to her new maidservant, together with one of her own kirtles; presumably the kirtle of strong cloth was meant for household duty, the mistress's cast-off for Sunday best.[91] Three other Kentish testators, John Alfegh, Sir John Fyneaux and Richard Martyn, gave livestock to their servants.[92] Several testators gave to a particular servant the horse on which he was 'wont to ryde'.[93] In his will of 1527 John Cheyne esquire of Sittingbourne bequeathed his shares in a ketch and a ship to Thomas Chapman, one of his servants, presumably with the intention of establishing him in trade or fishing.[94]

The death of the master could have been an alarming prospect for his servants if it meant that his household would be dispersed immediately afterwards. However, a number of gentry testators took pains to postpone the dissolution of their households so that their servants had the opportunity to find new employment before being cast out. Some, including Sir John Fyneaux, had clauses in their wills to the effect 'that my householde be kept holy an hole yere next after my decesse to thentent that my servantes may provide in that mean tyme for their

---

88 See the wills of of Sir John Fyneaux (PRO, PCC 1 Porche), Sir Edward Poynings (PCC 21 Maynwaryng), and Sir John Scott: PCC 15 Logge.
89 Rede: Weaver and Beardwood, *op. cit.*, pp.42–6. Sutton: Irvine, *op. cit.*, pp.41–6. Both William Lovelace in 1495 and John Thornbury in 1473 left land to their servants: Fleming, op. cit., p.203.
90 PRO, PCC 12 Wattys.
91 PRO, PCC 6 Porche.
92 Alfegh, 1488: PRO, PCC 18 Milles. Fyneaux, 1525: PCC 1 Porche. Martyn, 1499: PCC 38 Horne.
93 See the wills of Richard Haute, 1492 (PRO, PCC 21 Dogett), Hamnet Harrington, 1527 (Piccope, *op. cit.*, pp.29–32), and Sir John Speke, 1516: F. W. Weaver, *op. cit., 1501–1530*, pp.189–90.
94 PRO, PCC 21 Porche.

further lyving as they shall thinke best'.[95]

Many may have found new employment fairly soon after their master's death, since experienced servants, used to responsibility and of proven worth, were probably in demand. Certainly, some gentry testators were prepared to offer inducements to certain of their more valued servants in an effort to persuade them to stay in the family service. In 1502 the executors of John Digges were instructed to provide Richard Hunte, one of his servants, with his clothes, accommodation and board for life if he would stay in service in the Digges mansion in Kent, and in his will of 1492 Sir Richard Haute instructed his wife to pay 40s to William Gayman if she could retain his services.[96]

But for many, the role of servant would have been but a first stage in their careers. Well-born youths entered service partly to lessen the burden on their parents' finances, partly to have their rough edges knocked off, but also to find opportunities for self-advancement.[97] The writers of courtesy books were quite frank about this:

> For your preferment resorte
> to such as may you vauntage:
> Among gentlemen, for their rewards;
> to honest dames for maryage.[98]

And after dwelling on death and dissolution, the subject of career advancement allows us to finish with a success story. Among the Stonors' servants during the 1470s was a bright, legally-trained young gentleman called Thomas Wood.[99] In 1471 he acted as an attorney to Thomas Stonor to receive seisin of land in Buckinghamshire, and four years later his name was included on a list of expenses of Stonor servants, which recorded that five yards of cloth had been bought for him.[100] He

---

95 PRO, PCC 1 Porche. Similar arrangements were made by Sir Edward Poynings in 1521 (PCC 21 Maynwaryng), Sir Piers Legh, 1522, and Sir Richard Sutton, 1523 (Irvine, *op. cit.*, pp. 33–6, 41–6), Sir John Wadham, 1501, John Brent, 1524, and Sir George Speke, 1528 (F. W. Weaver, *op. cit.*, *1501–1530*, pp. 28–30, 229, 275–8), and Sir Simon Fitz Richerd, 1527: C. W. Foster (ed.), *Lincoln Wills*, II (Lincoln Record Society, X, 1918 for 1914), pp. 49–50.

96 Digges: Kent Archives Office, PRC 32/7/66. Haute: PRO, PCC 21 Dogett.

97 Girouard, *op. cit.*, p. 17.

98 Furnivall, *Manners and Meals*, p. 141.

99 For accounts of Thomas Wood's career, see E. Foss, *The Judges of England*, V (London, 1857), pp. 80–1; and J. C. Wedgwood, *History of Parliament: Biographies of the Members of the Commons House, 1439–1509* (London, 1936), pp. 967–8. Wood was described as a gentleman in an indenture enrolled in 1473: *Calendar of Close Rolls, 1468–1476*, no. 1204.

100 *Sl*, nos. 114, 147.

was a beneficiary by the will of Edmund Stonor, probably written before he went to France in 1475, and the following year Elizabeth Stonor wrote in anxious tones to her husband William that Thomas Wood 'hys very sore syke [with the pokys] at the Sworde in Flete strete'.[101] He recovered, and within a year he was escorting Elizabeth Stonor from London to her home in Oxfordshire.[102] By 1477 he was practising law.[103] In 1478 he began a career as a Berkshire JP that was to last for the rest of his life, and in the same year he represented Wallingford in parliament.[104] He was appointed a serjeant-at-law in 1485 and a king's serjeant the following year, and from 1487 he was active on the south-western circuit, and as a justice of gaol delivery for Reading, Winchester, Windsor, Salisbury, and Wallingford.[105] In 1495 he became a justice of the Common Bench, in 1496 he was one of the feoffees of the King's will, and in 1500 he was appointed Chief Justice of Common Bench, his career being crowned with a knighthood the following year.[106] He died in 1502.[107]

Thomas Wood maintained contacts with the Stonor family until at least the mid 1490s.[108] From servant to justice in twenty years is not quite an overnight success, but it is impressive nonetheless. He probably came to the Stonors already trained in the law, and as such he would have been a valuable member of their household. In 1483 – although he had left the Stonors' household service by this date – he gave Sir William Stonor the benefit of his legal opinion regarding the inheritance of Anne Neville, Sir William's third wife.[109] In return for his services, the patronage of the Stonor family probably helped him lay the foundations of his brilliant career.

101 *Ibid.*, no. 170, II, p. 186.
102 *Ibid.*, II, p. 20.
103 Foss, *op. cit.*, p. 80.
104 *Calendar of Patent Rolls, 1476–1485*, p. 554; Wedgwood, *op. cit.*, p. 967.
105 *Ibid.*, and Foss, *op. cit.*, pp. 80–1. See also, *Calendar of Patent Rolls, 1485–1494*, *passim.*
106 Wedgwood, *loc. cit.*, and Foss, *loc. cit.* He was appointed Chief Justice on 28 October 1500: *Calendar of Patent Rolls, 1494–1509*, p. 214.
107 Foss, *loc. cit.* His wife, Margaret, died in 1498 seised of lands in Berkshire which she held as jointure from her first husband, Robert Leynham esquire, by whom she had a son, Henry; her inquisition *post mortem* is in *Calendar of Inquisitions Post Mortem, Henry VII*, II, no. 374. She is buried at Tidmarsh: *Victoria County History of Berkshire*, III, p. 436.
108 For Wood's association with Joan Ingaldesthorp, a kinswoman of the Stonors, see *Calendar of Inquisitions Post Mortem, Henry VII*, I, no. 1085. In 1490 he was on a commission of gaol delivery with Sir William Stonor, and Stonor's cousin and servant Walter Elmes: *Calendar of Patent Rolls, 1485–1494*, p. 348.
109 *SL*, no. 328.

The members of a gentry household – from the master's wife and children, through his upper servants, perhaps even to his very scullions – would have considered themselves part of one *familia*, with a shared interest in its prosperity, and unified by affective as well as economic bonds. Naturally, all was not always harmonious. There were occasional outbreaks of ill-feeling between master and servant but, from the non-literary evidence, it seems that these incidents were no more frequent than is to be expected as normal in most families.[110]

With the presence of gentle-born, young and related servants, there is unlikely to have existed a stark division between the master's kin and his servants within the household. The gentry's keen sense of lineage, their careful noting of cousins up to and beyond the fourth degree, may actually have discouraged the erection of barriers between kin and servants. Certainly, the gentry household was hierarchical, but it seems that every link had ready communication with those immediately above and below it, to form an unbroken chain from the solar to the kitchens. This is far removed from the environment of the later upper-class household, with its strict separation of family and servants.

By the Yorkist and early-Tudor period the transformation of the household from 'medieval' to 'modern' had already begun – even Langland had complained that the rich were lately dining apart from their servants – but, right up until the eve of the Reformation, gentry households were still essentially 'medieval'.[111] Perhaps this transformation can be seen as reflecting in microcosm changes in the rest of society – changes which may not all have been for the better – but that is another question, and perhaps another article.

---

110 For a dispute between the Stonors and Thomas Pratt, see *SL*, no. 214.
111 Quoted in M. Wood, *The English Mediaeval House* (London, 1981 edn.), p. 91, and see also *ibid.*, pp. 91–4.

Feasting in an Early Tudor College:
The Example of Merton College, Oxford

J. M. FLETCHER AND C. A. UPTON

Tempora cum causis Latium digesta per annum
lapsaque sub terras ortaque signa cano

The life of any pre-Reformation society, religious or educational, was strongly affected by the ecclesiastical calendar. Members of such institutions recognised that their normal routines would be disrupted or transformed by a more ancient and higher obligation to celebrate and commemorate the life of Christ and his saints. Indeed, it has long been recognised that the need to change or overturn the mundane pattern of life on such occasions was a necessary factor in maintaining it and that such a need long predated the Christian era. It had both a religious and a social function.

The societies established in the medieval universitites were a recognised part of the European church. The college year at Oxford and Cambridge, therefore, included several occasions, varying from institution to institution, when the members of the community could expect to commemorate anniversaries associated with the birth, life and death of Christ, saints' days and notable domestic events. What began in the church's year as simply the recording of a 'religious day' – *festum* – soon became extended to include the provision of special food and drink on some occasions. The church itself recognised greater and lesser feast days for its many saints. Colleges seem to have followed this practice by naming certain festive days as being worthy of 'appietancia maior' and others of 'appietancia minor'. The association of particular church festivities with the provision of extra or different food and drink perhaps came from the desire to delineate carefully such days from those dates or periods of time when christians were required to abstain from certain foods. The festivities associated with the Annunciation, the vigils of Easter, Easter day and the third day of Easter must, for example, have brought to the college fellows some relief after the long period of abstinence from meat during the period of Lent.

Nevertheless, the very concept of 'feasting' in an early Tudor college needs to be justified. Colleges in England were founded to give poor students the opportunity to further their studies at the university, especially to assist them to proceed to the degree of master of arts and the higher doctoral degrees in law, medicine and theology. Certainly there was no intention to allow college members to indulge in extravagant living. Accommodation was not luxurious, even by the standards of the times, and fellows usually shared a suite of rooms. The weekly allowance for food and drink – commons – was fixed by the statutes and their subsequent modifications; it was not over-generous. Any extra items eaten or drunk by a particular fellow were charged to his personal account. As late as 1582, the warden of Merton could insist in a letter to the Visitor, the archbishop of Canterbury, that the whole fellowship of the college should be 'poore scholares'.[1] It would seem, therefore, that opportunities for excesses in food and drink in such institutions were extremely limited. There was also the persistent belief that 'poverty' and 'learning' were somehow linked: that if scholarship was used simply for personal gain, or 'turpe lucrum' as the late medieval commentators wrote, it was akin to prostitution. Students should, as many detailed statutes of the European universities record, show by their outward appearance, dress and behaviour a contempt for the vanities of this world.

The weekly accounts kept by the stewards of hall at Merton College, Oxford, indicate that, for the early Tudor period, the fellows could not be accused of extravagant living.[2] The steward of hall – *senescallus* – was responsible for the supply of food and some drink to the fellows, servants, certain guests and workmen who ate in hall. The warden with his small household ate separately in his own lodgings. To the items purchased for daily consumption in hall we must add those donated to the college as gifts by visiting farmers and well-wishers, and vegetables, fruit or meat drawn from the college garden or from animals kept by its servants. Such items imposed no expenditure on the steward and so do not appear in his account. It would seem from the stewards' regular purchases that the fellows in hall ate, at least on Tuesdays, Wednesdays and Thursdays, a substantial but rather monotonous diet of beef and mutton accompanied by bread, beer and such vegetables as were in season. Fridays and Saturdays were fish days, but here salted fish, dried fish or smoked fish formed the staple diet. The regular, daily lists of food purchases at Merton show no evidence of luxury; the fellows ate the mutton and beef that the Cherwell valley and the Cotswolds produced in relative abundance, and added to this the produce of the

1 J. M. Fletcher, *Registrum Annalium Collegii Mertonensis 1567–1603*, (Oxford: OHS, 1976), p. 145.
2 The stewards' accounts are at present kept in unsorted bundles in the college sacristy. We are gradually dating and numbering these documents.

local pools and rivers and the neighbouring fields. They supplemented their fish and meat with large amounts of bread and washed down their food with considerable quantities of beer.

The few occasions that were set aside for special meals must have come as some relief to the college fellows, and, perhaps, to the college cooks who would have been hard-pressed otherwise to provide a varied menu. By the close of the fifteenth century, it had become customary at Merton to celebrate particular dates each year that were of significance to the college. The fellows could normally expect to receive extra food allowances only on these days. Some were classed as 'major' feasts, others as 'minor'. From the surviving stewards' accounts, we are able to reconstruct the pattern of these festive dates as they occurred during the academic year, which at the college began with the election of new officers on 1 August. On 15 August the Assumption of the Virgin was celebrated as a major feast; on 8 September her Nativity followed, classed as a minor feast. On 29 September the feast of St Michael was a minor and on 1 November the feast of All Saints a major celebration. The college commemorated the dedication of its own chapel on 6 November, a date established in 1426 when the archbishop of Canterbury moved the celebration from 7 January;[3] this was a minor feast. St Catherine's feast was marked on 25 November with a minor celebration. The second bursar's term of office began with the commemoration of St Nicholas on 6 December with a minor feast and of Christmas day on 25 December with a major feast. Christ's Circumcision was celebrated on 1 January as a minor feast and the Epiphany on 6 January as a major feast. The virgin Mary's Purification was marked on 2 February with a minor feast and her Annunciation on 25 March with a major feast. Easter was fittingly commemorated with a minor feast on its vigils, a major feast on Easter day itself and a further major feast on the third day. Ascension day was another major feast, as was Pentecost. Two lesser feasts on Trinity Sunday and on the feast of Corpus Christi followed. Finally, to end the academic year, the college celebrated on 24 June the major feast of St John the Baptist and, on 29 June, the minor feast of St Peter. The fellows could, therefore, expect to celebrate ten major and eleven minor feasts in each academic year.

The dates given above are those that are specifically recorded in the surviving stewards' accounts for August–March 1490–1, and for April–July 1497. Other accounts from the fifteenth and early sixteenth centuries indicate that such feast days were little altered during this

---

3 *The Victoria History of the Counties of England. Oxfordshire. vol. III. The University of Oxford*, (London, 1954), p. 101 n. 32.

period. In October 1489,[4] however, the warden and fellows had determined that in future the date of the dedication of the chapel and the feast of Corpus Christi would be marked as 'dies appietancie' – that is days when the extra allowances for feast days were given. At the same time, Christmas eve and the eve of the feast of Pentecost were demoted. Apart from these minor changes, the days reserved for feasting at Merton remained the same throughout the reign of Henry VII.

From this reference of 1489 in the college register it is apparent that a third category of provision must be added to the 'normal' and 'festive' types we have discussed, since this entry notes that the two upgraded days had been previously 'dies allocacionis tantum' and that the two downgraded dates would in future hold only this status; it would appear that on some days an additional allowance was granted to the fellows. Clearly, this amount was less than normally allowed for even a minor feast day. The various stewards' accounts indicate that such a payment was made. It is not certain that these 'dies allocationis' were always recorded by the different stewards, but we do have indications of payments on the feasts of the Conception of the Virgin, 8 December, on Christmas eve and on the vigils of Pentecost. Amounts allowed varied. We have notes of 3s 4d, 5s, 4s 6d and 3s being paid. Such extra provision was not insignificant if the normal assignment of just one shilling to a fellow to cover his commons for a whole week is kept in mind.

On the days appointed for minor or major feasting, the college also modified its eating arrangements. Normally the warden, the subwarden and the three senior chaplains ate apart from the fellows in the warden's lodgings. On feast days, however, this company joined the others in the college hall and presumably all ate at the same table as the fellows. Not surprisingly, it seems also to have been the practice to invite guests to attend such celebrations; they ate either with the fellows or at the servants' table, no doubt according to their social status. Such arrangements seem to have been accompanied by special financial provision to cover the extra expense involved. Unfortunately, we are not yet able to describe precisely what occurred here. The warden was entitled to a special allowance known as 'sowcark', but what this involved is nowhere made clear. It would seem that it was taken in food rather than cash, for in several of the stewards' acounts a list of items with their cost is given under the heading 'sowcark' on the same page where details of a particular feast day are written. However, not every feast day has such a list nor does it occur only when the warden was then present. Perhaps the allowance was made to his household rather than to the warden

4 H. E. Salter, *Registrum Annalium Collegii Mertonensis 1483–1521*, (Oxford: OHS, 1923), p. 126.

personally. Certainly the amounts given as 'sowcark', noted below, are sizeable, equalling or exceeding the total allocation made to the college fellows on the special 'dies allocationis'.

For the subwarden and chaplains we have a note that they took two dishes at the fellows' table. Invited guests also took two dishes either with the fellows or with the servants. A second dish was provided for the fellows and servants; this would appear to indicate that at normal meals one dish only was allowed to them. A note from the record of a chapter meeting in January 1501 suggests that two fellows shared this one dish provided.[5] On some occasions, the warden's servants were given a small amount to provide for them some refreshment; the word used here, 'iantaculum', had probably lost its original association with a 'breakfast'. Also, lesser payments were made to the postmasters, the Merton undergraduates supported by the college, and to the laundress. When such allowances were made, who exactly was entitled to receive them and whether they were all taken in cash or kind was probably determined by college custom rather than by any detailed written record.

From the accounts for 1490–1 and 1497 it is possible to go beyond a simple recitation of the financial arrangements made for these feast days and give details of how the allowance was used by each steward. Again, we must emphasise that we have here only the named items on which money was actually spent. Any items reaching the college table at no cost to the steward would not be recorded in his account. Nor have we separate figures for the consumption of beer and bread at such celebrations since for such bulk items the steward gave only a total weekly figure of his expenditure. Missing from the accounts, therefore, are references to anything produced from the college garden, which would probably include certain culinary herbs, vegetables and some fruits, the flesh of swans, which the college kept, and some items of game which we know from the bursars' accounts were occasionally donated to the college. However, even if these limitations are borne in mind, the details of the accounts can give us a fascinating glimpse into the celebration of feast days in this Oxford college in the early Tudor period.

The feast of the Assumption fell, in 1490, on Sunday. The warden on this major occasion joined the company with his household. For his 'sowcark' 5s 0½d was spent on mutton, goose, veal, duck, lamb, small birds, capons, marrow bones, eggs, spices, butter and 'quaccum' – probably some type of curd. Ten pence was also spent on wine. Five guests joined the fellows and three ate with the servants. The steward spent 11s 8d on food for this feast, purchasing milk, and 'frumentum' – perhaps frumenty, mutton, goose, veal, lamb, duck, rabbit, small birds,

5 Ibid., p. 250.

calf's feet, beef, butter and spices. Some idea of the scale of the expenditure may be obtained from a comparison with the amount spent by the preceding steward a week before on his Sunday meals, 4s 4d.

The lesser feast of the Nativity of Mary fell on Wednesday, normally a day when the fellows ate frugally. The warden did not attend this celebration, but three guests ate with the fellows and three with the servants. The steward spent 7s 8d on frumenty, beef, mutton, pork, small birds, goose, chicken, marrow bones, butter, eggs and spices. On the previous Wednesday, the steward had spent 1s 9½d on the meal.

For the lesser feast of St Michael, again on a Wednesday, the warden was present and 7s 6½d was spent on his sowcark of which 3s 1½d was needed to purchase wine and spices. He also ate beef, mutton, capons, lamb, small birds, veal, duck, 'quaccum', marrow bones, eggs and trout. The feast cost 8s 5½d and the company ate frumenty, beef, lamb, small birds, mutton, veal, duck, calf's feet, butter, chicken, with wine and spices. Six guests joined the fellows and six the servants.

The warden was absent from the celebrations for All Saints' Day, a greater feast which fell on a Monday. Four guests ate with the fellows and five with the servants. The food cost 14s 7d and consisted of necks, beef, mutton, goose, lamb, rabbit, duck, 'quaccum', eggs, spices, butter, pork and marrow bones. Again the warden did not attend the festivities to mark the dedication of the chapel, but three guests were present with the fellows and four with the servants. The feast was given on a Saturday and 9s 1d was spent. It was customary at Merton for fish to be served on Saturdays and the company ate salt fish, pike, pollard (chub), salmon, stock fish, eels, herrings, butter, pears, wine, spices and eggs. The dependence of the town of Oxford, so far from the sea, on supplies from pools and rivers and on preserved fish is clearly shown here. The other ingredients of the meal also indicate how the food may have been prepared and that the feast possibly ended with a dessert.

The last feast day in the period of office of the first bursar was that of St Catherine, a minor celebration which fell on Thursday. The warden was again absent. Four guests were entertained by the fellows and five by the servants. The meal cost 13s 1d and was of a very varied nature. Necks, beef, mutton, goose, woodcock, rabbit, 'currus' (perhaps a 'cur', a fish or duck), pork, salt fish, eels, pike, pollard and spices were purchased.

The second bursar took office just before the season of Christmas and Epiphany and so during his first months his stewards of hall were required to provide for a number of important feast days. First, on 6 December, the minor feast of St Nicholas was celebrated. In 1490 the warden was present; five guests ate with the fellows and four with the servants. The warden's sowcark consisted of beef, goose, rabbit, chestnuts, larks, capons, 'caruca', marrow bones, veal, 'quaccum' and eggs, wine and spices, flour and wine. On this 6s 4½d was spent, and 1s on the wine. For the hall meal the steward purchased at a cost of 14s 4d necks, beef, mutton, goose, rabbit, woodcock, larks, small birds, piglets, pork, veal and spices. As this feast fell on Monday, the company was given a no doubt welcome change from the usual simple fare served on that day.

Christmas day fell on a Saturday in 1490, and, although it was a major feast, does not not seem to have attracted a lot of attention. The warden was not present; only one guest was at the fellows' table although six ate with the servants. At a cost of 17s 2½d the steward served necks, beef, mutton, piglets, pork, chicken, chestnuts, birds (aves), rabbit, veal, suet, eggs, wine and spices. An apparent reference to 'boar' has no cost associated with it. Shortly afterwards, Christ's Circumcision, a lesser feast, was celebrated on 1 January, a Saturday. The warden was not present, but four guests ate with the fellows and six with the servants. A fish meal was provided for 10s 3½d and consisted of salt fish, eels, fresh salmon, haddock, 'albicus', 'thornebak' – perhaps some small river fish, eggs, spices and herrings. A few days later, the major feast of the Epiphany on Thursday 6 January again found the warden absent but with four guests at the fellows' table and four eating with the servants. The company ate boar, necks, mutton, veal, beef, larks, 'currus', rabbit, pork, piglets, calf's feet, suet, eggs, eels, salt fish, roach, wine and spices at a cost of 11s 11½d. The references to the serving of 'boar' here and earlier is presumably an indication of the ceremonial presentation of the boar's head, a popular tradition in England at certain feasts.

On 2 February and on 25 March followed the two Marian celebrations of the Purification and the Annunciation. For the first, a minor feast, which fell on a Wednesday, the warden was provided with boar, beef, rabbit, marrow bones, piglets, calf's feet, wine and spices, capons, lamb, 'currys', larks, 'quaccum', eggs, duck, salt fish, haddock, salmon, eels, shellfish (conchys), butter and flour costing 11s 3½d, and with wine purchased for 1s 7d. Six guests ate with the fellows and nine with the servants. The steward purchased boar, necks, pork, beef, mutton, rabbit, veal, marrow bones, piglets, cockerels, sausages (sawsegges), calf's feet, wine and spices, and spent 13s 1d. For the second, a major feast which was celebrated on Friday and so was a fish day, the warden was absent; four guests ate with the fellows and four with the servants. At a cost of 11s 11½d the steward provided salt fish, salt eels, red herrings, pike, fresh eels, stock fish, oil, salmon, almonds, honey, spices and mustard.

At the feast of the Annunciation or on the Friday nearest to it the third bursar took over his duties, as the church began the commemoration of the Passion, Easter and the Resurrection. With the loss of his stewards' accounts for 1491, we must depend on those surviving from the same period for another year, 1497. In his first week of this year, the third bursar's steward of hall was required to provide for four feasts: the greater feast of the Annunciation, the lesser feast of the eve of Easter, the greater feast of Easter day itself and the greater feast celebrated on the third day – *tercia feria* – of Easter. The warden does not seem to have been present at any of these celebrations. Although the particular steward's account records details of all four feasts, it is probable that the fellows benefited from three occasions only since, in 1497, the feast of the Annunciation fell on the same day as the eve of Easter. Certainly, the daily expenditure of the steward for that week would indicate that three days only attracted abnormal expenditure. The eve of Easter and the Annunciation fell on Saturday 25 March 1497. The steward notes for the Annunciation feast the payment of 3s for two dishes for the subwarden, three chaplains and two guests at the fellows' table, 4s for a second dish for sixteen fellows, 1s 9d for two dishes for six guests at the servants' table and 10½d for a second dish for seven servants. In addition a collation was provided for the warden's servants and the usual minor payments were made to the laundress and postmasters. For the Easter vigils, three guests ate with the fellows and six with the servants. On this fish day, the steward purchased salt fish, fresh salmon, 'albicus', pike, eels, oil, almonds, and sugar, with two items that cannot be read, at a cost of 11s 10½d. Perhaps two substantial meals were provided on this day, but the amount spent for what was both a major and a minor feast was not much greater than the expenditure for Easter day, a major feast.

On Easter day, three guests ate with the fellows and seven with the servants. The steward provided necks, beef, mutton, veal, lamb, capons, spices, sugar and raisins costing 10s 7½d. On the third day, four guests dined with the fellows and seven with the servants. They ate necks, beef, veal, lamb, capons, mutton, eggs, butter, spices, marrow bones and sugar at a cost of 12s 3d. At the foot of his detailed list of the attendance of the four celebrations, the steward records also an expenditure of 3s 6½d in wine. There is no indication of whether this was for drinking or for cooking, but the considerable expense would suggest that during this special week of the church's year, wine could have been provided with the meals.

For the major feast of the Ascension on Thursday 4 May with the warden again absent, three guests joined the fellows and six the servants. They were provided with frumenty, 'quaccum', beef, mutton, veal, goose, lamb, small birds, marrow bones, spices, sugar, eggs and butter costing 12s 11¼d. Shortly afterwards, on Sunday 14 May followed Pentecost, another major feast. The warden was not present. Four guests ate with the fellows and five with the servants. The steward lists for this feast frumenty, 'quaccum', beef, mutton, chicken, lamb, goose, marrow bones, eggs, butter, spices and sugar for which he paid 12s 1½d. During the next week, the two minor feasts of the Trinity, on Sunday 21 May, and of Corpus Christi, on Thursday 25 May, were celebrated. The warden was absent from both. At the first, the fellows entertained two guests and the servants five. They were given frumenty, beef, mutton, lamb, goose, small birds, chicken, mustard and flour costing 8s 5½d, which is exactly the same amount as the steward recorded as spent on extra dishes and allowances for this day. At the second, three guests ate at the fellows' table and five with the servants. They were offered frumenty, mutton, lamb, marrow bones, eggs, mustard and spices, with several indecipherable items, costing 10s 10d. The academic year ended with the major feast of St John on Saturday 24 June and the minor feast of St Peter on Thursday 29 June. The record of the first celebration is damaged so that the attendance of the warden cannot be ascertained; he was present at the St Peter's day feast. On 24 June, seven guests dined with the fellows and four with the servants. The steward served eels, salt fish, scallops, pike, crayfish, pulses, chub and spices costing 14s 9d. He also noted the provision of wine for 5s 2d, presumably to be drunk with the meal. On St Peter's day nine guests ate at the fellows' table and six with the servants. They were provided with frumenty, 'quaccum', mutton, goose, veal, lamb, marrow bones, chicken, eggs, spices, sugar and mustard for 11s 8½d. Below the two notes of expenditure on extra dishes for these feasts is a list of 'sowcark' which cost £1 1s 10d. The items given are most varied, including fish, meat, fruits and other foods: frumenty, 'quaccum', capons, perch, crayfish, plaice (schuler), goose, quails, peacock, duck, spices, 'stynkoks', rabbit, pike, cherries, strawberries, beef, marrow bones, mutton, veal, lamb, eggs, sugar, butter, wine and flour.

Six feast days occurred during each of the terms of office of the first and second bursars and the remaining nine in that of the third bursar. At this stage of our investigation, with only a small proportion of the stewards' accounts transcribed, it is not possible to indicate exactly how the feasting at Merton was financed, what exactly was the relationship between the amounts recorded by the steward as allowances for extra dishes, those to the warden's household, guests and others and the amount noted as spent on the day itself. The role played by the special allowance of 'sowcark' to the warden also remains unclear. When a detailed analysis of all surviving Tudor steward's accounts is completed, we may be in a better position to understand what are at present often only a series of unrelated figures of expenditure.

The particular feasts days discussed above must also be seen in the wider context of college activities throughout the year. Other convivial occasions at Merton included the famous celebration of the election of the 'King of the Beans', so often noted in the college register. The fellow who was chosen for this post was expected to entertain the company; the election usually took place on 19 November. Also a further convivial gathering for the fellows could be expected when the *Ignis regencium* was held; apparently here the senior regent was expected to make some provision of food and drink for his colleagues. Individual masters occasionally provided hospitality for members of the college, usually in the form of refreshments around the hall fire – hence the title 'ignis' for such celebrations.[6] Also, benefactors sometimes instructed their executors to provide special food and wine to the company, usually after fellows had attended particular services in the college chapel held as trentals or obits to commemorate the deceased person. Some benefits to the fellows were small: beer and wine provided by the new warden, FitzJames, in 1483, or the wine given to the warden and fellows 'secundum antiquam consuetudinem' by inceptors.[7] Others were more considerable: Thomas Pash, a former fellow, provided an 'appietancia' worth 17s 5d, a notable amount, probably on his death, for the second bursar spent this 'de pecuniis magistri Passh' in 1489–90.[8] However, such advantages were usually only of temporary duration or did not impose a permanent charge on the college. The feast days that we have already recorded were those that fellows could expect regularly as a benefit from their membership of the college society.

The stewards' records of their expenditure and purchases, even before they have all been fully examined, tell us more of the character of these feast days. It would appear that sometimes expenditure was held back or brought forward so that it could then be associated with a particular feast day. For instance in 1490 on the day following the feast of St Nicholas the steward records only the purchase of liquorice for ½d; on the day before the feast of the Epiphany the steward purchased only pork for 1s 10d. Again, on the day before the feast of the Purification liquorice at ½d was purchased and also on the day before the feast of the Annunciation. There is clearly no need to assume that all the food purchased on any feast day was necessarily eaten on that day, or that no produce purchased earlier was used on such days. Items such as spices, cheese, flour and such like that would keep for some time were probably purchased in bulk and used as required.

The stewards' accounts are records of purchase and expenditure. They tell us nothing of the social consequences of the celebration of

6 Ibid., pp. xviii–xxi.
7 Ibid., pp. 12, 178.
8 Merton College Record (MCR) 3806B.

feast days at Merton. It does seem that occasionally the celebrations may have degenerated to produce unseemly behaviour. In December 1484 certain fellows were accused of celebrating 'immoderate or indiscrete vigils' on evenings of recreation to the annoyance of those performing ecclesiastical offices in the chapel; shortly afterwards, in January, junior fellows were blamed for too much noise 'in noctibus solemnibus'.[9] William Ireland, in February 1500, had apparently celebrated the vigils of the Purification too well for he roused the fellows and chaplain with his noise, his banging on their doors and his indecent singing; some fellows tried to take their meals on feast days elsewhere than in the college hall.[10] The register also contains many references to fellows prolonging their drinking sessions – *biberia* – and the consequent disorders that arose from this. We are probably seeing here some of the results of the difficulties of limiting the tendency of young men in their early twenties to take what enjoyment they could in a somewhat sober and restrictive environment.

Another disadvantage of the method of presenting the daily purchases followed by the Merton stewards is that we are unable to allocate any particular purchases to any particular meal. In fact, the whole question of meals and meal times at the college is especially vague. It has been suggested[11] that Merton provided four meals each day, an early 'biberium', a meal around lunchtime (prandium), an early evening meal (cena) and a late 'biberium'. The earliest and latest meals were probably taken in the buttery as light repasts. How the various items purchased on feast days were distributed, we cannot say. Perhaps two good meals were provided on such days, but there is a possibility that the extra allowance could have been used for only one of the two meals. As usual, when we attempt to go beyond the general records to trace the details of the daily life of the medieval university and its students, we find little concrete evidence to guide our investigations.

Merton was, of course, not alone amongst the Oxford colleges in celebrating festive occasions with special allowances for an improvement in the provision of food and drink. How individual colleges commemorated these anniversaries and the extent of their expenditure were dictated by the size and wealth of the particular society. Feasting at Lincoln College, for example, seems to have been on a much less lavish scale, limited by its relatively poor endowments and small company maintained in the early years. Here feasting took the form usually of the purchase of extra supplies for the society from

9 Salter, *Registrum Annalium 1483–1521*, pp. 56, 58.
10 Ibid., pp. 239, 304.
11 Ibid., pp. xxxiv–xxxv.

increased commons allowed to the fellows. Also, at certain dates, gifts of food and drink from college tenants were required by the leasing arrangements and these helped to add variety to the fellows' diet. Certain payments to which the college was entitled were also spent on food; a quit-rent paid by Queen's College provided oysters in Lent in the sixteenth century.[12] Queen's itself was allowed by its statutes to add an extra, third, course with wine to those normally provided for its fellows on the five feast days of Christmas, Easter, Whitsuntide, the Assumption and All Saints' Day. Later benefactors added extra provision on other feast days; John Pereson, a former provost, for example, left money for a second course for the fellows on the festival of the Epiphany.[13] For the monastic institution of Canterbury College at Oxford, there was a series of celebrations for the monks at Christmas, Shrovetide, Easter, Pentecost and perhaps Michaelmas. Of more interest to us is the appearance, as at Merton, of special feast days of particular importance to this community: 7 July, the Translation of St Thomas and 29 December, the date of his martyrdom, together with 21 March, the feast of St Benedict. On all these days either a supplement was made to the commons granted to individual members of the college or the warden made a payment 'pro gaudiis'.[14] These are just a few examples from the published records of the Tudor Oxford colleges. Feasts were also organised in the colleges at Cambridge. We have, for example, the grants, each of 6s 8d, to increase the commons of the members of Trinity Hall on the days when their obit was celebrated from two fifteenth century masters Simon and William Dalling.[15] Such a supplement was a valuable asset to the scholars of what was a smaller college than Merton.

The custom, therefore, of celebrating important festivals of the church and dates particularly cherished by some colleges with a feast was not confined to Merton. By the early Tudor period, any statutory provision made by founders to increase commons on certain days had been expanded by the generosity of individual benefactors who bequeathed property, the income from which was often partly to be used to enable the community to dine more lavishly on named dates. However, such evidence from both English universities gives usually only details of how feasting was financed. Only rarely are we able to say

12 These arrangements are outlined in V.H.H.Green, *The Commonwealth of Lincoln College, 1427–1977*, Oxford, 1979, ch. v.

13 J.R.Magrath, *The Queen's College*, (Oxford, 1921), i.55; J.R.Magrath, *Liber Obituarius Aulae Reginae in Oxonia*, (Oxford, 1910), p.73.

14 W.A.Pantin, *Canterbury College Oxford*, ii. (Oxford: OHS, 1947), 169, iv. (Oxford: OHS, 1985), 112, 115.

15 A.W.W.Dale, ed., *Warren's Book*, (Cambridge, 1911), pp.230, 232.

how this money was spent and how the types of food eaten differed from those normally presented. In this respect, the Merton evidence is of great interest. Not only can the scale of expenditure on any special day be compared with that on another normal day, but both menus themselves can often be examined. Such material enables us to see more clearly what significance such feast days held for those participating.

Certain college members also celebrated at other times with more and different food and drink. By the beginning of the Tudor period, the practice at Merton of holding regular 'chapters' to examine the behaviour of the warden, the condition of the college estates and the possibility of electing new fellows had become formalised. At some time during this chapter meeting the college provided a special meal or meals. No mention of such feasting is made in either the college statutes or the college register. The unpublished bursars' accounts, however, contain occasional references sometimes under a separate heading to expenditure in connection with this feasting: *Liberata in tempore capituli*. We are not assisted in tracing the exact nature of this feasting by apparently contradictory wording in these accounts. The bursars' expenses are entitled 'pro iantaculo capitulari' or 'pro prandio capitulari'; the evidence discussed below, however, seems to indicate that at least one full meal rather than a breakfast, if the word 'iantaculum' did retain this meaning, was provided. We have, then, the amount of money expended on chapter feasting by certain bursars. Happily, there survive a few full lists of purchases for these occasions so that we are able to fill out the details of some of these special feasts. We do not know where and when the food was taken, but it may be significant that it was the bursar and not the steward of hall who kept this account. Some light may be thrown on this problem if a steward's account for the week in which a chapter feast was held is found at Merton. It should then be possible to examine the expenditure on food of that day by the steward to learn if the chapter meal supplemented or replaced that normally taken by the fellows involved. At present we have no such material available. It would seem strange, however, if those participating in the chapter meeting took this special food in addition to that served in hall on that day.

To turn now to an examination of the bursars' lists of items purchased for the chapter feasting, we may here restrict ourselves to a discussion of the six documents that survive for the reign of Henry VII. In considering these details, we have the advantage of knowing that the food and drink obtained was intended to serve nine fellows or ten, if the warden participated in the meal. The bursars' lists also give separate expenditure on beer and bread for the chapter feast, so we are now able to give some estimate of the costs of those basic items for every fellow. If we keep in mind that fellows at Merton were each allocated commons of

1s per week, although this figure was usually exceeded and could be raised in time of scarcity, we shall have some conception of the value of this allowance at the chapter feast to the participants.

Chapters could be held at any time of the year. The arrangement of any particular meeting presumably depended on whether the fellows thought it necessary to discuss then the state of the manors or the need to elect new members. For the chapter meeting of 1 June 1489, the third bursar spent 9s 6½d on general food items with 7½d on bread and 8d on beer.[16] He purchased milk, beef, mutton, veal, goose, piglets, lamb, capons, rabbit, marrow bones, vinegar, flour and spices; he also spent 6d on fuel. For the following year, for the chapter feast of 22 February, one total for all purchases including bread and beer was recorded.[17] The second bursar then spent 10s 7½d on general food items, 6½d on bread and 7d on beer. He purchased beef, veal, piglets, capons, cocks, chestnuts, marrow bones, calf's feet, flour, lamb, eggs, pears, butter, milk and 'quaccum', lard and spices. On 18 August 1497,[18] a Friday, so requiring the bursar to serve a chapter feast without meat, the members at the meeting ate bread costing 10d and beer costing 1s 2d. Their food was purchased for 9s 11d: salt fish, conger eel, butter, pike, chub, roach, perch, crab, crayfish, tench, eels, spices, sugar and mustard.

The next account takes us into the sixteenth century with the list of expenditure of the second bursar for the chapter feast of 21 January 1501.[19] Bread costing 1s 6d and beer 1s 4d was provided. A varied menu was, on this occasion, presented by the bursar for 18s 9½d; wine, boar, beef, mutton, veal, pork, capons, cockerels, lamb, rabbit, chestnuts, partridges, larks, marrow bones, milk and 'quaccum', flour, lard, eggs, butter, calf's feet, wine for the kitchen, mustard, spices (in aromatibus), cheese and salt. In this total were included also payments of 1s 6d for faggots and fuel (in fassiculis, in focalibus). We have also an account for the chapter meal for the following year. This accompanied the meeting of 20 January.[20] Bread cost 7d and beer 8d. For the feast mutton, veal, five cockerels, six 'curr', suet, necks, pork, raisins, spices, sugar and flour were provided for an expenditure of 6s 6d. Three, presumably bundles of, faggots were needed and these together with fuel (in carbonibus) cost 9½d.

Finally, for the reign of Henry VII, we have the list of purchases for the chapter feast of 11 July 1504.[21] Milk and 'quaccum', beef, mutton,

---

16 Salter, *Registrum Annalium 1483–1521*, p. 120; MCR 3807.
17 Salter, *Registrum Annalium 1483–1521*, p. 129; MCR 3806B.
18 Salter, *Registrum Annalium 1483–1521*, p. 212; MCR 3811.
19 Salter, *Registrum Annalium 1483–1521*, p. 250; MCR 3842.
20 Salter, *Registrum Annalium 1483–1521*, p. 260; MCR 3813.
21 Salter, *Registrum Annalium 1483–1521*, pp. 291–2; MCR 3816.

veal, goose, lamb, piglets, capons, marrow bones, suet, eggs, butter, sugar, pepper, raisins, currants, prunes, dates, cloves, saffron, almonds, sweet wine (bastard), flour and cheese were obtained at a cost of 15s 1d; bread was purchased for 1s, beer for 1s 4d and faggots for 3d. Here, the interesting details of the procurement of the various accompaniments to the meats gives us some indication of what exactly was prepared for the feast. It would seem that some type of dessert was served in addition to the meat and poultry dishes.

The survival of these details of feasts prepared for a limited number of fellows enables us to analyse more closely the nature of the celebrations at Merton. Most surprising is the lack of consistency in these records of the chapter feasts. The bursars spent at the least 6s 6d on food and at the most 17s 3½d. We can offer no explanation, at the moment, for this variation. Nor does there seem any correspondence between the cost of the general food items supplied and the cost of the bread and beer that accompanied them. When, in February 1490, the bursar spent 10s 7½d on food, he also spent 6½d on bread and 7d on beer. In January 1502, the bursar spent only 6s 6d on food but 7d on bread and 8d on beer. Nor are the seasonal factors the reason for these different feast provisions; the two payments for the January chapters that we have are of 17s 3½d for food – the highest of the surviving records – and of 6s 6d – the lowest. The variations may be the result of temporary high or low prices in the local markets, but we have, at present, no further evidence to confirm or disprove this. The items of food purchased do not present any problems except that some lists do show a surprisingly high expenditure on spices, 2s 4½d, 3s 1d and 2s 9d and others a surprisingly low outlay, 4½d (with sugar) and 2d. It is difficult to account for these divergencies unless the bursars were, when small purchases were recorded, using mainly items they held already in stock. We have only one occasion when the purchase of wine for drinking as distinct from its use for culinary purposes is recorded. The amounts spent on the chapter meals compare very favourably with those spent on the provisions for the much larger company that ate in hall on the greater or lesser feast days which we have already examined in detail.

One of the most important events in the financial year of any well regulated institution was the general audit of its accounts. Oxford and Cambridge colleges were required to present their records for examination at various times of the year to particular auditors as determined by their statutes.[22] It soon became usual for the audit to be accompanied

22 For a discussion of the practices of some Cambridge colleges and the unusual situation at the King's Hall, see A. B. Cobban, *The King's Hall within the University of Cambridge in the later Middle Ages*, (Cambridge, 1969), p. 162.

by some kind of special celebration, usually involving the provision of food and drink. By the early Tudor period, the somewhat spartan allowances had been expanded so that the community, or that part of it involved in the audit, could expect some kind of feast at this time. The society of Lincoln College, Oxford, for example, had increased its original consumption of wine, fruit and cakes on audit day, 22 December, so that by the 1540s it was eating a special breakfast, a large dinner and supper with wine; this was taken in the rector's chamber.[23]

The audit in July at the end of the Merton year was an important occasion. It was, as usual, accompanied also by the provision of feasting for those involved. The third bursars' accounts, which survive, note the special expenditure on this feasting as *Liberata pro communiis tempore compoti*. From these accounts we are able to list their amounts during the reign of Henry VII:

1488	£6 3s
1489	£5 14s 11½d
1490	£6 12s 5d
1497	£8 14s
1502	£9 7s 0¼d
1504	£5 8s 2½d
1506	£3 11s 10d
1508	£7 1s 3½d
1509	£7 6s 7d

The audit procedure, as other records and also the surviving details of the particular expenditure show, lasted for two weeks so that each of these payments is for meals for fourteen days. References also in the accounts of the third bursars indicate that the auditors met, as least for meals, in the warden's lodgings, for the record of the expenditure for the two weeks' commons is noted as being 'in domo domini custodis'. Who was eligible to attend the annual audit and so benefit from the feasting is not clear. The five senior fellows appointed as auditors must have been present, but the subwarden and the three bursars were also apparently entitled to attend since the election of July 1486 notes that they have the right to be there: 'de iure statuti habent interesse'. Presumably the warden, when in residence, also attended such an important occasion, especially as it was associated with his lodgings. Whether any of the 'farmers' dined with the auditors as they presented their accounts, we cannot at the moment determine. Fortunately, we are able to go beyond the simple figures of the two weeks' cost given by the

23 *The Commonwealth of Lincoln College*, pp. 110–11.

bursars to look at the details of expenditure on food and drink each day. This may assist us to establish how the different aspects of these payments compare with those for the feast days and other normal days in the college year. We should then be able perhaps to indicate the number of people involved in the audit procedure and its accompanying festivities.

Of the nine accounts of the third bursars which, as noted above, give details of the expenditure on the audit feasting, seven provide also examples of the detailed cost of the food and drink provided; the records of 1497 and 1506 only are without these particulars. These seven documents, usually appended to the bursars' accounts, provide details for each week of the amounts spent on 'the kitchen' – *summa coquine*, on bread, on beer and, sometimes, on fuel – *pro focalibus*. They are as follows:

	KITCHEN			BREAD		BEER		FUEL	
1488(1)	£1	18s	11½d	8s	6d	8s	2d	2s	8d
(2)	£2	10s	7½d[24]	5s	11d	8s	2	–	
1489(1)	£2	0s	2½d	6s	2½d	8s	4d	–	
(2)	£2	9s	1½d[25]	5s	1d	6s		–	
1490(1)	£2	11s	2d[26]	6s	6d	8s		–	
(2)[27]									
1502(1)	£3	9s	8½d[28]	10s	3d	12s	5d	–	
(2)	£3	0s	1d[29]	11s	10½d	13s	5d	6s	4d[30]
1504(1)	£3	12s	6d[31]	15s		16s	2d	–	
(2)	£3	19s	11½d[32]	14s	1d	14s	2d	–	

24 This total includes an amount spent on fuel: Sunday 3½d, Thursday 2d, a total, therefore, of 5½d, giving a payment for the two weeks of 3s 1½d.

25 This total includes an amount of 3s 1d spent on Friday partly on fuel, presumably the expenditure for the two weeks.

26 This total includes an expenditure of 8d 'in carbonibus' on Friday, presumably the cost of fuel for the week.

27 The account is damaged and the totals of the second week and much of the expenditure for certain days have been lost.

28 To this total must be added 1s 4¾d for the purchase of salt, flour, candles and cheese. The total includes 11d spent 'in fascibus': 3d Sunday, 2d Monday, 3d Wednesday, and 3d Thursday.

29 To this total must be added 1s 6½d for the purchase of cheese, salt, flour and candles. The total includes 9d spent 'in, fascibus': 2d Monday, 1d Wednesday, 2d Thursday and 2d Friday.

30 4s 'in carbonibus' and 2s 4d 'in focalibus', presumably the total for both weeks.

31 These totals include payments of 6½d 'in fasciculis' 2d Sunday, 1d Monday, 1½d Wednesday and 2d Thursday, and a payment on Friday 'in carbonibus' of 2s 8d

32 This total includes payments of 7½d 'in fasciculis' 2½d Sunday, 1d Monday, 1d Tuesday and 3d Thursday, and a payment on Friday 'in carbonibus' of 2s 8d.

1508(1)	£2 0s 11d	9s 6d	13s 8d	–
(2)	£2 17s 9½d	9s 9d	9s 8d	–
1509(1)	£1 17s 10d	5s 7½d	11s 8d	–
(2)	£3 13s 3½d	6s 10d	11s 4d	–

If these figures are adjusted to take into account the various anomalies to which attention is drawn in our annotations, we have the following details of expenditure in the six accounts, excluding the one damaged document, on the three important items, the kitchen, bread and beer.

	KITCHEN	BREAD	BEER
1488	£4 9s 1½d	14s 5d	16s 4d
1489	£4 6s 3d	11s 3½d	14s 4d
1502	£6 11s 0¾d	£1 2s 1½d	£1 5s 10d
1504	£7 5s 11½d	£1 9s 1d	£1 10s 4d
1508	£4 18s 8½d	19s 3d	£1 3s 4d
1509	£5 11s 1½d	12s 5½d	£1 3s 0d

Since we are unable to say exactly who was present at these audit feasts and how far the attendance in different years rose or declined, we cannot attempt any detailed analysis or comparative study of these figures. However, it will be interesting to give some of the amounts spent at a similar period at the weekly meals for the fellows, guests, workmen, servants and others in the college hall, where they can be discovered. The stewards responsible to the third bursar in 1488, for example, spent on kitchen expenses for the two final weeks of their terms of office £1 12s 4d when there were twelve fellows in residence each week. For the preceding two weeks they had spent £2 11s 11d when there were twenty and twenty-one fellows in residence; no feast days occurred during these four weeks to distort the rate of expenditure. For the two weeks of audit feasting at about the same date, the bursar spent £4 6s 5½d in kitchen expenses. Toward the end of the century, in 1498, the stewards acting for the third bursar spent in the first three weeks of his period of office £1 9s 2¾d with twenty-one fellows in residence, £1 3s 6d for nineteen fellows and £1 3s 8d for twenty-two fellows. In 1502 the bursar spent £6 11s 0¾d for the two weeks of audit feasting. Clearly, without adducing further comparative examples, it is apparent that a considerable gulf divided the special audit expenditure on food from that made normally on behalf of the fellows and others eating in hall. As would be expected, the cost of beer and bread supplied at the audit feasts seems very roughly related to the expenses of the kitchen.

54

In general, our figures for the expenditure on the audit feasts suggest that either a considerable number of fellows, guests and officials were regularly entertained, or that more expensive food was provided, or that a combination of both factors explains the relatively high expenditure at this time.

We are able to carry this discussion further by an examination of some of the details of purchases for the audit feasting. The earlier limitations we have noted, the absence from these lists of items obtained without cost, still apply here, but the more unusual and more expensive food and drink supplied is certainly likely to be recorded here. Space does not allow us to consider every surviving menu for the audit in detail. That of 1504 is undamaged and so gives us full menus for each of the fourteen days of the audit. On Saturday of the first week we see the purchase of milk, salt fish, stock fish, pike, eels, roach, perch, fresh salmon, conger-eel, scallops (in pectinibus), crayfish, eggs and butter, tench, chevin and spices; on Sunday frumenty, beef, mutton, veal, goose, capons, rabbit, small birds, flour and spices; on Monday beef, mutton, veal, rabbit, flour, milk and spices; on Tuesday beef, mutton, veal, lamb, chicken, small birds, rabbit and spices; on Wednesday beef, mutton, beef's tongue, veal, lamb, young heron, chicken, rabbit, flour and spices; on Thursday beef, mutton, veal, lamb, capons, young heron, chicken, rabbit, flour, butter and spices; on Friday oysters, salt fish, pike, scallops, chub, chevin, eels, perch, sole, crayfish, peas, mustard and vinegar, spices, cheese, salt and flour. For the second week was provided on Saturday milk, green fish, pike, chub, chevin, perch, scallops, crayfish, eggs, butter, peas, tench, stock fish, eels and spices; on Sunday frumenty, beef, mutton, veal, capons, rabbit, small birds, piglets, 'quaccum', mustard and spices; on Monday beef, mutton, veal, capon, rabbit, small birds, mustard and spices; on Tuesday beef, mutton, veal, capons, rabbit, duck, chicken, small birds, mustard and spices; on Wednesday peas, salt fish, green fish, pike, chevin, chub and roach, eels, stock fish, perch, tench, gudgeon, butter, eggs, and spices; on Thursday beef, mutton, veal, lamb, capons, rabbit, young heron, chicken, suet, small birds, flour, sweet wine, almonds and spices; on Friday oysters, salt fish, pike, chevin, perch, eels, salt, tench, crayfish, mustard and verjuice, spices, cheese and flour.

Clearly the amount and variety of food provided at these audit feasts was far superior to that regularly eaten in the college hall on normal days. If 'farmers' and other estate officials were present during the audit, it was important that they should be properly entertained and should leave with a good impression of the college. We must not take each day's expenditure as indicating that all food obtained was necessarily eaten on that one day; the purchase of cheese on one day, for example, probably records a bulk purchase which was consumed throughout the period of the audit. The holding of the audit during the months of the summer must have eased the bursar's task in obtaining a variety of supplies. Some accounts mention the purchase of strawberries and cherries. Most striking is the appearance of unusual dishes, such as young heron, which were certainly not seen by the fellows eating in hall. Fish days also present a much greater variety of provision than we normally find. The absence of wine as a regular drink is also noticeable. Where we have mention of various types of wine in these audit accounts, the small amounts spent suggest that this was purchased for use by the cooks rather than for drinking with the meal. However, the occasional use of sweet wine, bastard, often noted in conjunction with ingredients such as flour and almonds, indicates that a drink with some kind of dessert was sometimes offered.

From this short discussion on feasting at Merton College in the early Tudor period some general conclusions may be drawn. First, the fellows and their guests could expect each year a more generous supply of food and drink on some occasions, reasonably scattered throughout the year. Such provision probably reflects the long-established character of the college with its relatively rich endowments. The chapter feasting and the audit meals represented special occasions on which the senior fellows especially could expect to benefit from a much more ample and varied menu. Oxford colleges were, of course, limited by their environment as to what their cooks could produce, but, accepting this restriction, at Merton the full resources of the area, its fields, rivers and streams were fully utilised. If we add to the lists of fish and meat provided, the flesh of the swans kept by the college and the occasional piece of venison and other fishes or meats presented by well-wishers, the college regularly feasted in some style.

What makes the Merton material so unusual, perhaps unique, is, as we have noted, the itemising of commodities for a single day's consumption, even allowing for the possibility that certain purchases, like cheese, were carried over to a subsequent day. When we look at evidence from other institutions, it becomes clear that such accounting procedures were not followed elsewhere. Nevertheless a necessarily very cursory consideration of some of these sources can throw some light on the Merton accounts. What survives is chiefly from three areas: monastic records, household accounts and borough records.

The mid-thirteenth century account book of Beaulieu Abbey[33] seems to have been drawn up as a guide line for subsequent accounting.

33 S. F. Hockey, ed., *The Account Book of Beaulieu Abbey*, Camden Soc. (London, 1975).

Expenditure on food and drink is given under a variety of headings, distinguished both by the nature of the produce (bread, beer, spices) or by the recipients (refectory, infirmary or guest house). There is, however, no indication here of when individual foodstuffs were eaten. But in the account headed 'Refectorium', the writer indicates when the refectory was expected to provide not only for the monks but also for the lay brothers (*Qualiter et quando conversi grangiarum veniunt ad abbaciam*). There follows a list of some twenty-five days from the feast of the Circumcision to the Exaltation of the Cross, most of which are familiar from the Merton accounts. On these days and all Sundays the lay community and the monks dined together. Clearly dining was closely associated with the religious celebrations that preceded. Again there is no indication that the diet varied on such occasions; perhaps the very presence of guests served to make the occasion different.

Under the heading 'Tabula hospicii' are outlined the annual expenses in the guest-house. Once more the accountant gives a general outline of procedures, specifying when individual items might be provided for guests or visitors. Here all the items could be produced from the cellars and again there is no indication that the provision of wine, for example, accompanied an unusually lavish supply of food, though this seems likely. What we see at Beaulieu is an institution regulating its pattern of dining according to a fixed ecclesiastical calendar but the question of the variation of diet is not one which the account book can answer.

It would be useful to find evidence from an institution nearer to that of Merton, both geographically and chronologically. The account rolls from the Benedictine monastery at Abingdon,[34] surviving from the early fourteenth century to the late fifteenth may be an appropriate source of comparison. The impact of feasts, both ecclesiastical and culinary, upon the Abingdon community was considerable, though again it is difficult to link foodstuffs, which are listed in some detail, to specific occasions. The Kitchener's Account of the 1370s lists the purchase of food in two sections, the second of which is devoted to spices and desserts. Comparing the lists with the Merton evidence, we may imagine that figs, raisins, almonds and the like were not part of the day to day diet but were used on feast days. However a reference elsewhere to 103s 'in expensis autompnalibus', that is, to the autumn feasts, suggests considerable expenditure on these occasions without detailed itemising of purchases. Was the monastery attempting to use perishables before they were ruined by the onset of winter? The cooks received a payment of 7s 4d 'pro festis principalibus', perhaps to reward their

34 R.E.G. Kirk, ed., *Accounts of the Obedientiaries of Abingdon Abbey*, Camden Soc., (London, 1892).

extra efforts on such days. The kitchener himself and his assistant received 3s for the feast of St Thomas. In addition to the general reference to the autumn celebrations, a number of other named days are associated with additional expenditure, including the feasts of St Martin, St Paul and All Saints. That such references appear in the Kitchener's Account suggests that they may be associated with food and drink.

The Chamberlain's Account of 1417–18 gives some indication of the situation in the Convent. Here on named feast days (Nativity of the Virgin, St Michael, St Thomas, St John the Baptist and the Annunciation) payments 'pro speciebus' are recorded for the abbot and various other senior members. We may here be dealing with an allocation for feasting transmuted into a simple monetary gratuity. Monastic and college accounts often conceal this distinction.

Evidence of feasting at noble houses needs to be divided into, first, regular annual occasions at which the Lord entertained and, second, extraordinary visits, perhaps from royalty, at which elaborate banquets had to be prepared speedily. Three times of the year seem to be associated with feasting in the Tudor nobleman's house: Christmas, Easter and Whitsuntide.[35] On such occasions extra dishes had to be hired – there is evidence of this also at Merton – and more food purchased, the cellars being unable to provide for such additional consumption. Household and borough accounts contain frequent references to gifts of food, normally unusual items such as dessert, fruits or game, to the nobility. It is likely that such presents were often made to an individual or institution about to prepare a lavish feast. Clearly there would be little point presenting to a large institution one swan or deer. The gift must be associated with other similar presents or purchases. Funeral feasts or the entertainment of royalty are occasions particularly associated with such gifts. The events of course would be widely known and some assistance from neighbouring estates expected.

Borough records suggest a similar arrangement. The Mayors' Accounts at Leicester[36] record gifts of wine, capons and other unusual items to the Earl, frequently associated with specific feasts like Candlemas or St Valentine's day. In addition the mayor was able to provide for entertainment on a considerable scale if circumstances demanded. On the visit of the King's Marshall in July 1317 four days feasting was funded, with the purchase of geese, salmon, strawberries, saffron and the like. Again staff associated with the event frequently received a gratuity.

---

35 T. Percy, ed., *The Regulations and Establishment of the Household of Henry Algernon Percy, 5th Earl of Northumberland* (London, 1827).

36 M. Bateson, ed., *Records of the Borough of Leicester 1103–1327* (London, 1899).

The considerable detail of the Merton records, therefore, greatly extends the evidence that can be drawn from such essentially financial accounts. Even at the present state of investigation of these documents, we are able to look beyond the simple expenditure of officials and understand something of the exploitation of local resources by stewards and cooks. Feasting at Merton had its religious, social and economic aspects as well as providing some welcome relief to the company.

We must acknowledge with gratitude the financial support given to our research work by the British Academy, the Social Science Research Council, Merton College, Oxford, and the Department of Modern Languages of Aston University. Without the interest and help of our secretary, Mrs Françoise Bannister, the production of this piece would have been much retarded.

A Sixteenth-Century Library: the Francis Trigge Chained Library of St Wulfram's Church, Grantham

JOHN GLENN

1. *The Early History*

By a quadripartite indenture dated 20 October in the fortieth year of Elizabeth I (1598) Francis Trigge, rector of Welbourn in Lincolnshire, entered into agreement with the Alderman of Grantham, the two prebendaries of Salisbury Cathedral who held the Grantham livings, together with their two vicars, to endow a library for the use of the clergy and others dwelling in the Soke of Grantham. The library, set up in the room over the south porch of the church, is thus the first in England to be endowed under civic authority and outside an institution. An attached schedule of rules requires the two vicars and, for good measure, the master of the school,[1] to swear an oath before the Alderman that they will 'be true to the said library and not to imbesill or deface or consent to be imbesilled or defaced anie booke..' In return, each of them has a key; a fourth key is to be kept 'for ever in the custodie' of the Alderman.

The indenture was signed by Trigge, by William Barkesdale, one of the prebendaries – the other, Abraham Conham, did not sign and was presumably not present – and by the vicars Robert Bryan and Stephen Lodington. It was sealed and delivered 'per me Galfridum Bordman' in the presence of four named witnesses. There are slits for the seal tags. These are missing; but from the patches of better colour left on the otherwise rather grubby parchment one imagines that they were cut off fairly recently by some unscrupulous collector.

Both documents appear to have been put in the Borough archives and forgotten. There is no surviving reference to them until 1957, when they were found by C.P. Willard, the Borough Librarian. In response to a request from the late Neil Ker, who was collecting material for his book *The Parochial Libraries of the Church of England*,[2] Willard had the documents transcribed by Dorothy Owen of the Lincolnshire Archives Office.

---

1 Now the King's School, Grantham.
2 N. Ker, *The Parochial Libraries of the Church of England* (1959). The entry for Grantham is in two hundred words only and is now in need of amendment.

With them, also on parchment, was the consent, in Latin, of the Bishop of Lincoln, William Chaderton, to use the porch room as a library. This is dated 8 November 1599, more than a year after the original agreement. There is also one oath in the required form, dated 23 September 1611; but no earlier or later oaths have survived. This one, on paper, was sworn by the vicars Thomas Deane and Thomas Dillworthe, with Hugh Wilkinson, who was Master of Grantham School from 1605 to 1645. It is signed and witnessed by Ralph Clark, Alderman, and four burgesses.

Finally there is, on parchment, a *Catalogus Librorum* of February 1608 which lists the contents of the library at that date. Ker repeats a typing error in the Owen transcription which dates the list as 1609.

All four documents are now in the Lincolnshire Archives office,[3] although photographic reproductions are held in the church vestry. All material sent to Ker was deposited by him in the Bodleian.[4]

In the year 1606 Francis Trigge died, leaving thirteen named titles to the library. Most of these are grouped together in the 1608 *Catalogus*, a fact that suggests a possible arrangement of the library. His will was proved on 23 May 1601 and is also in the Archive Office.[5]

The five documents mentioned are the only primary sources extant for the first years of the library. The endowment is noted on the church Benefactions Board set up in 1661 and also in the entry for Trigge in Wood's *Athenae Oxoniensis*,[6] which quotes verses said to be on the library wall. They run

> Optima Franciscus donavit Biblia Triggus
> Welbourniae quondam concionator amans.
> Plurima permultis largitus munera sanctis,
> Thesaurum nobis condidit usque sacrum.
> Sic pie talis opus valuis, sic pignus amoris,
> Sic Christum coluit, sic docet esse pium.

Presumably *pie talis* should be *pietatis*. There is now no trace of these lines.

There is also an amusing entry in the Grantham Hall Book for 1642[7] which shows that the library was in use, although, perhaps significantly, only clerical users are mentioned. In that year Edward Skipworth or Skipwith gave fifty shillings 'to find a fire in the librarie'. It was given by him 'out of his love and well wishing to learning, the better to inable and

---

3 Ref: Grantham (St Wulfram) Parish. 23/ miscellaneous.
4 Ref: MS Eng. Misc. C. 360.
5 Lincoln Consistory Court Wills 1606, fo. 1252.
6 Anthony Wood, *Athenae Oxoniensis. An exact history of all the writers and bishops who have had their education in Oxford*, 1691, vol. I, p. 284.
7 Grantham Hall Book entry for 16 November 1642, f. 108v. (per W. A. Couth).

encourage the vicars of Grantham in the winter and colde tyme of the yeare to follow theire studdies'. The yearly interest of four shillings – eight per cent – is to be 'bestowed in some fitte and convenient firewood by the discretion of the churchwardens for the tyme being', and this is to be used in maintaining a fire in the library when 'either of them [the vicars] shall give note or require during the tyme of theire studdie'. The present writer, who worked in the library during the winter of 1986, tried without success to encourage the discretion of the churchwardens for the time being; but in the end had to thaw out at intervals in the *calorarium* amply maintained in his vestry by the Verger.

After Wood the library disappears from written record until the nineteenth century, although its existence is acknowledged by the addition of some books during the seventeenth century, notably the works of Henry More, the Cambridge philosopher who was a native of Grantham and a pupil of the school. These include More's account of the mechanics and optics of Descartes, which were later to be demolished so effectively by another old pupil of the same school, Isaac Newton. The More volumes are marked 'ex dono auctoris' in the hand of the parish clerk of the time. Two or three volumes were added in the eighteenth century, but no details are known.

2. *The Provenance of the Collection*

Because the books span the period from 1472–1600, their status as a sixteenth-century collection would be enhanced if we knew exactly how they were assembled. It would be fascinating to know that this was part of the private library of a provincial clergyman whose own publications make his theological leanings apparent. Before the documents were found and published it was always assumed by local writers in the nineteenth century that Trigge gave all or part of his own library, but this is nowhere confirmed.

Evidence on the assembly of the library can only be circumstantial. The relevant passages from the indenture and the schedule are as follows.

> i. ... the said Frauncis Trigge hath of late for the better increasing of learninge and knowledge in divinitie & other liberall sciences and learning by such of the cleargie & others as well beinge inhabitants in or near Grantham & the soke thereof as in other places in the said countie at his own charges and expenses endevored to have a lybrary erected in the said towne of Grantham & hath provided or intendeth to provide at his like costs for the furnishinge thereof bookes of divinity and other learninge to the value of one hundereth poundes or thereabouts...

ii. ...(Trigge) promiseth to the said Alderman & Burgesses & the said prebendaries & vicars and their successors that necessary places in the said library for the placing of the said bookes being prepared and made fit in all thynges at the costs and charges of the said Alderman and cleargie adioyninge to the said towne of Grantham or some of them, to furnish the same with these bookes hereafter named and with such other bookes as he shall please.

iii. Item that a dubble regester be made one to remaine in the Chapter Howse at Lincoln the other amonge the town recordes of Grantham wherein shalbe entered all the bookes bestowed and hereinafter to be beestowed in the said library...

I think the phrase 'hath provided or intendeth to provide' is only a legal formula, since Trigge is unlikely to have provided the books before signing the indenture. In any case the permission of the bishop for the proposed use of the room over the porch was not obtained till November 1599, and the preparation of this room at the costs and charges of the Alderman, which could hardly have been begun without permission, was a stipulated prerequisite.

Moreover, a donor intending to give all or part of his own collection would probably not choose the wording 'to provide at his like costs ... bookes ... to the value of one hundereth poundes or thereabouts'. Although Trigge undertakes to furnish the library 'with these bookes hereafter named' there is no list, as there probably would have been had the books been in his possession at that time; and there is no sign of the 'dubble regester' having been kept or even started. A possible lapse of a couple of years between preparing the indenture and setting up the library after getting belated permission might explain this. The Charter Trustees of the former Borough of Grantham can find no trace of such a register, which would, had it existed, have made the 1608 *Catalogus* unnecessary: and indeed this list may have been compiled in a tardy effort to meet Trigge's wishes. If a copy ever went to the Chapter House at Lincoln (where, of course, such records would never have been stored in any case) the Diocese has no knowledge of it.

I conclude that it is unlikely that Trigge stocked the Library from his own shelves, even if two of the volumes do carry his signature. To suggest how it was assembled we have to fall back on the evidence of the books themselves, whose presence in 1608 is guaranteed by the *Catalogus*. This lists about 250 volumes of which all but 23 are still extant – a very reasonable conservation of stock for a 400-year-old library!

Of the identifiable bindings we have three by Thomas Thomas, one by Garrett Godfrey, both of Cambridge, and a number of binders either anonymous or known only by initials, who according to Oldham[8] were

8 J. B. Oldham, *English blind-stamped bindings* (Cambridge, 1922). All bindings

active either in Cambridge or London, from whence of course, books might be expected to travel to Cambridge. Moreover, about a quarter of the books are secondhand, often with signatures and marginalia in early sixteenth-century hands. Where provenances can be traced, these, too, often lead to Cambridge. We have, for example, a Duranti: *Rationale Divinorum Officinorum* (Lyon, 1499) signed by William Irland of St John's College, who died in 1571. The copy, incidentally is the only one of this edition recorded in any British library, and could well have been offered secondhand in Cambridge in 1600.

Even if the association with Cambridge is a coincidence and the books were assembled from other centres, a survey of the contents of the library suggests rather forcefully what may have happened. The bulk of the collection is theological, but indiscriminately so. We have Lutheran propaganda, extreme Calvanistic preaching, bitter refutations of Protestant heresies by Catholic theologians – all the arguments and recriminations that went on over the turbulent period when the Reformed Church was breaking away from the Church of Rome and later developing sects of its own. We have, in fact, a cross section of the writings of the men who brought about the Reformation and of those who sought to oppose it.

We have, as one might expect, many biblical commentaries both Catholic and Reformed, but they are ill assorted. There are, for instance, no less than five commentaries on the Psalms and five on Genesis, but only one, and that written in the thirteenth century by Albert the Great, on the gospel of St Mark. One does not see an attempt to bring together a library as useful and comprehensive as possible for the provincial clergy who would be its main users. We have three large volumes, dated 1488, 1505 and 1515, of Catholic Canon Law with commentaries, and these must have been quite irrelevant to the needs and interests of the vicars of North and South Grantham in 1600. One of the volumes, the compilation made by Gratianus in the first half of the twelfth century and set in type in Paris in 1505, has the title 'papa' after the names of popes deleted untidily and hurriedly throughout the text. Each deletion has set-off onto the adjoining page as the leaves were flipped over. It is difficult not to assume that such volumes came on the secondhand market after the Dissolution. Indeed, we have a copy of John of Damascus: *De orthodoxa fide* (Paris, 1512) with an inscription linking it with the Augustinian friary at Hull, the last house of this order to yield up to the King's officers at the Dissolution.

What is now one of our most treasured books, the *Repetitiones* of

---

identified are given their Oldham numbers in the proposed catalogue.

Lanfranc de Oriano, printed in 1472 at the first press set up in Venice by Vindelinus de Spira, written in a heavily contracted Latin almost incomprehensible to anyone not familiar with the vocabulary of medieval Roman law, is a collection of ancient legal cases heard in Padua, Siena and Venice in the late fourteenth and early fifteenth centuries. It is hard to imagine a use for this in a Lincolnshire wool town in the last years of Elizabeth I. We have several other legal volumes, the English Year Books dating from 7 Edward III to 21 Henry VII, as printed by Pynson, Tottel and others towards the middle of the sixteenth century. They are, however, odd volumes, some bound with years out of order or missing. The ones we have are all in the 1608 list and do seem to have been picked up at random. Apart from a copy of Gerard's Herbal no longer extant there is little likely to have been of interest to laymen of unpractised latinity dwelling in the Soke of Grantham. At this date, for example, Calvin's sermons were available in English translation and widely read, but apart from a collection on Deuteronomy and one on Job (which do seem well used and now rather tattered) all Calvin's works are in Latin, even those originally in French.

We come, then, to a reasonably tenable conclusion, not that Trigge supplied the books himself, but that an agent was sent to Cambridge with instructions to buy up to the required sum, and that he did this without much discernment, taking what theological works were on offer, new and secondhand, making up with a small job lot of legal texts, a few miscellaneous volumes of classical authors and some works of reference. It would probably have been a three day journey each way by carrier's cart, so I think it reasonable to assume that the library was assembled at one purchase rather than piecemeal after 1599. The discovery of direct evidence is now very unlikely.

3. *The* Catalogus Librorum *of 1608*

This is the key document for a description of the original library. It is written, not in the court hand of the other documents, but in a well-formed and legible italianate script with headings in larger and bolder characters. It is clear that the writer, however good his penmanship, was not an experienced scrivener practised in making lists, and began without ruling up his parchment or even, it would seem, counting the titles to be entered. He evidently meant to set them out in three neat columns under author headings, but towards the end of the first began to realise that he had more books than room for them. The writing becomes progressively smaller and more closely spaced as the work proceeds, and finally he had to squeeze in a fourth half-column. The list ends 'Exscript per me' with a signature in an elaborate monogram that has so far not been deciphered and the date February 1608. The writer might well have been Wilkinson's usher at the school.

The list has some 228 titles, some of them in more than one volume and some bound in with others. Apart from the grouping of works by the same author the order appears to be arbitrary; but while Joan Williams of the Lincoln Cathedral Library was preparing, with N. Bennett, a new and more exact transcription of the list in 1986 she noticed that the list was divided into four parts by the numbers [1], 2, 3, 4, not noted before, and suggested that this was how the books were arranged on or above the four benches which may have been the original furniture. Whoever made the list simply noted the titles in order as stored. The books from the Trigge bequest were put down together, and thus are listed together, as mentioned earlier. It is possible that the arrival of the Trigge volumes triggered the compilation of a belated attempt at the register already stipulated.

There are a few mistakes. The *Imago Mundi* of Petrus Alliaco is ascribed to Gersonus, whose contribution to the work is only a final short section added by the printer, and Calvin's two English volumes are entered as if in Latin. Apart from two early Bibles recently donated all extant books printed before 1600 are listed, together with twenty-three titles of works now missing. These could have been broken up by constant use, of course, but it is much more likely that during the past four centuries they have been 'imbesilled'. The transcribed list, with reference numbers to the works still extant, appears as an appendix to the catalogue of the Library published in 1988.[9]

4. *The Trigge Bequest*

Francis Trigge's death in 1606 added titles to the library, but the relevant section of his will does not make it completely clear which volumes were already nominally in the collection. It runs:

> I giue to the Librarye at Grantham my Theatru[m]vitae humanae, and Scotus his works, and all Antoninus, and my great Pagnen his lexicon, Concordantiae grecae Phillipus de dies his postell with that p[ar]te wh[ich] Mr Pontell of Carleton hath of it, Vigeas vpon the Revelation, Fox vpon the Revelation and Catholicon beesides such books as I haue at home from thence wh[ich] are Cheaned

9 J. Glenn (with D. Walsh), *Catalogue of the Francis Trigge chained library* (Cambridge, 1988).

and Baronius uncheaned and Ferus his postill and Hugo Cardinalis wh[ich] Mr Mills of Stamford hath and Willett his Synopsis and Tetrastulon.[10]

There are other books bequeathed to various persons and the remainder go to 'Sir Smith'. It is clear that Trigge had some of the books from the library at home, but it is not clear whether the named authors from Baronius to Willett are to be included among these. They are all credited to Trigge in the provenance index added to the 1988 Catalogue. All but two of the titles can be matched up to entries on the 1608 list. We have six works by Ferus listed and extant but none of them has the word 'postilla' in the title, but since any one of the six could be so described the discrepancy is annoying rather than obviously significant. However, of Hugo Cardinalis there is no trace: it is neither listed nor extant. One concludes that Mr Mills of Stamford failed to return it! Our most regrettable loss from the bequest is Trigge's 'great Pagnen his lexicon', listed as *Thesaurus Lingue s[an]c[t]e Autore Pagnino*. This would be a useful volume to borrow surreptitiously and fail to return.

5. *The Library in Chains*

The original schedule of rules requires that 'the bookes be kept continually bownd with convenient chaines to the staples devised and placed in the library for that purpose'. Examination shows that many books in their original bindings were never chained, and that many books that were have had the chains ripped off. When Canon Nelson described the library in 1893/4 he noted that there were loose covers still in chains, books stacked up without covers, and chains with no books attached. His repair programme recovered a few books completely and left others with patches where chains had been. All that one can now say is that there are eighty-two books with chains attached and four loose chains, two in the library and two that have found their way into the stock of the local museum. The chains were probably made in one batch by one blacksmith. Each link is about 43mm x 13mm with slight variations. One end has a double tongue fastened with two rivets to the fore edge of the front cover of each book, the other in a swivel which would have been fixed to the staple. Most of the swivels are now missing, and the chains end in modern split rings.

The chains have been far from 'convenient' and have been responsible for much damage over the years. The rivets may have been all right in oak boards, but in the soft boards made up from old paper they have

10 Transcription by Dorothy Owen.

pulled away, tearing both leather and board. Removal of volumes has often scored the leather on the rivet heads of adjacent books, and even more unfortunately the inside of the fastenings have sent ironmould through end papers, title pages and preliminaries, rotting the paper so that the centre of the discoloured areas falls away; a process now under control since the roof no longer leaks. The chains are of wrought iron and have thus resisted rust very well, and have been cleaned up by rubbing the links vigorously between fingers made slightly greasy with lanoline.

6. *Sixteenth-Century Price Codes*

The use of price codes by booksellers in the sixteenth century was discussed recently by J. Blatchley, the Curator of the Ipswich Town Library, which has some twenty volumes with markings that can be interpreted as prices.[11] These marks are handwritten letters usually beside or below the imprint on the title page. By assuming a simple code a = 1, b = 2, ..., i = j = 9,... Blatchly obtained prices in fair agreement with some available records of the purchase of books. We have no similar records in Grantham, but search of the volumes turned up about sixty with this assumed coding. With a couple of exceptions all the books were printed after 1560 and indeed forty-two of the sixty after 1580; so it is likely that they were new when bought in 1600. Although the style of the letters is not quite uniform there is sufficient likeness from one book to the next to make one guess that many came from the same bookseller.

The Blatchly code translates the marks convincingly into prices. We have, for example, a number of books with the marks **nd, fh** and **cd**, which would correspond to 13/4, 6/8, 3/4, and surely can only be one Scottish mark and its fractions, coins then commonly in circulation. As at Ipswich multiple volumes carry the letters on the first volume only. There are no separate marks which can be read as £ s d, but it is usually clear from the context which would be which. The six volumes of Baronius, *Annales Ecclesiastici*, marked **e** would presumably be £5, an octavo Zanchius with the same mark 5 shillings. A list of the marked books is added as an appendix to the Catalogue.

An interesting result is obtained by adding up the assumed price equivalents for the sixty books, which arrive at £25 in round figures, for about one quarter of the collection. If, albeit as an unsupported hypothesis, we take the price of the sixty to be a fair sample of the price

---

11 J. B. Blatchly, Ipswich Town Library, in *The Book Collector*, vol. 35, no. 2, Summer 1986, pp. 191–8.

of the lot we get a possible shelf value for the Trigge library in 1600: about one hundred pounds. This is the sum Trigge offered to meet. If this is a coincidence it is worth recording anyway!

7. *Items of Note*

A few works in the library have already been mentioned since they seemed relevant to establishing a general provenance for the collection. We also have some items of interest in themselves. The *De orthodoxa fide (1512)* already noted has, as end papers, four leaves in conjugate pairs, ff. 69/74 and 68/75, from Cornelius Roelans, *De aegritudinibus infantium* (Louvain, 1486). These come from a section of the original work that has not survived, although two other leaves are recorded.[12] Our leaves include directions for the weaning of infants, telling us that when their teeth begin to show they should be given small quantities of food, 'bene masticatum' moistened in 'aqua ubi sit modicum de vino'.

Bound in with our Lanfranc de Oriano are two other works of legal 'repetitiones', both printed in Naples by Jodocus ˙Hohenstein c.1476. One of these, by Marianus Soncinus the Elder, *Repetitio capituli sententiam sanguinis super materia irregularitatis*, is known only in one other recorded copy, at the Biblioteca Capitolare in Atri. The other, Stephanus de Caieta, *Repetitio c. quoniam, in qua tractatus materia iurispatronatus*, is known to have been printed but a copy is not recorded elsewhere than in the Trigge Library. Both works were originally identified by Dr D.E.Rhodes of the British Library.

We also have, among our Year Books, the second year of Richard III, printed by Henry Smythe in 1543, which does not appear in Pollard and Redgrave's *Short Title Catalogue*.

Full details of these, and some other works that are rare or do not appear in standard catalogues, are given in our own catalogue.[9]

8. *The Library after 1600*

After the brief notice in Wood's *Athenae Oxoniensis* there is no further written record of the library till the nineteenth century, when it began to be mentioned, usually by local writers. Few of the notices extend beyond a line or two and give little useful information exccept to make it clear

---

12 D.E.Rhodes, A volume from the monastery library at Hayles, in *Trans. Cambridge Bibliographical Soc.* VIII, 1985, pp.598–603.

that the room and its contents were in a state of dilapidation. In 1884 a new floor and roof were provided by Samuel Rudd, a churchwarden and local builder, who also installed three sets of shelves which now house the books. There is, unfortunately, no record of the old furniture that he cleared away during the restoration. The split rings already mentioned were added at this time to allow the chains to run on rods fixed to the shelves. The books were now dry and protected from leaky roofs and windows, but they were shelved without other attention and the furniture beetles continued to feed on their oak covers.

In 1893 Canon Hector Nelson, former Principal of the Lincoln Diocesan Training College, came to live in Grantham. He took the library in hand and saved it from terminal disintegration. Many of the original oak covers were completely worm-eaten and fell to pieces; but the leather, perforated but otherwise sound, was replaced either on new oak or board. Almost two hundred volumes were repaired or given some sort of attention by William Mouncey, a local bookbinder whose normal trade was in account books and ledgers.

Examination of the volumes today shows that the books were, over the centuries, stacked and restacked and generally roughly treated. Under some of the replaced and repaired covers, title, preliminary and end leaves are dirty, torn or missing, while the body of the text is pristine; so that one appears to be turning the pages for the first time. Evidently the 'studdies' of the vicars did not continue far beyond the early years of the endowment.

From the end of the nineteenth century the library has attracted a few visitors who came to look at the church. During the 1920s and for over thirty years the books were cared for by the late Mrs M. A. Phipps, who initiated a regular programme of cleaning and inspection. It is now hoped that under a new programme which has included full cataloguing,[9] Francis Trigge's endowment will escape further deterioration and be preserved as an example of a sixteenth century provincial library.

Humour and Folly in English Misericords of the First Quarter of the Sixteenth Century

CHRISTA GRÖSSINGER

This article will concentrate on four interrelated themes: the World upside-down, the Power of Women, the Ape and the Fool. It will restrict itself to Manchester Cathedral, 1506–8, Durham Castle Chapel, c. 1515, Beverley Minster, c. 1520, Bristol Cathedral, c. 1520, and Westminster Abbey, c. 1510–20, where these themes are best represented at the beginning of the sixteenth century.[1]

The carvers of all these stalls made use of prints, which played such a great part in popularising the themes of humour and folly mentioned. Furthermore, there was an extensive workshop of carvers centred on Ripon Minster at the end of the fifteenth century which influenced the whole north. Thus, patterns for misericords in Manchester Cathedral can be traced back to Ripon Minster (1489–94). They were carved under the wardenship of James Stanley, 1485–1506, who left Manchester to become Bishop of Ely in 1506 and died in 1509. Many of the Manchester misericords, including the shape of the misericords themselves and the arrangement of the supporters are found again in Beverley Minster, c. 1520. The Ripon workshop was still going in 1520, when William Carver, alias William Bronflet is still mentioned at the head of a group of craftsmen. The influence of his workshop therefore was very long lasting and strong and can also be seen in some of the misericords now in Durham Castle Chapel, those which originally came from Auckland Castle and were made in the reign of Bishop Ruthall (1508–22). Some of these are nearly identical with misericords in Manchester Cathedral and I would like to date them after the Manchester Cathedral misericords and before those in Beverley Minster, i.e. c. 1515.[2] They are close to the Ripon misericords in the arrangement of the supporters and yet have novelties like the house introduced in Manchester in scenes such as the pig playing the bagpipes to the piglets.[3]

---

1 For a catalogue of English misericords, see G. L. Remnant, *A Catalogue of Misericords in Great Britain*, 1969, with an essay on the iconography of the misericords by M. D. Anderson.
2 F. Bond, *Woodcarvings in English Churches, I. Misericords*, 1910, p. 227 dates them 1512.
3 Also associated with the northern workshop are the misericords in Richmond, St Mary's, brought from Easby Abbey after 1515.

In Bristol Cathedral the initials of Robert Elyot, abbot of St Augustine's, 1515–26, are on several of the stalls and they are dated to c.1520. Here especially, extensive use has been made of prints, discovered by M.D.Anderson.[4] Even here, some of the misericords are the same as in Beverley Minster, illustrating the very wide-spread use of prints by this time.

The Westminster misericords are the most sophisticated in style and some of the carvers may well have come from the Continent. It can be shown that they used prints by Israhel van Meckenem and Albrecht Dürer.[5]

The World upside-down

Also called the topsy-turvy world, it inverts the natural state of affairs of the world and thus upsets the divinely rational order. The theme goes back to Antiquity, Sumerians and Egypt in the New Kingdom[6] and the Christians saw the destruction of the rational order through the fall of Lucifer and Adam and Eve, thus resulting in˙ sin and disorder. Illustrations of the world upside-down therefore also point to a moral and can be used as proverbs. Pieter Bruegel the Elder in his Proverbs of 1565 painted the symbol of the world turned on its head, with the cross pointing downwards. Thus, the world turned on its head represented the foolish world and often it is difficult to separate the topsy-turvy world from that of folly. The clear-cut examples of the world upside-down are the crasser ones which depict a type of black humour. They often show animals taking over the roles of human beings, e.g. the ox who slays the butcher or the hares or sheep who roast the hunter. Also, there is the reversal of roles of children and parents, e.g. the child rocks the parents in the cradle, masters and servants exchange roles as, above all, do men and women.[7] With the advent of popular broadsheets a whole series of such examples could be published[8] and, as William Coupe says,[9] the popular print here takes over from the fool, who was earlier

4 M.D.Anderson, *History and Imagery in British Churches*, 1971, p.215.
5 G.L.Remnant, *op cit.*, p.98 and J.S.Purvis, 'Use of Continental Woodcuts and Prints by the "Ripon School" of Woodcarvers', *Archaeologia*, LXXXV, 1936, p.125.
6 H.Grant, 'The World Upside-down', *Studies in Spanish Literature of the Golden Age*, ed. R.O.Jones, 1973, p.104.
7 The exchange of roles of servants and masters, rich and poor, goes back to the Roman Saturnalia. *ibid.*, p.119.
8 For illustrations, see 'The Topsy-Turvy World', Exhibition of the Goethe-Institute, (London, 1985).
9 W.Coupe, *ibid.*, p.39.

allowed to castigate, so that the print came to act as the moralistic judge.

One of the most popular illustrations of the world upside-down was that of the revenge of the animals in the hunter turned hunted. This is found on a misericord in Manchester Cathedral, showing the *hares roasting the hunter*.[10] The carver has portrayed the scene in detailed realism; the hunter with his bugle dangling from his belt has been tied to the spit and is being turned over the fire. Water is being boiled in large cauldrons and already the huntsman's dogs are being boiled and seasoned, while more dogs are carried in. This scene, as Canon Purvis discovered,[11] must have been copied from a print by Israhel van Meckenem, who came from Bocholt on the Lower Rhine. The scene retained great popularity and can be found on playing cards, e.g. by Erhard Schön, c. 1528.[12] In Germany many of the woodcuts were inspired by the satirical poems of Hans Sachs at the beginning of the sixteenth century. It was a time too when animals could be used to satirise social conditions and highlight political controversies, especially at the time of the Reformation when, for example, Luther had the Pope portrayed as an ass. In Germany, in the first half of the sixteenth century, the reversal of the world became very real because of the Peasant Revolt. Thus in the hares roasting the hunter, it is possible to see an element of social criticism, with the oppressed for once gaining the upper hand and taking revenge. In the woodcut of such a scene by George Pencz to the text of Hans Sachs, the execution of the huntsman is seen as a just punishment for tyranny.[13] He is tortured by the hares in the foreground, then an order of execution is made out and he is turned on the spit in the background. In the world of misericords the criticism is usually mingled with such humour, brought about by the juxtaposition of animals and human beings in situations which are ridiculous and yet tinged with a sense of apprehension. The humour thus spiced with criticism cannot create spontaneous laughter but induces relief from tension because the laughter is often used to enforce a moral lesson.

A typical example of the inverted world is still well known as a proverb, *putting the cart before the horse*, of which there is an example on a misericord in Beverley Minster (pl. 1). Malcolm Jones has found the first English attestation of this proverb in literature to be exactly contemporary:[14] 'that teycher setteth the cart before the horse that preferreth imitacyon

---

10 For an illustration, see J. S. Purvis, *op. cit.*, p. 122, fig. 6.
11 J. S. Purvis, *op cit.*, p. 122.
12 For an illustration of the print, see M. Geisberg, *The German Single-leaf Woodcut 1500–1550*, 1974, G. 1308, p. 1260.
13 *Ibid.*, G 1014, p. 970.
14 Personal information from Malcolm Jones, Matlock, Derbys.

before preceptes', from Whittington, 'Vulgaria' 36, 2–3. This proverb, as William Coupe says, is a genuine world upside-down situation, where the inversion is independent of the will of the individual concerned.[15] He differentiates this situation from that which he calls perverted which is the result of the will of the individual, thus making him into a fool. The right supporter in the same misericord may depict such a foolish situation, for although it looks as though the woman was milking a cow, there is no sign of an udder.[16] The woman is therefore trying to do the impossible, i.e. *milk the bull*, a world upside-down motif that goes back to Classical times. The same scene appears on a playing card designed by Schäufelein, c. 1535, where a woman is trying to milk a furiously glaring bull.[17]

Another motif of the world upside-down in Beverley Minster, depicting the foolishness of man, is the *shoeing of the goose*. This represents a foolish, because useless, activity as is made clear in a misericord of the same subject matter in Whalley Abbey (Lancs.) which has an accompanying text, saying, 'Whoever meddles in other people's affairs is sure to make a failure of it',[18] meaning that everyone should keep to his or her own trade. The supporter on the other side of the Beverley misericord depicts the owl, an animal of sin and evil, because it does not see the light and therefore Christ and is thus as foolish as the man shoeing the goose. The geese taken in by the fox in the central part of the carving are equally blind and foolish and in peril of their lives.

Animals are also used to satirise the behaviour of man, when it does not come up to expectations. Man is supposed to be strong, reliant and rational. Thus, his cowardice is illustrated by turning the tables once more and having him run away from the otherwise weak and fearful animals, often the hare. In the same way, it does not take any courage to be brave in the face of a snail, and in the left supporter of a misericord in Beverley Minster, *a man stabs a snail* with exaggerated force. Lilian Randall[19] writes that by the late thirteenth century the motif of the snail referred to the Lombards who were very unpopular in northern Europe (because many acted as pawnbrokers and userers) and who became proverbially known as cowards, an accusation which went back to their flight from battle before Charlemagne in the eighth century. The snail combat thus came to be seen as an example of cowardice and

---

15 W. Coupe, *op cit.*, pp. 41, 42.
16 Personal information from Malcolm Jones.
17 For illustration, see M. Geisberg, *op cit.*, G. 1112–17, p. 1064.
18 'Who so melles hy(m) of y al me(n) dos let hy(m) cu(m) heir and shoe ye ghos.'
19 L. Randall, 'The Snail in Gothic Marginal Warfare', *Speculum*, XXXVII, 1962, pp. 358–67.

this would explain the action of the man in the right supporter, who is putting his head into a sack.

The Power of Women

This theme is related to that of the World upside-down, because here too the roles can be reversed and the woman can put on the breeches or take up arms to go off to war. *The battle for the breeches* was a theme especially popular in Netherlandish art, e.g. a misericord at Hoogstraten, 1530s. The idea behind this is that the man will submit to the woman and carry out her task, i.e. spinning. The woman is seen as the virago who fears no one, not even the devil, whom she subjugates and ties down, as in *Mad Meg* by Pieter Bruegel the Elder.[20] She is therefore rather different from the ideal picture given her in a woodcut of 1525 by Anton Woensam[21] or another attributed to Cornelis Anthonisz, second quarter of the sixteenth century, where the symbols attached to the woman indicate her qualities. Thus, she must have eyes like a falcon to keep clear of shameful behaviour, the key in her ear stands for her willingness to listen to the word of God, the lock in her mouth prevents her from using bad language or talking unnecessarily and the mirror wards off pride; the turtle-dove on her breast indicates that she will let no other man but her husband near her, the serpents around her waist demonstrate that she will speak to no one except her husband and the jug she carries indicates her charity towards the poor, while her horses' hooves symbolise her unshakable chastity.[22] Above all, therefore, a woman was to be chaste and have the correct attitude towards her husband: that of humility and deference to him in all things. The relationship of women to men found on misericords is rather different, however. There, the most popular illustration is that of the woman grabbing the man by the hair and belabouring him with a washing-beetle or her distaff, the emblem and weapon of the housewife. In Manchester Cathedral the battle representing the *marital discord* is enacted over a broken pot from which spills the broth, whereas in Beverley Minster (pl. 2), the man has been caught by the hair while the dog is diving for the left-overs in the pot and in Bristol Cathedral (pl. 3), the man has been caught in the very act of taking food from the cauldron. In all three examples, therefore, the domestic strife has been caused by the greed of

---

20 Antwerp, Museum Mayer van den Bergh.
21 For illustration, see M. Geisberg, *op cit.*, G. 1558, p. 1511.
22 I. Veldman, 'Lessons for Ladies: a selection of sixteenth and seventeenth-century Dutch prints', *Simiolus*, 1986, p. 113.

the man who has invaded the woman's domain, resulting in her quick burst of temper and the use of distaff and utensils as weapons and flying objects. To the man, to be pulled by the beard meant great humiliation and loss of honour, because the beard stands for his strength and virility. It is an extremely sensitive part when in a fight, and Sebastian Brant in his 'Ship of Fools' says that to grab someone by the beard is an unforgivable offence. Lawrence Stone writes: 'The extraordinary amount of casual inter-personal physical and verbal violence, as recorded in legal and other records, shows that at all levels, men and women were extremely short-tempered. The most trivial disagreements tended to lead rapidly to blows and most people carried a potential weapon, if only a knife to cut their meat. The correspondence of the day is filled with accounts of brutal assaults at the dinner-table or in taverns, often leading to death. ...Quarrels, beatings and law-suits were the predominant pastimes of the village.'[23]

As Kunzle says, the literary satire on the vices and wiles of women is a world-wide, age-old phenomenon,[24] and looking at misericords, it was a subject matter already treated with much gusto by the fourteenth-century misericord carvers. Denunciation of women was not only a common trait in the late Middle Ages, but also found in Humanist literature of the sixteenth century, often in very strong language. Judging from sixteenth-century German prints, the anti-feminist feelings were especially strong there, with some extremely rude and coarse illustrations. It is difficult to say though, to what extent this satire was meant to be taken seriously, or whether it was just intended as light entertainment. In real life, it was probably a lot of wife battering rather than husband bashing that took place.

One of the German prints which became extremely popular both in Germany and England is by the so-called Master bxg (pl. 4) and it was copied by the Ripon carver.[25] This shows *the woman transported in a wheelbarrow*, in this case in a three-wheeled one; she holds a bottle in one hand and a twig in the other. What, however, was really happening originally can be gleaned from a French Book of Hours from the end of the fifteenth century, depicting the Labours of the Months and illustrating the story in its unpolluted state.[26] The woman is there holding a pitch fork and flail in one hand and a bottle in the other,

23 L. Stone, *Family, Sex and Marriage*, 1973, p. 93.
24 D. Kunzle, *The Early Comic Strip c. 1450–1825*, 1973, p. 222.
25 J. S. Purvis, *op cit.*, pp. 121, 122, and C. Grossinger, next BAA Trans. on Beverley Minster, 'The Misericords in Beverley Minster and their relationship to other misericords, and fifteenth century prints'.
26 Paris, Bibl. nat., MS.lat. 1173, fo. 4 (August), Book of Hours of Charles d'Angoulême, probably workshop of Jean Bourdichon.

meaning that she was being taken to work in the fields by force, to do the threshing in August.

The composition by the Master bxg is further adapted on a misericord in Durham Castle Chapel (pl. 5), where the woman is wheeled along in an ordinary wheelbarrow and holds the twig very much like a weapon with which to strike the man. This belligerent attitude is also found on a misericord in Beverley Minster, where the woman in the wheelbarrow turns back to torment the man. This threatening gesture can be found in another print by the Master bxg of a woman heaved along in a wicker basket.

In Westminster Abbey there are two misericords which show the *men down on the ground and beaten up by women*. In the one example the man is on his back, while the woman wields her distaff over him and in the supporters, jesters grin with glee and make gestures (pl. 6). In the other misericord the situation is even more humiliating for the man, because he is down on his knees and has his bared bottom birched while he holds the spindle, symbol of his total submission[27] (pl. 7). Both these situations are in full accord with representations of late fifteenth-century German prints by such masters as bxg and Israhel van Meckenem. An engraving by Israhel van Meckenem (pl. 8) shows the woman gripping a man by the arm and beating him with her distaff, as is the case in the first misericord. In addition, she puts her foot on his, thus subjugating him, and his breeches, the cause of the battle for power, lie on the ground. The composition of the second misericord can again be found on a playing card of c. 1528 by Erhard Schön (pl. 9), thus illustrating once more the use of the same model in print and carving.

The battle of the sexes could also be depicted as a *tournament*, as seen on a misericord in Bristol Cathedral (pl. 10). Here, a man comes charging on a sow, with a broken-off staff, possibly originally a hay-fork, as a weapon, while the woman rides on a goose, armed with a broomstick and another standing upright behind her. Vices are traditionally seen to ride on animals and the pig is a symbol of gluttony and unchastity; the goose too has sexual connotations. The broomstick, like the distaff is the housewife's tool and weapon and because of its roughness she is likened to it.[28]

Thus, the picture we get from the misericords is one of continual strife between men and women where, mostly, the women are victorious.

27 The story of the hen-pecked husband goes back to Ovid who tells that Hercules was imprisoned by Omphale, Queen of Lydia and dressed as a woman and made to spin, as seen in paintings by L. Cranach the Elder.

28 On a misericord in Manchester Cathedral a wild man and woman ride against each other on a camel and horse respectively, a composition which derives from a print after the Master E. S.

Man's greatest fear was to be humiliated by an adulterous wife and all women were considered unreasonable, prone to lose their tempers, uncontrollable and gossips. It was common knowledge that the fabled beast Chichevache (Pinch Belly) was as thin as a stick because it fed on obedient wives, whereas Bigorne (Fillgut) had well-rounded proportions because its diet consisted of obedient husbands, e.g. misericord in Carlisle Cathedral. Alison Stewart writes that there was a greater proportion of women to men in the late Middle Ages and that the proportion rose with every decade of the age.[29] This too may have added to the anti-feminist feeling and men's fears. Women often had to marry old men, because marriages were based mostly on economic considerations, or else there was a choice between life in a convent or a brothel. The property classes certainly did not indulge in love marriages and arranged marriages were common. The situation is best reflected in art in the theme of *unequal couples*, which was extremely popular at the beginning of the sixteenth century and of which there is an example on a Westminster Abbey misericord (pl. 11). There, an old and bearded man sits next to a younger woman and puts his arm around her waist. On closer scrutiny, we notice him dipping his left hand into his purse and realise that the woman is selling her services to the lustful old man. The carver copied this scene from Dürer's print of c. 1495 (pl. 12).

The contrast between true and false love greatly preoccupied the early sixteenth century. Much was made of romantic love and sexual intrigues in sixteenth- and early seventeenth-century poetry, but in reality it was only allowed to flourish in the households of princes, where it had been the popular theme since the twelfth century as L. Stone explains.[30]

A misericord in Westminster Abbey shows *two young lovers*, where the man puts his hand up the woman's skirt while she wards him off and turns away, similar to the engraving of the lovers on a grassy bank by the Master E.S. However, she could also beat him off, as seen on another misericord in Westminster Abbey.

It was always the woman who got the blame for man's downfall, because Eve was the first woman to tempt Adam and since then, man has succumbed to women's wiles. In the woodcut to Sebastian Brant's 'Ship of Fools' Lady Venus, representing false love, has all the male fools on a leash, while Cupid shoots his arrow blindfolded and Death lurks behind her back, thus also making her into a personification of Vanitas. The company also includes the stupid and lecherous donkey and the lustful monkey.[31] Thus, Venus rules men according to her

29 A. Stewart, *Unequal Lovers*, 1977, p. 102.
30 L. Stone, *op cit.*, p. 103.
31 No. 13.

whims and leads them to death and damnation. The same moral becomes even more obvious in a misericord in Bristol Cathedral,[32] where *a nude woman is welcomed into the jaws of hell by the devil, the apes in tow*. There is a well-known proverb, *To lead apes to hell*, frequently used in Elizabethan literature from c. 1570 onwards to describe the dire fate of old maids.[33] It means to attract lecherous males. Therefore, if the woman had been unchaste on earth, she was forced to continue likewise in hell, with rather unpleasant partners. This is similar to a late fifteenth-century engraving by the so-called Master of the Power of Women, where men in fool's caps and apes are led by Dame Folly, riding on an ass and carrying a cuckoo. The inscription reads: 'An ass I ride whene'er I will/ A cuckoo is my hunting bird/ With it I catch many a fool and apes.'

The Ape

The ape was the perfect example to mimic human beings, to show them up as fools. Janson writes that the Ancients thought the ape to be ugly and evil but with the advent of Christianity, it was also considered sinful and thus threatened by eternal punishment. It was associated with sexuality and therefore seen as an unclean beast. In sixteenth-century England it had the reputation of being the embodiment of male sexual rapacity.[34] It could also be seen as the devil, as in Chaucer's Friar's Tale, where the devil tells of how he comes to earth in different shapes: 'sometimes it's like a man, sometimes an ape'.[35] In the sixteenth century, however, the ape was viewed with more tolerance and seen to express the 'all-too-human' mentality of man by the northern Humanists.[36] The playful humour was already well represented in marginal illuminations, showing depictions of the ape parodying the behaviour of human beings. Its association with them is seen in its fondness for human babies whom it steals, as found in the supporters of misericords in Manchester Cathedral and Beverley Minster where, also, the ape is seen inspecting a urine bottle, thus satirising the profession of the medical men.

Because of its great vanity, the ape could easily be caught by a hunter with a mirror, and an engraving by Israhel van Meckenem shows apes much preoccupied with self-adoration and grooming. Temptation was therefore great to *ransack the pedlar's pack* which contained such objects as

32 See C. Grossinger, next BAA Trans. on Beverley Minster, *op cit.*
33 H. Janson, *Apes and Apelore in the Middle Ages and the Renaissance*, 1952, p. 207.
34 *Ibid.*, p. 208.
35 On the ceiling of Peterborough Cathedral the ape as the devil hunting souls is seen riding on a goat, holding an owl.
36 H. Janson, *op cit.*, p. 199.

combs, mirrors, ribbons and belts, and in the margins of the Smithfield Decretals, c. 1340, the napping pedlar is bereft of all his goods.[37] Apart from creating a humorous situation, there would thus be the moral in the pedlar found sleeping and punished for his sloth. The scene of the pedlar asleep while apes rifle his pack is found on misericords in Manchester Cathedral, Beverley Minster and Bristol Cathedral.[38] The carvings in Manchester Cathedral and Beverley Minster are very similar and derive from the same model. The monkeys admire themselves, make off with combs and search through the pedlar's pack. The humour of the situation is increased in Manchester Cathedral, where one of the monkeys is not able to resist the pedlar's hair for a delousing session.[39] In Beverley Minster, the situation has got out of hand, because the monkeys have become quite aggressive and pull at the pedlar's hair, while in Bristol Cathedral, the monkeys have become so violent as to have woken up the pedlar in an attempt to pull his pack off his back while threatening him with sticks.

A misericord in Westminster Abbey shows *a nursing female ape handing an apple to her male companion* and, once more, the carver has turned to Israhel van Meckenem for inspiration and copied the bottom left pair of the Four Pairs of Monkeys, including all the details (pls. 13 and 14).

The Fool

Janson says that the ape as a domestic pet was the counterpart of the fool or jester and the jesters were put in charge of the apes.[40] Thus, they both point to the foolishness of mankind. The fool observes human weaknesses and comments on the world upside-down, on it being out of joint; he is the very opposite of what a good burgher should be, because he is ruled by his passions in sexual matters and he is haughty, greedy, lazy and gluttonous as well.

The misericords in Beverley Minster above all show a delight in carvings of jesters. It may be that the Feast of Fools, celebrated in

37 MS Roy.10 E.IV, fols. 149r–51r. Also see K.Varty, *Reynard the Fox* 1967. H.Janson, *op cit.*, p. 211, thinks that because this depiction does not tell a tale but presents us with a situation, the origin is pictorial rather than literary and that the subject may have developed from the story of the treacherous boots which trapped the ape when he put them on, preventing him from getting away quickly.

38 For illustrations see next issue of BAA Trans. on Beverley Minster.

39 In the left supporter of a misericord in Beverley Minster showing a monkey riding on a horse, followed by a running man, the monkey uses a comb to groom a cat.

40 H.Janson, *op cit.*, p. 211.

Beverley every Christmas, when the clergy and others dressed up as fools and held mock services, was responsible for this predilection for the Fool.[41] The Fool was first popularised in the Carnival plays of the fifteenth and sixteenth centuries, where he either acted a part or commented on the action as narrator or herald and where he was an eager servant to Lady Venus, who really represented Dame Folly. Carnival time was a period of unruliness, of the world upside-down, of dancing and dressing up, until the Fool's rule came to an end on Ash Wednesday. In one of the misericords, *three fools in fools' caps and motley gowns dance* in the centre, while flute and tabor are played by a jester in the right supporter and another is bent double in the left supporter, pointing with his finger, probably at the foolish behaviour, and holding his bauble, the repository of the fool's innermost thoughts (pl. 15). An engraving by Israhel van Meckenem (pl. 16), c. 1480, which depicts a Morris Dance, can be well compared: the dancers move around in wild contortions and include a flute and tabor player and a jester with his bauble. In the case of the print, the Morris dancers are incited to their wild abandonment by the woman who tempts them with a ring as the prize. A similar engraving of c. 1490 by Israhel van Meckenem[42] is found in the form of an ornamental frieze with dancers, musicians and jester gyrating within the prickly tendrils of a tree that encases a temptress who this time holds out an apple, the symbol of carnal pleasure. Thus, as in the last engraving, the men are fools, fighting over the woman, as indicated by the prickly growth and the dog at her feet, fiercely guarding its bone.[43] Although there is no woman present on the Beverley misericord, a woman probably is meant to be the cause of the fools' gyrations, as the fool was included increasingly often in the theme of the Power of Women and was well known as the servant of Venus; all the prints and drawings of similar scenes include the woman.

Three other misericords in Beverley Minster concentrate on the fools' faces, smiling and making rude gestures (pl. 17). Jesters belonged to every lordly household in the Middle Ages and the Renaissance and acted as a reminder of the foolishness and vanity of all earthly power and glory. Emperor Maximilian I on the balcony in Innsbruck, c. 1500, is flanked on either side by good counsel: his chancellor and his fool. The fool is looking out at the world critically, gesturing and commenting on

---

41 F. Bond, *op cit.*, p. 110. The Feast of Fools was finally abolished throughout England by royal proclamation in 1542.

42 Illustration in *The Illustrated Bartsch*, vol. 9 (formerly vol. 6, pt. 2), ed. W. Strauss, 1981, p. 191, no. 201 (280).

43 It is interesting that the same ornamental pattern is used for a Tree of Jesse by Israhel ven Meckenem, where the tendrils are without thorns and bear fruits. (*The illustrated Bartsch*, p. 192, no. 202 (281).

what he sees, whereas the chancellor is persuasively and thoughtfully turning towards the Emperor. Thus the fool is always reacting with the world and usually laughing at it, making a fool of it and making a face at it, as in the misericord in Beverley Minster. To pull a face and stick one's tongue out as an expression of mockery and derision is a gesture commonly used by Christ's tormentors, e.g. at the Mocking of Christ or the Carrying of the Cross.[44]

From the end of the fifteenth to the sixteenth century there was much more emphasis on the foolishness of people, as opposed to their sinfulness. The sense of humour changed with the introduction of drolleries into the margins of manuscripts and a new playfulness began. The Devil himself was turned into a comic character, a fool, an object of laughter, funny and repulsive at once. Although the monsters and devils still abounded, there was also the belief that Christ would be able to overcome them. Saints and devils were humanised and, with a greater sense of the individuality of each person, everyone was thought responsible for his or her actions and sins. It was therefore believed that foolishness and lack of knowledge led to sin. Thus the 'Ship of Fools' became a popular theme, best known from Sebastian Brant's version of 1497, where all humanity in fools' dress and bells sets out on a rudder-less boat for the Never-never Land. Sebastian Brant takes on board all the foolish behaviour of the world and both castigates and smiles at the human weaknesses. Basically, he is a moralist and the humour, as in the misericords, has elements of criticism in it. However, inspite of the inherent morals, humorous depictions could be greatly enjoyed. Alison Stewart says that in the fifteenth and sixteenth centuries there was a much more tolerant view towards rude and licentious behaviour than nowadays[45] and L. Stone[46] emphasises the, to us, amazing inquisitiveness of people in the late Middle Ages. He talks of the lack of privacy and of people gossiping freely about the most intimate details of domestic relations: 'One gets the impression of a society in which privacy was non-existent, spying and prying and questioning was a universal pastime, especially of the women, and tongues were continually wagging about the shortcomings and moral lapses of others in the village.'[47] The misericords in their rudeness therefore express this much greater openness and totally different sense of fun, often considered obscene by later generations.

44 Malcolm Jones believes the misericord in Beverley Minster to be a reference to the proverb 'Shall I stand still, like a goose or a fool, with my finger in my mouth?' (*OED*, under 'goose').
45 A. Stewart, *op cit.*, p. 108.
46 L. Stone, *op cit.*, p. 93.
47 *Ibid*, p. 98.

A towel-rail, c. 1540 by Arnt van Tricht,[48] sums up the type of humour popular in the early sixteenth century with carvers and printmakers (pl. 18). The woman and fool are tightly enclasped, the woman's breasts are bulging and new baby fools appear from everywhere. The humour also lies in the fact that this is a towel-rail, an object usually found in scenes of the Annunciation and thus in connection with the purity of the Virgin and the Immaculate Conception.

With the advent of printed pictures in the second half of the fifteenth century, such themes as the Power of Women, already well known from fourteenth-century misericords, could find even wider circulation and the satire itself could be expanded on. The prints could then be used as patterns by artists of all media, including the carvers. Israhel van Meckenem, whose prints, as seen, were used by the carvers, himself copied from other engravers, such as the Master E.S. and Dürer. Playing cards too were effective transmitters of patterns. There was therefore a new accessibility and an increased interest in secular and satirical subjects. The popular comic types represented were those who were in reality weak, who had little power but who could best be used to demonstrate human weaknesses and animality, i.e. peasants and women. Animals behaving like people were also used to satirise life. Misericords contain many examples of this, such as the sow playing the bagpipes to her dancing piglets, in Manchester and Beverley Minster.

In spite of frequent moralising, the carvers of misericords were capable of real jokes, such as one in Beverley Minster:[49] *a monkey playing bagpipes on a dog* – a juxtaposition so ridiculous that it causes surprise and induces pure laughter (pl. 19).

48 In the Town Museum Haus Koekkoek, Cleve. Arnt van Tricht was active in Calcar from c. 1530.
49 Right supporter of misericord showing man on horseback leading three muzzled bears.

The Act of Resumption of 1515

S. J. GUNN

Historians can be readily forgiven for passing over the act of resumption of 1515 in almost total silence; most contemporaries did the same. In a reign full of momentous parliamentary activity, the session of February–April 1515 was one of the least memorable, and even at the time most observers thought other legislation or other debates in that session more important than the act of resumption. Edward Hall, the London chronicler, picked out as statutes 'much spoken of' an act of apparel, and one fixing wages for artificers and labourers.[1] Many churchmen had their minds on the parliamentary ramifications of the suspicious death of Richard Hunne, found hanged in the bishop of London's prison in December 1514: there was discussion both inside and outside parliament of the specific issue of benefit of clergy in cases of murder, and of the general issue of the liberties of the church. The remainder of the session's business was very ordinary, with acts for the maintenance of archery, the regulation of the cloth industry, the restoration of disinherited royal servants, and the ratification of the king's grants to newly endowed noblemen.[2] We might be forgiven for finding the 'grett & weighty maters' of parliament in spring 1515 as dull as did those 'dyvers knyghtis of shires, citizens for cities, burgyses for boroughes & barons of the Synk Port[es]', who 'long tyme before the end of the seid parliament, of their owne auctoritees depart & goeth home into their countrees', and had to be statutorily threatened that they would forfeit their wages if they did so on subsequent occasions.[3]

Those who played truant probably missed the bill of resumption, since it did not appear in the house of lords until 2 April, the session's fifty-seventh day.[4] By 5 April, when parliament was prorogued, it had

---

1 E. Hall, *Hall's Chronicle* (London, 1809 edn.) p. 581; *Statutes of the Realm*, ed. A. Luders et al. (11 vols., London, 1810–28), 6 Henry VIII c. 1, 3. I am grateful to Dr G. W. Bernard, Mr C. S. L. Davies, Mr P. J. Gwyn and Dr S. J. Payling for their comments on this paper, and to Professor Sir Geoffrey Elton for advice about parliamentary procedure.

2 6 Henry VIII c. 2, 8–9, 11–13, 19–22.

3 6 Henry VIII c. 16. Punctuation and capitalisation have been modernised in all quotations, as has the use of i, j, u and v.

4 *Journals of the House of Lords* (10 vols., London, 1846), i. 41–2. The ambiguities of the sources, and the present lack of detailed research on early Henrician

collected nine provisos, and passed smoothly through both houses and on into an obscurity almost immediate and almost complete, but not quite. One contemporary, in about 1526, made prominent use of the claims 'We begon fyrst to move o[ur] prince to call in a generall resumpsion', and 'We have begon to put in use the grawnt off the generall resumption'.[5] These were the first points of John Palsgrave's comprehensive and mockingly hostile rehearsal of the achievements of Wolsey's ministry, and it is on the act of resumption, as a governmental measure and political ploy of some importance in the early years of Wolsey's greatness, that the rest of this paper will concentrate. At the start of 1515 Thomas Wolsey was archbishop of York, a successful military administrator and diplomat, and *primus inter pares* in the king's council. By the end of the year he was cardinal, lord chancellor, and indisputably chief minister, and the act of resumption and the policies it represented played an important part in that consolidation of his power.

By 1515 bills and acts of resumption had a history over a century long. In origin they were highly controversial measures, taking back for the crown – resuming into the king's hands – patronage previously distributed. Several times in the reigns of Edward III and Richard II the house of commons had pressed on the king the importance of conserving his income, to pay for wars and great affairs of state, and so lessen the burden of taxation on his subjects.[6] In two successive parliaments in 1404, Henry IV, faced with revolts that had necessitated extensive military expenditure, and with the urgent need to buy and retain political support through the generous distribution of patronage, found the commons demanding legislation to resume royal grants. At the Coventry parliament that autumn, Henry bowed to the pressure of the commons, and an act of resumption was at last passed. Henry doubtless disliked being dictated to by parliament, and in the act's implementation he almost entirely negated its purpose, reducing it from a cancellation of all grants of lands and annuities since 1366, to a one-year suspension of annuity payments, and a promised conciliar review of patronage which never took place. Henry repudiated the

---

legislative procedure, make it hard to present a definitive account of the act's passage.

5 Public Record Office (hereafter PRO) SP1/54 fo. 251r (*Letters and Papers, Foreign and Domestic, of the Reign of Henry VIII*, ed. J.S.Brewer et al. (22 vols. in 36, London, 1862–1932) (hereafter *LP*), IV, iii.5750); J.Palsgrave, *The Comedy of Acolastus*, ed. P.L.Carver (Early English Text Society 202, 1937), p.xli.

6 For what follows, see B.P.Wolffe, *The Royal Demesne in English History* (London, 1971), pp. 73–87.

letter of the statute, but not its spirit. From 1404 crown lands ceased to be alienated except to the royal family, and from 1406 grants of new annuities that diminished royal revenue were largely curtailed.

From 1404 resumption was established as part of the give-and-take of the late-medieval constitution. Not surprisingly, it became a prominent issue in the late 1440s and 1450s, when the political dissidence of Richard, duke of York lent weight to parliamentary criticism of royal patronage.[7] The most effective act of resumption ever passed was that of March 1451, and the reasons for its success are plain: the government had collapsed, through defeat in France, popular rebellion and the murder of the leading ministers; the house of commons contained very few patentees who would suffer from resumption; and where Henry VI and his household servants, the main beneficiaries of his patronage, had blunted the effects of an almost identical act passed in May 1450, York's return from Ireland and assumption of a place in government prevented such evasion. The short-term results were impressive, for the resumed grants did improve crown finances, and the 1453 parliament was generous with taxation. The wider implications were more dangerous, for 1451 made resumption an attractive weapon for partisan politicians. The last of the Lancastrian acts of resumption was passed after the first battle of St Albans, by the Yorkist lords, eager to implement their victory over Henry VI's household men by stripping them of their royal grants.

From the accession of Edward IV, the character of resumption changed.[8] As the crown itself became one of the spoils of political and military victory, so the constitutional and the partisan aspects of resumption merged, and the sword wielded by critics of weak monarchs was beaten into a ploughshare of the new monarchy. Acts of resumption were used to assure the Yorkist and Tudor titles to the Lancastrian crown estate, and to facilitate the withdrawal and redistribution of patronage by kings who placed a premium on loyal service and sought ways to ensure it, at times utilising fear as much as gratitude. The impact on crown finance of the numerous resumptions of Edward IV and Henry VII was minimal, as was their role in the wider dialogue between crown and subject. Unlike Edward, Henry VII returned to the Lancastrian form for the acts, casting them as a petition from the commons to the king to keep up his household and foreign commitments, by resuming his ancestors' hereditaments. But these acts of

7 Wolffe, *Royal Demesne*, pp. 107–40.
8 M. A. Hicks, 'Attainder, Resumption and Coercion, 1461–1529', *Parliamentary History* 3 (1984); Wolffe, *Royal Demesne*, pp. 150–99.

resumption were clearly official measures, enabling the government to tinker with its own patronage.

In some ways the 1515 act was the culmination of this newer tradition. It resumed no grants of crown lands, not even of leases on the crown lands.[9] It concerned itself entirely with grants, since Henry VIII's accession, of offices, annuities, advowsons, and customs licences. Annuities were revoked only if they were unattached to the performance of an office. Grants of office were revoked only if they were of certain types: grants in reversion after the current occupant; grants in survivorship to two occupants, to last until the second of them died or resigned; grants of constableships of castles which did not require any activity by the patentee or his deputy (usually because the castle was ruinous); all grants of constableships of castles in North Wales and Cheshire; and grants which gave the occupant wider powers of patronage over his subordinates, or higher fees, than were current in the last year of Henry VII. The impact was lessened still further by the fact that many of these offices were to remain in the hands of the holders without the need for any regrant, but with fees reduced to the old level, or with additional patentees under grants in survivorship deprived of their rights. It was an act with very few teeth, and we might wonder why it was passed at all.

One answer that would have occurred to those sitting in the lords on 2 April was that Thomas Wolsey wanted it passed. When the bill came up from the commons it was read twice, and then handed over by Wolsey to Sir Robert Sheffield, speaker of the commons in the previous parliament, for some redrafting.[10] This unique recorded intervention by Wolsey in the business of the session linked him closely with the resumption, though admittedly he may have been handling all government business in the lords in the absence of Lord Chancellor Warham. In the matter of customs licences too – one addressed by the act – there is clear evidence of Wolsey's special responsibility at this time, in the form of a surviving 'declaration for my lord archbishop of York', expounding the disadvantages for the royal customs system of the licences held by one particular Italian merchant.[11] The act also fitted in closely with the policies of retrenchment and reform which Wolsey was beginning to make his own. Three times in his ministry, in the years 1514–16, 1519–21, and 1525–6, he produced and began to implement wide-ranging packages of policies designed to save the king's money,

9 6 Henry VIII c.25. The original act, with eight of the provisos attached, is in the House of Lords Record Office.
10 *Lords' Journals*, i. 41.
11 *LP* I, ii. 41.

improve the administration of justice, and revivify many areas of government.[12] Or so he claimed. Historians, like contemporaries, have varied in their reactions. For some Wolsey was a genuine, though cautious, reformer. Bishop Fox thought so too, praising in 1516 Wolsey's 'better, straighttar and spedyar wayes of justice, and mor diligence and labour for the kyng[is] right[is], duties and profitz...then ever I see in tyme past in any other'.[13] Others have followed the hints of George Cavendish, Wolsey's gentleman usher, that the minister's policies were less the visions of a statesman, than the tools of a cynical and manipulative politician: as David Starkey has put it, 'the rhetoric of reform was used to bend Henry to Wolsey's purposes'.[14] Perhaps the act of resumption can shed some light on this debate.

We must be wary of associating all the new governmental initiatives of 1513–16 with the advent of Wolsey. Rationalisations in the receipt of the exchequer which went through at this time were clearly the product of long-term developments within that department, and were implemented by the exchequer's own staff, while improvements in the administration of wardships from 1513 to 1515 can be attributed to Sir Thomas Lovell, one of the leading survivors of Henry VII's council.[15] But many of the government's moves do bear Wolsey's stamp. The spring 1515 parliament passed an act against the decay of tillage, a problem that Wolsey would shortly address through the enclosure commissions.[16] October 1514 saw a proclamation against unlawful livery and retaining, offences on which Wolsey would mount set-piece attacks in 1516 and 1519.[17] Retaining by badge was a problem intensified by the wars of 1512–14 with France and Scotland, and so was Wolsey's greatest concern in this first burst of reform: the parlous state of the crown's finances.

In 1514–16, as in 1525–6, Wolsey's reforms followed immediately on a protracted and expensive bout of international warfare. In part, this

12 D. R. Starkey, *The Reign of Henry VIII: Personalities and Politics* (London, 1986), pp. 79–80, 86–9; J. A. Guy, *The Cardinal's Court: The Impact of Thomas Wolsey in Star Chamber* (Hassocks, 1977), pp. 30–5, 45–8; A. P. Newton, 'Tudor Reforms in the Royal Household', in *Tudor Studies*, ed. R. W. Seton-Watson (London, 1924), pp. 231–56.

13 *Letters of Richard Fox, 1486–1527*, ed. P. S. and H. M. Allen (Oxford, 1929), p. 83; cf. J. J. Scarisbrick, 'Cardinal Wolsey and the Common Weal', in *Wealth and Power in Tudor England*, ed. E. W. Ives et al. (London, 1978), pp. 45–67.

14 Starkey, *Reign of Henry VIII*, p. 86.

15 J. D. Alsop, 'The Exchequer in Late Medieval Government, c. 1485–1530', in *Aspects of Late Medieval Government and Society*, ed. J. G. Rowe (Toronto, 1986), pp. 186–8; W. C. Richardson, *Tudor Chamber Administration, 1485–1547* (Baton Rouge, 1952), pp. 284–8.

16 6 Henry VIII c. 5; Scarisbrick, 'Cardinal Wolsey and the Common Weal'.

17 *LP* I, ii. 3353; Guy, *Cardinal's Court*, pp. 30–3.

may have been from a desire to take control of court politics as the political nation returned from its campaigning.[18] In part, it must have been because Wolsey was too busy running the war effort to do anything else until hostilities had ceased. But neither of these considerations should obscure the fact that warfare on the scale necessary to sustain Henry's hopes of conquest in France placed the English government under significant strain, especially in its finances. Wolsey sought real solutions to real problems. Reliable figures are hard to produce, but the war of 1512–14 cost at least £892,000 over and above the ordinary expenses of government.[19] For the latter the king's income from the customs, crown lands and other sources was comfortably sufficient, but war demanded taxation. Despite grants in parliament in 1512, 1513 and 1514, the net yield of taxation by spring 1515 was less than £180,000.[20] Though the rapidly evolving lay subsidy was proving an effective means to tap the national wealth, its yields fell far short of the king's needs, and even of the hopes of those drafting the subsidy bills. As a high-powered delegation from the lords explained to the commons on 10 February, the 1515 parliament had been called principally to make up the difference between the sums raised by the previous subsidies and the final cost of the war.[21] Both sessions in 1515 duly granted subsidies, but these between them brought in only some £90,000 net. The financial problem remained.

Clerical taxation, and benevolences probably taken by Henry from his subjects to support his personal invasion of France in 1513, helped to close the gap between income and expenditure.[22] So did the easily overestimated, but none the less significant, reserves left by Henry VII. Even so, the government had to search for ways to balance the books, and the search was led by Wolsey. Veterans of Henry VII's council like Sir Henry Wyatt and Sir Andrew Windsor spent most of 1515 auditing numerous accounts arising from the war, while the treasurer of the chamber, John Heron, continued to reimburse crown officials for their wartime expenditure.[23] But overall financial control was in Wolsey's hands, as Dame Elizabeth Southwell, widow of Sir Robert, knew when, in March, she handed over to the archbishop £200 in unpaid revenues from offices held by her husband. It was, indeed, Wolsey who had

18 Starkey, *Reign of Henry VIII*, pp. 86–9.
19 F.C. Dietz, *English Government Finance, 1485–1558* (Chicago, 1920), p. 91.
20 R.S. Schofield, 'Parliamentary Lay Taxation, 1485–1547' (Cambridge University PhD thesis, 1963), table 40.
21 *Lords' Journals*, i. 21.
22 B.P. Wolffe, *The Crown Lands, 1461–1536* (London, 1970), pp. 87–8.
23 *LP* II, i. 46, 254, 586, 710, 722, 751, 853, 1034, ii, App. 6; PRO E36/215 fo. 189v.

checked through and signed a compilation of Sir Robert's accounts following his death.[24] What remains of Wolsey's archive shows the serious intent with which he tackled the financial situation. Special abstracts were drawn up for him showing details of both expenditure and income: fees paid to the wardens of the marches at current rates compared with three dates in the previous reign, for instance, or the exact state of paid and unpaid customs revenue for Easter term 1515, as at 15 May.[25]

Wolsey's reforms were always marked by careful gathering of information, and in 1525–6 both the reorganisation of Welsh government and the restructuring of the household were based on the consideration of ample lists of offices and their incumbents.[26] At least in 1515 Wolsey's reforms were also marked by bold and decisive action. In January Lord Mountjoy was dispatched to Tournai as the new governor, with instructions for economies so drastic that they prompted an immediate mutiny among the garrison. By April Wolsey had made a cut still closer to the king's heart: the quiet abolition of the glittering royal bodyguard of a hundred 'spears', maintained since 1510 at a cost of over £2,000 a year.[27] Meanwhile he was doing his best to increase the king's income. On 4 August 1514 he was appointed, with Bishop Fox and John Heron, to negotiate with those who owed debts to the king and secure their repayment.[28] Earlier in the reign such matters had been handled by veterans of Henry VII's debt-collecting activities, notably Lovell, Heron and John Ernley.[29] They may have been behind the assurance of repayments totalling £690 a year by eight debtors, settled in summer 1514, but when Wolsey took the reins their efforts began to look paltry.[30] On 25 and 28 November the archbishop and his fellow-commissioners sat at the Savoy and called thirty-one debtors to account, securing promises of annual repayments of £4,050. We need not doubt that the occasion appealed to Wolsey's *amour-propre*: among the apologetic debtors were a duke, a marquis, four earls, nine barons and several leading courtiers. But the fact remains that the sums

24 Ibid., fo. 183v; E101/85/16, 22 (*LP* I, ii. 3313).
25 *LP* II, i. 1365; PRO SP1/10 fols. 201–4 (*LP* II, i. 544).
26 S.J.Gunn, 'The Regime of Charles, duke of Suffolk in North Wales, and the Reform of Welsh Government, 1509–25', *Welsh History Review* 12 (1985), 488; *LP* IV, i. 1939.
27 C. G. Cruickshank, *The English Occupation of Tournai, 1513–1519* (Oxford, 1971), pp. 68–77; Dietz, *English Government Finance*, p. 88; PRO E36/215 fols. 181r, 185r.
28 *LP* I, ii. 3226(8).
29 PRO E210/10103, E211/74. I am grateful for these references, and others in the same classes, to Dr R. W. Hoyle.
30 For what follows, see PRO SP1/9 fols. 179–82.

involved were a significant addition to the royal revenue, and one that Wolsey was determined to secure. The following two-and-a-half years saw many of those who appeared at the Savoy bound in indentures for these repayments, and transferring lands to royal feoffees to ensure that the money did reach the king.[31] In several instances the annual payments were to be smaller than the figures agreed in November 1514, but the final total for repayment was often larger: Wolsey was negotiating rather than dictating, but he was negotiating with serious intent. He may even have wished to pursue the debt question further in the spring 1515 parliament. One or more bills for the king's debts achieved a total of seven readings and several redraftings in the lords, but despite the house's agreement to appoint the justices and the king's legal officers to produce 'quendam actum pro securitate regia, pro debitis suis obtinendis', no legislation resulted.[32] Eleven of the peers who appeared before Wolsey in November were in the lords for at least one day of these debates; perhaps they spoke their minds.

1514–15 brought changes in the collection not only of the king's debts, but also of his landed revenues. In 1512 the general surveyors of crown lands had been restored in part to the position they had held under Henry VII, controlling the landed estate which had become so important a foundation of Yorkist and early Tudor government. In spring 1515 the act renewing their powers extended and exemplified them, partly as an administrative improvement, an improvement attributed by the historian of the crown lands to Wolsey.[33] But the change may have been as much occasioned by the death of Sir Robert Southwell, the general surveyor who seems to have exercised a roving supervision over many aspects of the financial system in succession to Sir Reynold Bray, and here we strike another general principle of Wolsey's reforms. He tended to institute structural change not for its own sake, but in response to the loss of key individuals. The *locus classicus* might be the remodelling of Welsh government in the wake of the death of the trusted Sir Rhys ap Thomas in 1525; a closer parallel to the changes of 1515 could be found in the reordering of chamber finance following Sir John Heron's retirement through ill-health in 1521.[34] Perhaps Cromwell tried harder to fit men to institutions, but the comparison should not make us disregard Wolsey's version of reform.

The documentation thrown up by the changes to the general surveyors must have made one fact painfully clear to Wolsey. On the income side,

31 PRO E36/215 fo. 306v; E210/10103, 10782; E211/74, 76, 152, 199.
32 *Lords' Journals*, i. 26–36.
33 Wolffe, *Crown Lands*, pp. 79–80; Richardson, *Tudor Chamber Administration*, pp. 248–57.
34 Ibid., pp. 233–7.

the difference between the royal affluence of Henry VII and the dire straits of 1515 lay largely in the £20,000 or more of crown revenue given away since 1509.[35] Almost half the king's estate income had been alienated in six years, and the commons of Henry IV's or Henry VI's reign would have been baying for resumption. Some of the dispersal, admittedly, was unexceptionable by fifteenth-century standards. Over £6,000 went to fund the royal household by assignment, lessening the burden of purveyance and royal debt; £4,000 formed a jointure for the queen. £2,500 was restored to the heirs of those attainted under Henry VII: such restoration was in a sense a spiritual duty to the late king, made sound political sense at the start of a new reign, and was further encouraged by Henry VIII's blood-relationship to the Yorkist royal family through his mother. Over £450 returned to families from whom it had been confiscated by Henry VII on grounds of lunacy or idiocy, and almost £250 was won back from the crown in the lawcourts. Most of these alienations could be forgiven a new king eager to make a good start. But Henry had also distributed nearly £1,000 in rents and nearly £3,500 in lands, plus over £5,800 in wages and annuities not paid by his father. It is not surprising that when Wolsey began to concern himself with stabilising Henry's finances, it was not only he who thought of an act of resumption.

Resumption seems to have been in the air at court as early as November 1514. On the 24th, Sir Ralph Egerton secured letters patent appointing him riding forester of Delamere Forest, Cheshire, which contained a special clause instructing that he be paid his fees any act, statute or restriction notwithstanding.[36] Similar phrases reappeared in grants of new annuities and offices liable to the resumption made in late April and early May 1515, once the statute had been passed and its provisions were clear.[37] In February and March, though, fears of a wider resumption prompted others to seek protection. Sir John Cutte wrote into his indenture with the queen on 17 March that no act of resumption should affect her life lease to him of the manor of Thaxted in Essex, nor the grant of the reversion of the manor in fee-farm after her death.[38] The councillors of Charles, duke of Suffolk – who was himself away in France – added to the bill confirming the king's landed endowment of the duke, introduced into the lords on 21 March, the provision that no act of resumption, nor any other act for the king made

---

35 For what follows, see PRO SP1/12 fols. 47–8 (*LP* II, i. 1363); SC11/837 (*LP* II, i. 1795); Wolffe, *Crown Lands*, pp. 83–4, 181.
36 PRO SC6/Henry VIII/344 m. 6.
37 PRO C02/419, 420.
38 *LP* II, i. 601.

or to be made, should threaten Suffolk's tenure.[39] The similar bill for the duke of Norfolk, introduced on the same day, did not mention an act of resumption, presumably because he was in England, in the lords, and in council, and knew better the government's intentions. We cannot know whether Wolsey ever considered resuming grants of lands, but it seems unlikely that it was a political possibility.

The rhetoric of full-scale resumption carried two different messages, but in 1515 neither would have appealed to Henry VIII. The Lancastrian acts spoke of a tension between crown and subject which encouraged the subject to question and constrain the monarch's patronage: a far cry from Henry's idea of kingship. They implied that the king was weak-willed – with the precedent of Henry VI, weak-minded too – and that those he had rewarded were self-seeking and unworthy. Henry was not likely to declare such things either about himself, or about the men whose fortunes he had helped to establish and who would remain the pillars of his regime, the two Thomas Howards, Charles Brandon and others. His early alienations had founded his rule on a bedrock of grateful loyalty not unlike that formed by Edward III when he created and endowed his own friends Montagu, Clinton and Ufford as earls in 1337. Edward III and Henry V may have been dangerous models of kingship for Henry VIII to follow, but they were better than Henry VI.[40] Equally inappropriate in 1515 was the pattern of Edward IV's and Henry VII's resumptions. No-one questioned Henry VIII's claim to the crown lands, and he judged it better that no-one questioned his sincerity in giving them away. Henry's rule by magnificence was a natural, and probably a necessary, reaction against his father's rule by suspicion; and when regional politics demanded a reorganisation of crown patronage, as they did in the late 1530s, Henry did not imitate Edward IV's tactic of 1473–4 in redistributing his patronage by act of resumption, but drew on his credit with the recipients of his favour – and the implicit threat that the uncooperative might forfeit the king's friendship – to persuade them individually to move with his plans.[41] Whatever his motives in so doing, Wolsey knew how to produce and present policies that appealed to the king, and in 1515 he surely knew that full-scale resumption was a non-starter.[42]

So why did Wolsey produce an act of resumption at all? One reason sprang from that same history of resumption that made it such a sensitive subject. Kings agreed to resumptions to show the commons

---

39 6 Henry VIII c. 20; *Lords' Journals*, i. 36.
40 Cf. S. J. Gunn, 'The French Wars of Henry VIII', in *The Origins of War in Early Modern Europe*, ed. J. Black (Edinburgh, 1987), pp. 36–40.
41 Hicks, 'Attainder, Resumption and Coercion', p. 26; S. J. Gunn, *Charles Brandon, Duke of Suffolk* (Oxford, 1988), pp. 167–70.
42 Starkey, *Reign of Henry VIII*, p. 63.

that they were doing their best not to misspend the nation's money; in response, the grateful commons granted taxation. It was surely no accident that the bill of resumption left the commons for the lords on the same day as the bill for the 1515 subsidy. The bill followed the early acts of resumption, in linking the king's re-assumption of control over his own revenues with his duty to place the welfare of the generality of his subjects above the favour of particular persons. In so doing, it echoed Warham's stress, in his speech at the opening of parliament, on the need to maintain the health of the commonwealth and avoid the avarice or ambition of evil counsellors.[43] Given the very limited terms of the bill, some of the commons doubtless thought these to be empty phrases. In the 1523 parliament they would take criticism of Henry's spending, and Wolsey's means of funding it, to great lengths, in the process gaining Wolsey a reputation as a haughty and ham-fisted manager of parliaments.[44] Wolsey's position was far more difficult in 1523 than in 1515, and he may have been growing rather over-confident;[45] at any rate, the 1515 act met the commons' criticism with some skill. Written into it was not only a resumption of all customs licences, but also a provision that all denizened foreign merchants were to pay customs at alien rates.[46] It would be no surprise if Sir Robert Sheffield's redrafting concerned these points. For Sheffield had until 1508 been recorder of London, and remained prominently involved with London's interests in parliament.[47] In the city, hostility to foreign merchants was building up towards the peak it reached in the riot of Evil May Day 1517; in the spring 1515 parliament five London bills had failed, though two of them placing restrictions on foreign merchants had reached the lords; and so sensitive was the proviso added to the act of resumption to save the privileges of the Hanseatic merchants, that the lords ordered it to be written onto the parliament roll without passing the commons, as they had in the case of a similar measure in 1512.[48]

In using the act of resumption to respond to some of the commons' clamour against privileged foreign merchants, Wolsey was successfully playing to the house. One might wonder if he was also doing so in the

---

43 *Lords' Journals*, i. 18.
44 M. A. R. Graves, *The Tudor Parliaments: Crown, Lords and Commons, 1485–1603* (London, 1985), pp. 43, 61–2.
45 I am grateful for discussion of the 1523 parliament to Dr J. A. Guy.
46 6 Henry VIII c. 25 s. 3.
47 S. T. Bindoff, *The History of Parliament: the House of Commons 1509–1558* (3 vols., London, 1982), iii. 304–5.
48 H. Miller, 'London and Parliament in the Reign of Henry VIII', *Bulletin of the Institute of Historical Research* 35 (1962), 140; G. Schanz, *Englische Handelspolitik gegen Ende des Mittelalters* (2 vols., Leipzig, 1881), i. 201–4, 420–4; *Lords' Journals*, i. 39, 41.

general thrust of the resumption. By the reigns of Mary and Elizabeth the commons were growing ever more irritable over the crown's attempts to interfere with private property: the former church lands, the property of protestant or catholic exiles, and so on. Such assertion of the common-law rights of private property against arbitrary 'tyranny' – and resuscitated feudal claims – was to climax under the Stuarts, but there were hints of it already in the reaction against Henry VII's policies. A resumption of lands might well have met with a more hostile reception in the 1515 commons than a resumption largely of offices, which never became private property in England as they did in France, and of annuities, which, though defensible at law, did not share the range of actions or the mystical sanctity of landed property.

The commons harboured no such protective feelings towards the foreign merchants blessed earlier in the reign with customs licences. But did Wolsey or the king? Here we reach the fundamental questions about the act. Was it merely a gesture to weary taxpayers, or did it achieve anything for the crown's finances, its freedom of manoeuvre in matters of patronage, and its political and administrative control of the nation? On the customs the impact was small. Between 1512 and 1517 the crown's total customs revenue never fluctuated outside the range £40,000–46,000, though the peak did come in 1514–15, when the withdrawal of licences would have had most impact.[49] By the end of 1516, at least fourteen individuals or syndicates, mostly Italians, had had anulled licences renewed, or had been granted new licences along the same lines as old (and possibly used-up) ones; completely new licences were also being granted out.[50] In some instances the merchants involved could offer special inducements to the government, like a commitment to import the saltpetre necessary for gunpowder manufacture, while in other cases the licences were bought, bringing the crown much-needed cash.[51] Some licences were renewed on terms less generous than those on which they had first been granted. But as licences from as long ago as 1512 were still being used at Southampton in January 1515, and renewed grants were being issued from June, it is no wonder that the act had little real effect.[52] As a declaration of intent, though, it signalled an important change in licensing policy. In 1514 licences were issued for the duty-free import of 10,680 tuns of goods. By 1517 the total tunnage licensed had fallen to 1,575 and it stayed below 2,000 every year until 1521, and did

49 Schanz, *Handelspolitik*, ii. 59.
50 For all grants and regrants, except where otherwise specified, see the calendars in *LP* I, II.
51 PRO E36 fols. 345r, 347r.
52 PRO E122/216/1.

not rise above 4,500 for the rest of Wolsey's ministry; meanwhile an act of the session of parliament later in 1515 declared void all licences unused by Easter 1516.[53] In customs licensing the government had followed the model of the first act of resumption, that of 1404: the act was not allowed to destabilise the existing balance of patronage, but did portend a significant change in long-term policy.

The same was true of the crown lands. In January and February 1515 the king signed away in perpetuity between £500 and £600 per annum of his landed estate.[54] From March 1515 to the end of 1516 he made fourteen grants of land, but two were in Tournai, one was in Ireland, and most were of small scraps or distant reversions. Only three were immediate alienations of one or more whole manors or equivalent units, and one of those three was merely for the life of the grantee and his wife.[55] There would be no further widespread distribution of lands from the king's hands until the fall of the duke of Buckingham in 1521, which enabled the demand for such patronage to be met without further encroachment on the landed estate inherited from Henry VII.[56]

Paradoxically, the areas of the act's greatest immediate impact were those of its least long-term significance. The total volume of crown annuities is hard to calculate, because of the different sources of income on which they were assigned: the exchequer, the chamber, the sheriffs, the customs, the hanaper of chancery, or various crown estates. But as with the customs licences, those who lost annuities through the act were quick to beg for their renewal, and frequently proved successful. By the end of 1516 at least eighty annuities had been regranted under the great seal to their original holders, constituting an annual expenditure of £1,465 12s 6d. Some of these were affected by the act only because they were not explicitly attached to an office, though granted for its exercise: the 50 marks each of the attendant esquires for the body, and the 40 marks each of the king's surgeons or his French secretary, were unlikely not to be restored to them. But many of these annuities were merely supplements to the income of past or present royal servants, and these were readily renewed too. In some instances the opportunity was taken to reduce them, but in others the recipients asked for, and got, higher pensions after the act than before it.

Some annuities were permanently abrogated, but all too few. At Tournai many fees had not been regranted by May 1516, but accounts do not survive to enable the savings there to be quantified.[57] At Calais,

53 Schanz, *Handelspolitik*, i. 370–1.
54 PRO SP1/12 fols. 174–5; *LP* I, ii. 57, 93, 94, 266.
55 *LP* II, i. 1695, 1713, 1850.
56 H. Miller, *Henry VIII and the English Nobility* (Oxford, 1986), pp. 214–15.
57 British Library (hereafter BL) MS Cotton Caligula EI fo. 99r (*LP* II, i. 1855).

whose financial officers had under Henry VII regularly paid a surplus of income over expenditure into the king's chamber, eighteen annuities totalling £235 17s 7d were handed out by the young Henry VIII. Twelve of these were renewed in time for their holders to be paid without interruption from Michaelmas 1514 to Michaelmas 1515; six, amounting to £86 a year, were withheld, understandably enough in four cases, since two of the holders had been given feed offices at Tournai, one had been promoted to be undermarshal of Calais, and one was dead.[58] In the accounts for Denbigh and Cheshire, two prime targets for annuity-hunters in the royal household, the figures were similar. Ten Denbigh annuities first granted by Henry VII were not renewed – rather a twisting of the terms of the act – leading to a long-term saving of £74 3s 4d a year out of an annuities bill of £172 6s 8d, though only one Cheshire pension was discontinued, saving £12 out of £97 16s 8d a year.[59] The one-third cut in the crown's spending on annuities suggested by the examples of Calais and Denbigh was not sustained for other revenues on which annuities were assigned, such as those of North and South Wales, the chamber and the hanaper.[60] While the duchy of Lancaster was affected by the act, many of the annuities paid from its estates, for instance from the honour of Tutbury, had been granted by Henry VII and were thus not resumed.[61] Lastly, at the receipt of the exchequer, the largest source for annuities, payments of annuities and wages in the year following Michaelmas 1515 were only £144 11s 9½d lower than in the year preceding that date.[62] Some of these payments were of arrears for previous years, and the difference between Michaelmas term 1514 and the same term in 1515 was more marked than that between Easter term 1515 and Easter term 1516, suggesting that these annual totals do underestimate the act's impact. None the less, from a total exchequer expenditure on wages and annuities of nearly £5,800, the act of resumption hardly produced dramatic savings.

It is true that the immediate effects on crown finance of the resumption of annuities were more beneficial than these figures might suggest. Many of those deprived did not secure renewal of their patents until it was too late for the suspended second half of their pension for 1514–15 to be paid, producing a partial stop on annuities from Easter 1515 reminiscent of that effected by Henry IV in 1404. The sums involved

58 PRO E36/270 fols. 529–45; Cruickshank, *Tournai*, pp. 46–7; *LP* II, i. 616.
59 PRO SC6/Henry VIII/344, 4993, 4994.
60 PRO SC6/Henry VIII/345 mm. 82–5, 96; E101/220/7; E36/215 fols. 185, 193v, 196r, 202r.
61 PRO DL29/406/6499.
62 PRO E405/88, 89.

were not large: £18 13s 4d on Denbigh, £30 1s 8d on Cheshire, £11 17s 0d on the hanaper, and so on, but they must have helped a little with the royal cashflow. Sooner or later, though, many annuitants obtained royal warrants restoring their pensions retrospectively for the period between Easter 1515 and the date of their new letters patent.[63] And new annuities were soon being granted out: 100 marks to the king's armour-gilder, 40 marks to the English ambassador to Denmark, £20 to William Coffin, one of the young men just starting to make his mark at court.[64] As in the distribution of lands, Wolsey could not really expect the king to disown all his previous acts of generosity, but by 1518–19 many of the crown estates were more burdened with annuities than they had been before the act, and by March 1521 Wolsey was again investigating fees and pensions.[65] Annuities were bound to be the hardest form of permanent patronage – gifts which were not merely one-off presents of money or goods – to restrict. For the king they were a more flexible way to reward his servants than office or land; for the courtier, afflicted like almost all his contemporaries by chronic shortages of ready cash, they were an attractive prize. Wolsey, caught between the king and his servants, stood little chance of making significant economies here.

The grand total of annuities Wolsey found in his 1521 investigation, including many fees directly linked to offices and thus untouched by the 1515 act, was £7,170 13s 6d. This was paltry compared with the annuities bills decried by the commons of Richard II or Henry IV, for Richard's had reached perhaps £20,000 at his deposition, and Henry's peaked at some £35,000, a quarter or so of royal income.[66] Richard and Henry retained the gentry directly, judging such expenditure worthwhile for the local political control it gave them. Edward IV largely abandoned such retaining, and in this the Tudors followed him.[67] But the Tudor state compensated the gentry in two ways, both relevant to the act of resumption. The retention of large estates in the crown's hands enabled the appointment of favoured gentlemen to stewardships, constable-ships, receiverships and other offices on the crown lands. These paid fees (which would not, for example, have appeared on Wolsey's 1521 list of annuities), enhanced the local power of the holder, especially through the right to raise the king's tenants for his wartime retinue, and tied him to the crown, paralleling and reinforcing the increased use of

---

63 E.g. PRO DL28/6/14 fol. 14v.
64 *LP* II, i. 455, 1771, 1949.
65 PRO SC6/Henry VIII/345 mm. 35r, 77, 89, 106v, 139; *LP* II, i. 2736.
66 C. Given-Wilson, *The Royal Household and the King's Affinity* (New Haven and London, 1986), pp. 136, 263–4,.
67 D. A. L. Morgan, 'The King's Affinity in the Polity of Yorkist England', *Transactions of the Royal Historical Society* 5th series 23 (1973), 13–14.

the gentry as JPs in local government. In one way this was only a modification of the old competitive retaining policy, for contemporary magnates were evading the legislation against liveried retaining by appointing knights, esquires, and even other peers to supernumerary and well-feed estate offices.[68] The crown's trump card was to concentrate the distribution of such patronage in a large, splendid and comparatively open court.

Though the dominance of the court in the political structure of early Tudor England can readily be exaggerated, there is no doubt that as a centre of royal propaganda and political control it was more important than it had ever been before. Local office was most easily won through the court, and when it was resumed it was most easily won back through the court. By the end of 1516, eighty or more office-holders deprived under the act of resumption had had their grants renewed, for constableships of castles, offices whose fees the general surveyors had refused to pay because they could not be found in accounts of Henry VII's reign, or offices granted in survivorship. The vast majority of those who gained these regrants were in some sense courtiers, and there is no sign that Wolsey tried to bypass the normal workings of the court to impede them. At the top there were the likes of Charles, earl of Worcester, the lord chamberlain, who obtained on 14 June, 1515, a grant renewing all the offices which made him the most powerful man in the Welsh marches, and as that was not enough to get all his £245 2s 0d fees paid, a warrant from the king to the general surveyors, commanding payment without objection, on 13 July, 1516.[69] The vice-chamberlain and captain of the guard, Sir Henry Marney, acted faster still, having his offices regranted on 11 May 1515, and then securing full payment of his fees for the period between Easter and the regrant under a privy seal letter of 6 March 1516.[70] Lesser men about the court often reached the king long before their superiors: Thomas Broke, serjeant-at-arms and a former yeoman usher of the chamber, gained the distinction of being the first person, after those who attached provisos to the act itself, to obtain the king's signature on bills confirming him in his offices, and these reached the great seal only eleven days after the closing of parliament.[71] And, as

68 B.J.Harris, *Edward Stafford, Third Duke of Buckingham, 1478–1521* (Stanford, 1986), p.137; M.E.James, 'A Tudor Magnate and the Tudor State: Henry fifth earl of Northumberland', in his *Society, Politics and Culture* (Cambridge, 1986), pp.51–2.

69 W.R.B.Robinson, 'Early Tudor Policy Towards Wales: the Acquisition of Lands and Offices in Wales by Charles Somerset, earl of Worcester', *Bulletin of the Board of Celtic Studies* 20 (1962–4), 421–38.

70 *LP* II, i.439; PRO SC6/Henry VIII/345 m.3v.

71 *LP* II, i.329, 330.

ever, the men closest to the king found it easiest to be importunate. The first two provisos to be signed by the king and added to the bill in parliament seem, from the notes on the originals, to have been those for Sir William Compton and Sir John Sharpe, two of the king's most intimate servants in the privy chamber. The aptly-named Sharpe also secured four confirmatory grants of office in April, one in June and one in December, plus a signed bill to the chancellor in September, commanding him to make as many grants as necessary to Sharpe and Sir John Pecche to restore them to all the offices and fees they held before the act.[72]

Since so many grants were renewed, the act had little effect on the structure of office-holding. Once again, upheaval would not necessarily have been in the king's best interests, for the office-holders constituted a royal affinity in the localities which the king would have been unwise to disown.[73] As in the case of annuities, the delay between resumption and regrant cut in half the fees paid on many positions for the year 1514–15, but they soon returned to normal.[74] The sealing fees on the many letters patent issued to confirm offices and annuities did boost the hanaper's income by £600 or £700 a year for two years, just as an anonymous advocate of acts of resumption suggested to Thomas Cromwell, probably in 1533, that in returning resumed grants 'the kynges grace shall & may take avauntage & profite by the seale'.[75] On the constableships of North Welsh castles there were some long-term savings: wages of nearly £370 a year for mainly non-existent soldiers manning Caernarvon and Beaumaris castles, granted to Charles Brandon and Sir Roland de Veleville early in the reign, and unselfconsciously referred to by Brandon as an augmentation of his fee, were not restored.[76] But once again, the act fell very far short of effecting major cuts in crown expenditure or increases in crown income.

The implementation of the act gave the general surveyors and exchequer officials a good chance to iron out some of the administrative confusions of the previous five years. The wages of the king's librarian were at length confirmed as a legitimate expense on the Bristol customs,

---

72 6 Henry VIII c. 25 s. 14; *LP* II, i. 347–50, 621, 930, 1289.
73 D. R. Starkey, 'Ightam Mote: Politics and Architecture in Early Tudor England', *Archaeologia* 107 (1982), 158–61.
74 PRO SC6/Henry VIII/345 passim.; cf. many other items in class SC6/ Henry VIII. For examples in print, see R. Somerville, *History of the Duchy of Lancaster*, i (London, 1953), pp. 388–654; R. A. Griffiths, *The Principality of Wales in the Later Middle Ages*, i (Cardiff, 1972); *Thirty-Ninth Report of the Deputy Keeper of the Public Records* (London, 1878), Appendix, pp. 1–306.
75 PRO E101/220/7; 'Four Early Tudor Financial Memoranda', ed. S. Jack, R. S. Schofield, *Bull. Inst. Hist. Res.* 36 (1963), 202.
76 PRO SC11/837; SC6/Henry VIII/5420 m. 5; Gunn, 'North Wales', 466–7.

for example, and Charles Brandon finally secured his fees for a set of stewardships for which he had obtained several unavailing royal grants since 1513.[77] Many reversions and grants in survivorship were abrogated, and this was a genuine success of the act. Certainly some such grants were renewed, and not only for teams of two or three auditors, for whom tenure in survivorship was an eminently sensible arrangement. New grants in survivorship were being made by February 1516. Yet their partial curtailment did enhance the crown's freedom to distribute its patronage, since, as Cromwell's anonymous correspondent argued, joint patents and reversions 'put' the monarch 'from his libertie'; such grants had been used all too often by one courtier to buy out another, or by a father to ensure his son's succession in the possibly distant future.[78] Similar improvements were the aim of another statute of spring 1515, which ordered that all those seeking grants of offices for which others already held patents should declare the details of the former grant, or their new grant would be void. Surprisingly few cases arise in the records of such chicanery, 'wherby', as the act put it, 'the said form[er] patentees have ben advoyded and put from th'advauntage of their said form[er] g[ra]unt[es] and patent[es] cont[ra]rie to th'entent and g[ra]unte of oure said sov[er]aigne lord'.[79] In the absence of a computerised patent roll, such problems were common to all late-medieval monarchies, and Wolsey the statesman was doubtless mildly pleased to ease them.[80]

But did Wolsey the politician have personal grounds to be satisfied with the act of resumption? What survives of his correspondence – a comparatively small proportion of the whole – suggests that he might have done. Those who could not plead their case for restoration to the king in person needed help to cope with the act, and some of them sought that help from Wolsey. Many of those who attached provisos to the act may have been sitting in parliament, but Sir Robert Wingfield was not. He was in Augsburg on embassy, and he knew whom to thank when he heard that 'by youre gratious favour it hath pleased the kynge to signe me a proviso for myn anewite and fees. My good lorde' he

---

77 PRO E159/294 Brevia directa, Hilary, 6r; E199/70/1/38v; Gunn, *Charles Brandon*, p. 19.
78 *Letters and Accounts of William Brereton of Malpas*, ed. E. W. Ives (Record Society of Lancashire and Cheshire 116, 1976), pp. 25, 27; 'Financial Memoranda', ed. Jack, Schofield, p. 202.
79 6 Henry VIII c. 15; D. R. Starkey, 'Court and Government', in *Revolution Reassessed: Revisions in the History of Tudor Government and Administration*, ed. C. Coleman, D. R. Starkey (Oxford, 1986), p. 49.
80 W. Paravicini, 'Administrateurs Professionels et Princes Dilettantes', in *Histoire Comparée de l'Administration, ive–xviiie Siècles*, ed. W. Paravicini, K. F. Werner (Beihefte der Francia 9, 1980).

continued 'it hath pleasyd you to taake that labour and payne for hym that is yours to his power, which youre lordship shall knowe by the proffe whanne so evyr it shall lyke you to comawnde or desyre eeythir service or ony oothir thingge that shall lygh in my power'.[81] Sir Richard Wingfield, at Paris, was briefer but equally submissive: 'My lord', he wrote, 'I counte to ha[ve] nothing but by yo[ur] good meanes'.[82] Sir Richard Whethill, at Tournai, called a spade a spade, and offered Wolsey anything he chose to the value of £20 to see him restored to his 40 marks annuity.[83] Lord Mountjoy at Tournai, Anthony Spinola at Paris, and Suffolk on his return from France, all sought Wolsey's help to have their grants renewed.[84] The act, in effect, gave the new minister a hand in redistributing much of the bounty dispensed by the king in the years before Wolsey's rise.

It would be unwise, though, to dismiss the act as merely a clever stratagem in the struggle for power and patronage. The correspondence of others who probably played a part in securing fresh grants for their clients as well as themselves – Sir John Sharpe, say, or Sir Henry Marney – does not survive, and without it we cannot evaluate accurately Wolsey's dominance of the regranting process. In any case, whatever the balance between the minister and other patrons, Wolsey cannot have hoped to take charge of the entire redistribution of patronage generated by the act. To do so he would have had to abrogate the king's freedom to grant – a gross contradiction of Henry's idea of kingship – and somehow abnegated the natural reaction of all Henry's subjects to the act, which was to petition the king. This was a healthy reaction in a personal monarchy, and one so ingrained in the officers of Calais that, when news of the act arrived, the deputy had to order them to stay in the town, rather than cross the Channel en masse to seek their regrants.[85] To interfere with the petitioning process would have created the same tensions between minister and courtiers which have been seen in Wolsey's later periods of reform, but of which there is no sign in 1515. Indeed, 1515 also shows little of the opportunism among courtiers which helped to undo Wolsey's work in the Welsh reforms of 1525.[86] Though new men were coming to the fore around the king – Nicholas Carew, Francis Bryan and others – they did not exploit the resumption to win themselves offices and fees. That this was not because Wolsey chose to exclude them, in favour of other candidates

81 PRO SP1/10 fol. 160r (*LP* II, i. 388).
82 BL MS Cotton Caligula DVI fol. 222v (*LP* II, i. 297).
83 *LP* II, i. 1437.
84 *LP* II, i. 297, 825, 946, 1622, 1855; PRO SP1/30 fol. 260 (*LP* IV, i. 182).
85 *LP* II, i. 297.
86 Gunn, 'North Wales', 489–91.

closer to himself, is suggested by the fact that the act occasioned so little overall change in the distribution of crown patronage. Even those far closer to the old king than to the new were only rarely pushed aside – Thomas, Lord Darcy, for instance, did not lose his £100 annuity from the duchy of Lancaster – and there is no evidence that Wolsey's friends prospered through the act.[87] We cannot tell how far it was Wolsey's ambition to channel royal patronage to his own ends, though it cannot be denied that he stood to gain power and wealth from the influence over the king which others begged him to use on their behalf. What seems clear is that to control patronage, even to make policy, for its own sake, was not Wolsey's only aim: to dismiss him as a mere power-broker is unfair. It is to the credit of Wolsey the statesman that Sir Richard Whethill did not get his 40 marks annuity, and that presumably Wolsey the politician did not get his £20 present.

We need not doubt that Wolsey enjoyed the exercise of power, and its rewards; but we must recognise that in 1515 he tackled serious problems with intelligent measures. In the short term the impact of his policies on crown finance was limited, but important. An effective stop on many payments eased the temporary crisis, while the resumption and its associated measures probably improved the balance of royal payments by something between £5,000 and £10,000 a year. The passing of the act smoothed the passage of the subsidy bill, and facilitated future restrictions on some forms of royal patronage. On the great problems of war finance and the protection of the royal livelihood against the constant pressure for expensive good lordship, Wolsey had achieved far less. But he had done well within the political and historical constraints placed upon him. A resumption which repudiated Henry's largesse and loyalty to his servants, or associated Henry with some of his most incompetent or unsettled predecessors, was as unthinkable as cuts in expenditure which seriously impaired the king's magnificence. Yet Wolsey turned resumption to serve the needs of the moment, to serve the deepest desires of the king and make himself the king's greatest servant. In 1515 the king still aimed above all at international greatness, and it is no surprise that whatever money Wolsey saved was soon paid over to shiftless Swiss mercenaries and the slippery Emperor Maximilian, in yet another attempt to make Henry VIII the arbiter of Europe. In many ways, the act of resumption of 1515 was not quite what it seemed to be, but in the dispersal of its profits it was true to its preamble: economies were made not for their own sake, but to enable Wolsey to spend ever more in the effort to make England and her king 'dradde of all outewarde nacions'.

87 PRO DL28/6/14 fols. 11v–13v.

The Ashwellthorpe Triptych

ANDREW MARTINDALE

The purpose of this paper is to make more widely known a remarkable altar-piece commonly known as the Ashwellthorpe triptych (pl. 1).[1] There are many points of interest about it which illustrate different facets of late medieval art and early Tudor history. It is, too, attractively painted and, in all, it deserves a wider public. It came to the Norwich Castle Museum in 1983. At that time, it had for some years been the property of different members of the same family to whom it had passed from the collection of Lord Lee of Fareham. The general outlines, though not the detail, of this recent history are clear and the painting itself appears in the 1923 catalogue of the Lee collection.[2] Before that it has a reasonably good pedigree back into the eighteenth century in the possession of the Wilson family, the Lords Berners.[3] For the connection with Ashwellthorpe, however, it is necessary to go back even earlier; and it is clear from the heraldry that the original owner was not a Wilson but

---

1 This paper in many ways merely consolidates research done by others and I am pleased to acknowledge this. During the negotiations surrounding the purchase of the triptych, Robin Emerson and Andrew Moore of the Castle Museum, Norwich did a substantial amount of initial research into the antecedents of the picture and of the Knyvetts – and this was 'published' locally at the time. I have used this as the basis for much of my own work. To David King I owe the correct version of the Le Neve document quoted in this article. Mr Tony Simms was a great help in trying to establish the Belgian end of the Van Assche connection. I have also helpful conversations and correspondence with Janet Backhouse and Ann Payne of the British Library, particularly with regard to the heraldry. Finally, Dr Roger Virgoe of the University of East Anglia has in hand a very substantial history of the Knyvetts for this period. It is largely the result of his work that the place of the Knyvetts in the framework of national history is much clearer; and also the place of the Clifton inheritance in the aspirations of the family. All these have been unfailingly helpful – indeed without this assistance, what follows would have been much less interesting.

2 T. Borenius, *A Catalogue of the pictures etc of 18 Kensington Palace Gardens, London, 1923 collected by Viscount and Viscountess Lee of Fareham* (Oxford, 1923) no pagination, no. 28. The painting's history between 1923 and 1983 is recorded in outline in the papers of the Castle Museum, Norwich.

3 In Borenius *op cit.* it is noted that the painting was 'until lately the property of the present Lord Berners'. I return to the question of its pedigree and descent below.

a Knyvett (although, as will be seen, the Wilson family inherited the barony from the Knyvetts by marriage and through an heiress).

The painting contains in its central panel representations of the Seven Sorrows of the Virgin Mary (pl. 2). The Virgin herself is seated in an attitude of humility in the foreground, her submissive posture being commonly associated with the scene of the Annunciation. The episodes of her sorrow are spread out in the landscape behind her. The left wing (pl. 3) contains a kneeling male figure in armour; he is presented by St Christopher. The right panel (pl. 4) contains a kneeling lady; she is presented by St Catherine. Both donors kneel before a misty blue landscape, both bear arms and, in addition, have their arms painted on shields which hang from trees over their heads. Both side panels contain elements which bind them indissolubly to the central panel.[4] There can thus be no reasonable doubt that the triptych was originally devised in this form.[5] The only additional subject matter – on the outer faces of the two wings – are the figures of St John the Evangelist and St Barbara (pl. 5). The altar piece is, on the whole, in good condition.[6]

The arms borne by the man are those of Knyvett and Clifton (pl. 6). The tinctures present an immediate and pressing problem. Clifton may be blazoned as *checky or and gules, overall a bend ermine*. It will be noted that the bend, while containing the black tails for the ermine, is coloured gold. Gilded ermine, termed *erminois*, is not normal for Clifton; and since the gilt is of a different character and quality from that of the *checky*

---

4 The temple of the Presentation spans the gap between the left and central panels; the mound of the Lamentation falls away into the landscape of the right hand panel.

5 Nobody between the time the picture was painted and the date of the Lee Catalogue either described or described correctly and completely the central panel. It is therefore necessary to emphasise its 'belonging' to the wings.

6 Ultraviolet photography confirms the generally favourable impression of its condition. The worst areas of damage are as follows:

Left panel: the head and neck of St Christopher have been largely repainted (this is now pictorially one of the weakest areas in the triptych). The donor's face has been much touched up in its central part and the hands appear to be repainted.

Centre panel: the mouth, left cheek and right eye of the Virgin have been repainted; also the face of the Magdalen in the Entombment (this, too, is one of the weakest areas in the triptych).

Right panel: this is in good condition and the two female heads seem to be the best preserved faces in the triptych (pl. 12).

Outer panel, left: St John's face and left foot and shin have been extensively repainted and there are numerous small areas of touching up.

Outer panel, right: rather better condition than the outer left panel, but with numerous small patches of repaint throughout.

design, it is clear that something has gone wrong with the colour at this point. However, turning to Knyvett is to be confronted by the same problem. A shield, correctly blazoned *argent, a bent and a bordure engrailed all sable*, turns out to be 'gilt' of the same quality as the adjacent *ermine*. The problem is to know what has gone wrong. The answer revealed as a result of scientific analysis carried out at the request of the Norfolk Museums Service, is that the original tincture was indeed silver; and that small traces of this exist, though these are now oxidised. Today what is chiefly visible is a ground pigment with some traces of yellowish overpaint. A similar problem arises in the heraldry of the opposite panel.

The other heraldic problem is the swan, to be seen in the centre of the shield. It might be expected to be a mark of cadency but no such mark is normal in English heraldry. Nevertheless, the donor appears to be a younger son. There are two pointers towards his identification, one positive and the other negative. When Le Neve saw the painting c.1700, he recorded on it the date 1519.[7] He gave no explanation where this was to be seen; but it is likely to have been on the original frame which no longer exists.[8] It would be exceedingly odd as a gratuitous invention, and, if genuine, must give some indication where to look on the family tree. The female donor equally indicates where *not* to look. The wives of all the principal Knyvetts are known; and consequently (see family tree) it can be said that the man is *not* Sir Edward Knyvett (who married a Le Strange) nor Edmund (he married a Tyrrell), nor Sir Thomas (he married a Howard) nor Edward (who married a Bourchier). In practice, this leaves younger sons. There was indeed a younger son called Christopher whose patron may be supposed to have been his name-saint (though this does not always follow). Unfortunately, the life of Christopher is obscure. There is very little to show that he owned property in England,[9] and he appears financially to have made his way as a servant of the King (as indeed did several other members of the family). From 1514 to 1520, he received a salary as a member of the royal household. He was in the Netherlands in 1512 on a mission to Margaret of Austria. In 1513, he was part of the military campaign

---

7 For the description, see below.
8 The present frame appears, as a piece of carpentry, to be entirely separate from the painted panels. It would appear to be an exceedingly handsome evocation of the period around 1500; and it is likely to have been made for Lord Lee.
9 Dr Virgoe has pointed out that Sir Christopher Knyvett was mentioned in Dean Colet's will (1519) and became in the same year the holder in tail of lands in Weldon (Northants) paying an annuity to John Colet's feoffees. This seems to be the only evidence of Christopher being 'landed'.

which captured Tournai. In 1515, he was rewarded with a grant of lands in Tournai. That is all that is known about him.[10]

If Christopher is indeed represented in the left wing of the Ashwell-thorpe triptych, his wife opposite can with some confidence be said to be a member of the Van Assche family from Brabant. Her identity has long been elusive, partly because so little is known about Christopher and partly because the heraldic evidence is ambiguous. It seems necessary at the start, therefore, to introduce into the discussion a book of genealogies now in the British Library (Add. MS 5530). This dates from the first half of the sixteenth century and has been attributed to Thomas Wriothesley, Garter King of Arms (died 1534). Several folios (ff. 146r–150v) are dedicated to the Knyvetts and their antecedents. Christopher duly appears, married to a lady described (without Christian name) as *filia et heres domini de Aske in Brabancia prope Brucellis*.[11]

The arms of the lady may be blazoned as *or, a fess azure overall a saltire gules* (pl. 7). Even at this stage of the description, problems arise since the *or* would appear to be in exactly the same condition as the errant argent/ermine of Knyvett/Clifton. It seems necessary to assume therefore that it was originally *argent*.[12] In its design, the blazon appears in origin to have belonged to

10 This information is all contained in J. S. Brewer, *Letters and Papers Foreign and Domestic of the reign of Henry VIII* vols. II and III (London, 1864 and 1867). R. Virgoe has pointed out that the accounts by which Christopher was paid his wages are deficient, leaving a strong likelihood that he was paid £20 p.a. continuously from 1514–20. He has also pointed out that Brewer's version contains an error (vol. III item 1114) where Christopher is apparently listed as 'the King's priest at Walsingham'. In the original, the entry is similar to that on III p. 1535 where (in 1519) Christopher received his usual £10 per half year; and the King's priest at Walsingham is clearly distinguished as a separate person immediately following. This is of some importance since it extends Christopher's life at least up to March 1520. Because of the deficiences in the series, he may have lived longer. On the other hand, his previous regular employment in the service of the crown makes it unlikely that he survived long after this date since he is never heard of again.

11 The confirmation that this lady was a Van Assche of Brabant removes an important area of speculation. English heraldic textbooks attribute these arms to the English family of Ashe, specifically of Somerset (J. Edmondson *A complete body of heraldry*, London, 1700, under *Ashe*). Up to now there has remained the possibility that Christopher was married to an English wife. This may now be discounted since it is entirely unlikely that the compiler of the genealogy would have manufactured the Brabantine connection.

12 When Le Neve (see below) saw the painting c. 1700, he blazoned the field of arms as *or* so that the colour change had already occurred. He also recorded the *fess* as *sable* though it is, at least on the lady's mantle, clearly *azure*. The colour change of the argent/or is to be seen most clearly on the shield in the tree, where it may, as in the case of Knyvett, be contrasted with the true *or* of Clifton.

the Lords of Grimberghen. By the late thirteenth century, it was used by the Lords of Assche, one of whom, John, is said to have been the uncle and heir of Robert of Grimberghen.[13] The escutcheon with a field of *argent* appears in the Camden Roll of Arms c. 1280, attributed to the Sire d'Asche.[14] Notwithstanding this, however, the Assche family by the late fourteenth century seems to have adopted the field of *or*. There is no problem about their centre of gravity. Grimberghen and Assche are both close to Brussels; and members of the Van Assche family (sometimes also called van Grimberghen) can be traced in Brussels in the position of *echevin* and bearing the same arms (with *or*) through the fifteenth and into the sixteenth century.[15] However, the compiler of the genealogy calls the Ashwellthorpe lady *filia et heres domini de Aske* which indicates a very important status. If the genealogy of the Van Assche family has been studied, it should immediately be possible to see where she fits into the family tree. The British Library Knyvett genealogy shows no children from the marriage to Christopher; and, as an heiress, it is quite possible that she married again after Christopher's death. (The fact that the author of Add. 5530 did not know her christian name suggests that she was no longer 'available' in England. She may, of course, have died.)

Nevertheless, the problem of the tinctures remains if the Ashwellthorpe shield was originally coloured *argent*. For there was in the fifteenth and sixteenth centuries a quite separate group of families Maelstede – Moerseke – Lessinghers who used precisely the same design but with an *argent* or *ermine* field. Neither their relationship to each other nor to the Lords of Grimberghen are clear; nor their centre of gravity. In fact, they appear to divide between Holland and Flanders.[16] It is most

---

13 On this J-Th. de Raadt *Sceaux armoriés des Pays-Bas et des Pays Avoisinants* (Brussels, 1898) p. 123 ff. under Grimberghe. See also under Assche p. 185.

14 G. J. Brault *Eight thirteenth-century rolls of arms in French and Anglo-Norman blazon* (Pennsylvania and London, 1973) pp. 68–76, the Camden Roll no. 56. There are a number of other Netherlandish arms including no. 57 'Munsire Louwis Bertout'.

15 See de Raadt *op cit.* pp. 185 and 516. The history of the Lordship of Grimberghen and of the Asshe family was related by the Brabant herald Edmond de Dynter down to c. 1420, see P. F. X. de Ram *Chronique des dues de Brabant par Edmond de Dynter* (Brussels, 1854–60).

16 According to de Raadt, *op cit.*, p. 598; the fourteenth-century herald Gelre attributed the *ermine* field to Maelstede of Holland. The *argent* and *ermine* alternatives are given to Maelstede (of Holland) in the armorial attributed to John le Fevre, Sire de St Remy, chief officer of Arms to the Order of the Golden Fleece sometime after 1440. (R. Pinches *A European Armorial*, London, 1971, pp. 66–7.) On the other hand, the same shields are illustrated but in a Flemish context in an armorial compiled c. 1562 (P Bergmans *Armorial de Flandre du XVI*ᵐᵉ *siècle*, Brussels and Paris, 1919 fol. 50v and fol. 55v) Rietstap (*Armorial Général* 1884) attributed it to Flanders.

unlikely that the information from the Knyvett genealogy is wrong. For one thing, if it was compiled c. 1530, its author was in a position to know the facts. (There were plenty of Knyvetts around.) For another, it would be a surprising piece of circumstantial evidence to invent. But the anomaly of the tinctures remains.[17]

The lady's arms have in the past appeared to present a further problem since her escutcheon, hanging on the tree, is lozenge-shaped. The standard works on English heraldry are clear about the meaning of this – the lady should be a widow, granted that she appears to be in the presence of her husband.[18] However, although it is very difficult to establish the continental conventions in these matters, it is noticeable that virtually all female arms painted in similar circumstances during this period are in lozenges; and since it seems statistically unlikely that we are confronted by a long sequence of widows, it seems more probable that in the Netherlands at least the lozenge shape was normal for a married armigerous lady.[19] This is of some importance since it has reasonably been suggested that the presumed fact of her widowhood might be used to explain both the date of the altar and its subject matter. Yet, as will become clear, a date in the 1520s is stylistically late for the altar in relation to others by the same hand; and the choice of subject matter is more likely to be properly understood in relation to a comparatively new Netherlandish devotional cult.[20]

Speculation about the wife of Christopher Knyvett tends to divert attention from the third coat of arms present in the triptych – that of Clifton. There was, of course, a Clifton marriage in the first half of the fifteenth century between Sir John Knyvett and Elizabeth Clifton (see family tree). By the second decade of the sixteenth century, however,

17 The anomaly of the tinctures is matched by the anomaly of the quality of the heraldic painting. This is decidedly inferior to that of the rest of the altar and likely to have been added by a different artist – presumably an heraldic specialist, who may have operated either in Brabant or in England. Notwithstanding Friedländer's approval of the heraldic work in the paintings of the Magdalen Master ('notably large and clearly done with loving care') the results here are murky and lack-lustre.

18 See A.C. Fox-Davies *A Complete guide to heraldry* revised and edited by J.P. Brooke. Litte (London, 1985) p. 410, and C. Boutell *Heraldry historical and popular* (London, 1863) p. 152. Both authors agree that a peeress in her own right may also bear her arms in a lozenge (respectively p. 409 and p. 153); but this is hardly relevant here.

19 The illustrations in Friedländer's early sixteenth-century volume (*Early Netherlandish Painting*) suggest that lozenges were the norm for female arms. I am very grateful to Ann Payne for confirming this impression from her professional knowledge.

20 See below.

that event was more than half a century away. The Knyvett family was certainly entitled to those arms; it may initially seem less clear why they continued to display them to the exclusion of many others.

It has recently become clear how crucial to the Knyvett family was the Clifton connection. The family tree (p. 114) shows how, by its means, doors were opened to power and influence which would otherwise have been firmly shut. It also provides the background to one of those late medieval property disputes in which a late starter comes up from behind the field to win the race.[21] It has long been known that, in East Anglian terms, the Knyvett family are comparatively recent arrivals. Originating from Northamptonshire, they made their first effective appearance in the eastern counties in the late fourteenth century. This was through a marriage which brought with it, amongst other things, the manor of Mendlesham in Suffolk. The first of these 'East Anglians' was buried in the church there in 1418. It was however his son's marriage to Elizabeth Clifton which was to give the Knyvett family in the course of the second half of the fifteenth century a position of exceptional prominence and power in Norfolk society. The lands at issue were the substantial remnants of the Tattershall inheritance. In the early years of the previous century, this had separated into two portions of which one, centred on Buckenham castle, descended through the Cailly family to the Cliftons. It was this portion which John Knyvett succeeded in securing in 1461 after a protracted legal battle which had lasted since the death of Sir John Clifton in 1447 and which had been carried on through the series of major military and political upheavals leading to the second battle of St Albans.

During the 1470s the Knyvetts also made good a claim to the remnants of the other part of the Tattershall inheritance. This had descended to the Lords Cromwell; and an earlier Clifton had married a daughter of the first Lord Cromwell. That legal battle was settled in 1476 though it was several years before the full benefits of the settlement was enjoyed. However, from this it will be seen how central to the fortunes of the Knyvett family was the Clifton marriage.

The evident importance of the Cliftons is to be seen also in the heraldic displays surviving in or on the churches connected with the Knyvetts at Old and New Buckenham. The shields round the west door of New Buckenham church are especially interesting since they illustrate

---

21 What follows abbreviates the extensive research of Dr Roger Virgoe into the history of the Knyvett family. It will appear in full in a forthcoming issue of *Norfolk Archaeology* and I am extremely grateful for his generous permission to use the typescript. The family tree represents a part of his research in a simplified form.

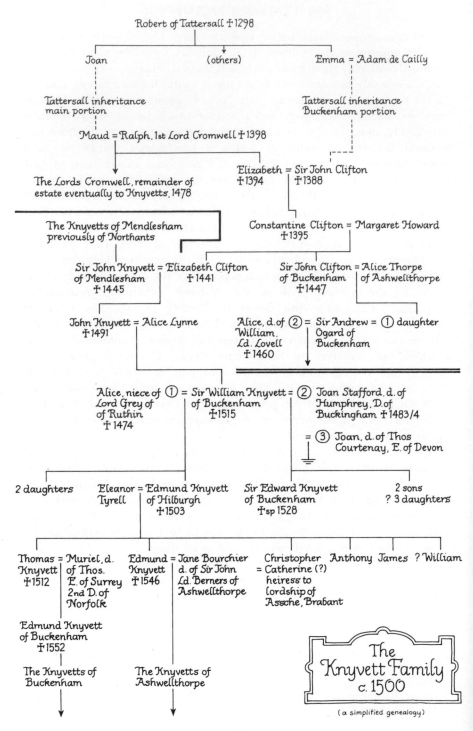

Robert of Tattersall ✝1298

Joan   (others)   Emma = Adam de Cailly

Tattersall inheritance
main portion

Tattersall inheritance
Buckenham portion

Maud = Ralph, 1st Lord Cromwell ✝1398

The Lords Cromwell, remainder of
estate eventually to Knyvetts, 1478

Elizabeth = Sir John Clifton
✝1394   ✝1388

The Knyvetts of Mendlesham
previously of Northants

Constantine Clifton = Margaret Howard
✝1395

Sir John Knyvett = Elizabeth Clifton
of Mendlesham   ✝1441
✝1445

Sir John Clifton = Alice Thorpe
of Buckenham   of Ashwellthorpe
✝1447

John Knyvett = Alice Lynne
✝1491

Alice, d. of ②= Sir Andrew = ① daughter
William,   Ogard of
Ld. Lovell   Buckenham
✝1460

Alice, niece of ① = Sir William Knyvett = ② Joan Stafford, d. of
Lord Grey of   of Buckenham   Humphrey, D. of
of Ruthin   ✝1515   Buckingham ✝1483/4
✝1474

= ③ Joan, d. of Thos
Courtenay, E. of Devon

2 daughters   Eleanor = Edmund Knyvett
           Tyrell   of Hilburgh
                   ✝1503

Sir Edward Knyvett
of Buckenham
✝sp 1528

2 sons
? 3 daughters

Thomas = Muriel, d.
Knyvett   of Thos.
✝1512   E. of Surrey
       2nd D. of
       Norfolk

Edmund = Jane Bourchier
Knyvett   d. of Sir John
✝1546   Ld. Berners of
       Ashwellthorpe

Christopher   Anthony   James   ? William
= Catherine (?)
heiress to
lordship of
Assche, Brabant

Edmund Knyvett
of Buckenham
✝1552

The Knyvetts of
Buckenham

The Knyvetts of
Ashwellthorpe

The
Knyvett Family
c. 1500

(a simplified genealogy)

what might be seen as an alternative armorial emphasis. The arms (pls. 8 and 9) are as follows (the shields have, of course, lost their original colour). Over the door:

1. Bohun – a bend cotised between six lions rampant
2. Bohun – as above (1)
3. Stafford – a chevron
4. Thomas of Woodstock[22] – quarterly, 1st and 4th France modern, 2nd and 3rd 3 lions passant gardent all within a bordure
5. Knyvett and Cailly quartered[23]
6. Knyvett quartered with ? (now unreadable)[24]
7. Knyvett and Cailly quartered (as for 5)
8. Lynne: a demi-lion rampant within a bordure charged with roundels

In the spandrels

9. Left, Knyvett and Clifton quartered[25]
10. Right, Albini – a lion rampant

The greatest political and social coup of Sir William Knyvett had been to marry, as his second wife, Joan, the daughter of Humphrey Stafford,

22 E. Farrer *The Church Heraldry of Norfolk* (Norwich, 1887) I. p. 60 gives this shield as Holland. In the context, this makes no sense.
23 The arms for Cailly are variously reported – most often as the same as those for Clifton. The alternative *bendy of five, argent and gules* (there are slight variations in the description) has no clear source though noted in both Rietstap and Edmondson, cited above; and accepted by Farrar (cited above) and Duleep Singh (cited below).
24 Farrer (*op cit.* above) says that Knyvett is here quartered with Bassett; and he blazons the shield as *Paly of six within a bordure charged with roundels*. It is now almost illegible; but the bordure with roundels may still be seen and within it vertical lines which may be the outlines of *pales* Blomefield gave this blazon and presumably the shield was in a better condition in the eighteenth century. Its identification as Basset of Weldon presents problems. The Bassets were a far-flung family; and the English textbooks give their main charge variously as *pales* and *piles*. The *Complete Peerage* (II p. 9), basing itself on glass in Great Weldon Church (Northants) opts for *or, three piles gules, a bordure sable bezantee* for the Bassets of Weldon. It is not clear therefore what heraldic advice was taken at New Buckenham c. 1500 since an allusion to Great Weldon is entirely in keeping with the other shields. The Weldon estates in Northants came to the Knyvett family in the second half of the fourteenth century by marriage to an heiress – a generation before the Knyvetts came to Mendlesham.
25 Farrer *op cit.* states that this shield is 'quite gone but it is given thus [i.e.: as Heveningham] by Blomefield'. However, the distinctive *bend* of Clifton is still discernible – which in itself makes it impossible for these arms to have been Heveningham (always given in Blomefield as *quarterly or and gules in a bordure engrailed sable eight escallops argent*).

duke of Buckingham. Descended from Thomas of Woodstock, son of Edward III and from Thomas' marriage with Eleanor de Bohun, Joan added to the Knyvett lineage a lustre which was otherwise totally lacking. The marriage in practice led to a schism in the family since the principal property of Buckenham was diverted to Joan's son Sir Edward, notwithstanding the existence of an elder son Edmund. In those circumstances the west door of New Buckenham could only have been erected for Sir Edward.[26]

It is nevertheless interesting that the principal arms in the spandrels are devoted to Knyvett and Clifton, and – in genealogical terms, a very long shot – Albini, the post conquest lords of Buckenham. This is apparently the side of the family stressed on the south (right) side of the upper row of shields. It also represents the connections stressed in the glass which survives at Old Buckenham.[27] The fact is that the Stafford alliance gave the Knyvetts 'class' but also a precarious political position. It was the Clifton alliance which had given them the stability of land upon which their influence depended.

The triptych was attributed by Friedländer to an unidentified painter whom he called the Master of the Magdalen legend or the Magdalen Master.[28] Of the group of paintings which he assembled, two triptychs stand out as being very close to the Norwich painting. One, now in Brussels, has as its central feature an *Annunciation* (pl. 10); the other (whereabouts unknown) had a *Lamentation*. In both the wings have kneeling donors whose arms are attached to the branches of trees above their heads. In both, the treatment of the central subject derives directly from ideas generated within the circle of Roger van der Weyden.[29]

In one sense, the Norwich painting looks more old-fashioned than either of those other two triptychs – namely, in its severe rectangular format which is instantly reminiscent of the fifteenth-century triptychs by painters such as Roger Van der Weyden and Hans Memlinc; and it

26 An almost identical set of arms is to be seen on the brass to one of Sir Edward's sisters, Elizabeth, buried at Eastington, Glos. (died 1518). See A. C. Fox-Davies *A Complete Guide to Heraldry* revised and annotated by J. P. Brooke-Little (London, 1985) p. 44. Roger Virgoe informs me that she belonged to the household of the Duke of Buckingham.

27 This was described by F. Duleep Singh, *Norfolk Archaeology* XV (1904) pp. 324–35, 'Armorial glass in Old and New Buckenham churches'. It includes Tattershall, Cromwell, Cailly, Clifton and Thorpe as well as Knyvett.

28 M. J. Friedländer *Early Netherlandish Painting* (Leyden and Brussels, 1975) vol. XII, pp. 13–17.

29 The format for the Annunciation devised in Roger's workshop probably as early as the 1430s was repeated throughout the fifteenth century in works of painters such as Bouts and Memling. The same is true of the Deposition/ Pieta theme.

will be necessary to return to this point. The treatment of the central panel is unusual. It offers a form of storytelling in which the viewer is invited to pursue a sort of visual pilgrimage through the landscape, pausing to meditate at certain chosen resting places. Although this type of composition received a powerful impetus from a number of prominent fourteenth century Italian mural paintings,[30] it was in fact not particularly imitated in the fifteenth century. Nevertheless, there survive two striking examples from the workshop of Hans Memlinc. One at Turin, dated 1470, shows the story of the Passion. The other in Munich, dated 1480, is more difficult to label but seems to combine the story of the Magi with the Joys of Mary.[31]

The Ashwellthorpe triptych has, as its theme, the Seven Sorrows of the Virgin. Taking its tone from the grisaille figure set in the architecture on the left of David lamenting over the head of Absalom, the spectator is invited to ponder, in turn, the Presentation, the Flight into Egypt, Christ seated amongst the Doctors, the road to Golgotha, the Crucifixion, the Deposition and the Entombment.

The iconography of the Seven Sorrows of the Virgin was of comparatively recent invention in the early sixteenth century. The veneration of the Virgin in her sadness was, of course, much earlier; and by the early fourteenth century certain image-makers had seized on Simeon's words 'Yea, a sword shall pierce through thine own heart' (Luke 2.35) to show, quite literally, the Virgin with a sword with its point entering her heart. That interpretation is invariably northern; and the regularisation of the cult of the *Virgin of Sorrows* appears to have taken place at the synod of Cologne in 1423, where it was a part of a small package of measures devised to counter the influence of the Hussites.[32] However, it seems agreed that a more significant development was the foundation of a Confraternity in Bruges which received papal authorisation in 1495. The object of its veneration was Our Lady of the Seven Sorrows.[33] Other

---

30 Notably the frescoes of *Good and Bad Government* by Ambrogio Lorenzetti in the Palazzo Pubblico, Siena (1338–9); and the fresco of the *Three Living and Three Dead* and of the *Thebaid* in the Campo Santo at Pisa attributed to Buffalmacco (c. 1340).

31 See M. Corti and G. T. Faggin *L'opera completa di Memling* (Milan, 1969) cat. nos. 9 and 42. The same technique of narrative painting is to be found in the Altar of the two St Johns and in the Lubeck altar (ibid. nos. 6 and 16, dated 1479 and 1491).

32 For the decisions of the Synod of Cologne see *Acta Conciliorum et epistolae decretalis ac constitutiones summorum pontificum* (Paris, 1714) vol. 8, cols. 1007–14, chap. XI.

33 For general accounts, see E. Mâle *L'art religieux de la fin du moyen age en France* (Paris, 1949) p. 122 ff; L. Réau *Iconographie de l'art Chretien* (Paris, 1957) vol II, pt. 2, pp. 108–10; E. Kirschbaum *Lexikon der Christlichen Ikonographie* (Rome, Freiburg, Basel, Vienna, 1972) vol. 4 pp. 86–7.

dedications followed and also altarpieces celebrating the cult. It is difficult now to know where the visual image was launched but the essential ingredients seem present in an altar ordered from Jan Joest for Palencia cathedral by the bishop in 1505.[34] In this altar, the central panel containing the Virgin comforted by St John (and with the kneeling donor) is surrounded by seven smaller panels, each containing a separate episode. Other altars from the first twenty-five years of the century adopt what became a more normal format for the image. The Virgin seated dolorously alone is surrounded by seven small roundels each containing a scene (the same format was used for the Seven Joys of Mary and also for our Lady of the Rosary). It is a simple device calculated to concentrate the devotions of the beholder as his eyes move in an orderly fashion round the picture from vignette to vignette.[35]

The Ashwellthorpe artist showed considerable originality in rejecting that common approach. He may have appeared old-fashioned; but in this case his idea of drawing his audience on a pilgrimage through a landscape has much to commend it. Emile Mâle showed considerable asperity towards the iconography of the Virgin of the Seven Sorrows, which he regarded as an uncouth Netherlandish invention incapable of being translated into high art. The Ashwellthorpe triptych surely shows him to have been wrong. However nobody imitated it; it remains unique.

The painting is, indeed, thoroughly conservative in its general approach and tone. Only in a few details of the architecture is there any suggestion that this is a sixteenth century rather than a fifteenth century work.[36] This is in keeping with the little that Friedländer deduced about the artist. He seems to have had a longish career from c.1490 to c.1525 and to have had a reputable court clientele at Brussels which included

---

34 See M.J.Friedländer *Early Netherlandish Painting* vol.IX, pt.1 (Leyden and Brussels, 1972) – Jan Joest, cat. no.2.

35 The chronology of this second type is less clear. A version said to date at least from 1505 attributed to Matsys (now in Brussels, Musée Royale des Beaux Arts) has six medallions floating in the air round a central Pietà group. The Virgin is pierced by a single sword (M.J.Friedländer *op cit.* vol.VII, cat.no.63). In an altar by C.Engelbrechtsz (now in Leyden and dated by Friedländer to c.1510) the central subject is a Lamentation group while the other 'sorrows' are contained separately within the (painted) gothic frame. In a diptych attributed to Ysenbrandt and probably dating from the 1520s, two separate representations of the Seven Sorrows show the Virgin seated in the centre and the seven sorrows accommodated within the architectural frame-work or structure against which she sits. (See Friedländer *op. cit.* vol.XI, cat.no.138.)

36 The 'renaissance' architectural detail amounts to a little more than the use of rectangular pilasters and lintels carved in low relief; a gable decorated with a large shell motif; and a roundel containing a relief bust.

members of the Hapsburg family. Some of his best painting is derived directly from his great predecessors in Flemish art. He possessed, for instance, a splendid ability to capture the misty blue of distant landscapes; and the sheen of armour is caught with all the panache of the Eyckian tradition.[37]

However, the orb (pl. 11) held by the Christchild on the shoulders of St Christopher needs special comment. Orbs, being a part of normal regalia, are generally painted as superior pieces of goldsmith's work – where they are characterised at all. Sporadically other possibilities appear. Both the Master of the Westminster Retable in the later thirteenth century and Simone Martini at Avignon c. 1340 portrayed orbs in which are to be clearly distinguished the sky, the land and the sea. At Westminster, the artist showed a small boat on the water; Simone Martini showed miniscule trees and mountains. After a quite different manner (and much later) both Jan van Eyck and Hugo van der Goes, painted the orb translucently as if it was made of crystal. The Magdalen Master combined both these ideas in the Ashwellthorpe triptych. One looks into a crystal orb and into a tiny independent world. A mysterious river wanders through a rocky valley with, on one side, a tiny church. Afloat on the water is an even tinier boat with a man in it. This is all the purest fantasy contained in an area about the size of a tenpence piece; it is, perhaps, a gesture towards the world of Patenir.[38]

The Ashwellthorpe Triptych fits into a clearly established pattern of Netherlandish domination of English patronage. This displacement away from France towards the Low Countries perhaps started in the fourteenth century with the marriage of Edward III to Philippa of Hainault and it persists through into the seventeenth century. The portrait of Edward Grimston (on loan to the National Gallery, London) provides an interesting illustration of this. One of the men of William de la Pole, Earl of Suffolk, he went to the Low Countries on a diplomatic mission in 1446 and presumably had his picture taken then (by Petrus Christus, successor at Bruges to Jan van Eyck). In the years c. 1475–80, another Englishman, Sir John Donne, also ordered a painting in Bruges – a triptych by the successor to Christus, Hans Memlinc. There are an amazing number of fifteenth century manuscripts made and decorated

---

37 Friedländer suggested that he might be one of the members of the De Coninxloo family, a prolific clan of painters. Of these he suggested Pieter de Coninxloo as a possibility; but no documented works survive as a basis for reconstructing his work.

38 Crystaline orbs are discussed briefly by J. Baltrŭsaitis *Le Moyen Age Fantastique* (Paris, 1981) pp. 195–9 who illustrates a very similar orb from a *Salvator Mundi* by Joss van Cleve (Paris, Louvre). Friedländer *op cit*. VII, p. 57 dated this c. 1515, in which case it would be very close in date to the Ashwellthorpe triptych.

in the Netherlands but for English patrons.[39] On a larger scale, the Eton College wall-paintings, the sculpture of Henry VII's chapel and the stained glass of Kings College, Cambridge, all testify to the powerful attraction of Flemish art. Even at an entirely local level, the influence is perceptible. It has recently been shown that the painter of a group of early sixteenth century Norfolk roodscreens had, as part of his equipment, an assortment of engravings by Israel van Meckenen (after Schongauer) and Lucas van Leyden.[40]

The rectangular format of the Ashwellthorpe triptych makes it in an obvious way similar to the Donne triptych. In fact, it is rather more like another formula for the private altar on which the central panel contains an event rather than a group of holy persons. Obvious comparisons with works by David and Memlinc merely reinforce the impression that, in the world of painting, it was with the style of Bruges that foreigners – or at least Englishmen – felt at home.[41]

Even so, the apparent date of the painting still remains an enigma. It has already been shown that the use of a lozenge does not seem necessarily to imply that the lady was already a widow. Moreover since Christopher Knyvett survived into 1520, the date 1519 reported by Le Neve cannot have any connection with his death. But the date 1519 itself remains a problem. By that time, the fashionable shape for the upper frame of a Netherlandish altarpiece was a curvilinear rather than rectilinear. The two comparable altars by the Magdalen Master follow that convention; and though 1519 is not impossible, the Ashwellthorpe triptych would at that date have seemed very conservative.

The survival of the Ashwellthorpe triptych is a matter for comment. In a sense, its history is clear. Commissioned for a Knyvett, it was in 1908 apparently still in the hands of a family which could claim the blood if not name of Knyvett. At almost every step of this chronological journey, however, there are uncertainties. In the first instance, granted that the circumstances of the deaths of both Christopher and his wife are unknown, it is not entirely clear why the painting came into the possession of the family of Edmund Knyvett of Ashwellthorpe rather than that of Edmund Knyvett of Buckenham, the senior branch (see family tree).

If, however, it is assumed that Christopher died c.1520–1, this would have been during the minority of Edmund Knyvett of Buckenham. It is

39 They have been 'collected' into a group by Nicholas Rogers.
40 For this, see the recent research of John Mitchell, shortly to be published.
41 For the closest comparisons, see the Reins triptych (1480) by Hans Memlinc; and the triptych of the Baptism of Christ by Gerard David (both in Bruges, Hospital of St John).

possible to imagine that Edmund Knyvett of Ashwellthorpe acted as administrator of Christopher's estate and acquired his dead brother's religious painting in the course of exercising those responsibilities. That the altarpiece became associated with Ashwellthorpe can now only be inferred from a note made by Le Neve c. 1700. This has already been quoted in part and the full text may now be given.

There is a fine old picture formerly at Ashwellthorpe dated 1519 now at Weston in Suffolk with a man in armour kneeling at an alter. Knivett and Clifton quarterly with a crescent. Against him a woman in a dress of that age on a lozenge behind her Knyvet and Clifton quarterly as before impaled with or a fess sable surmounted by a saltire gules. This by the pedigree is ... Clifton of ... and ... his wife daughter of...[42]

Perhaps at this point it would be convenient to complete the history of the painting. The best subsequent description was given by Thomas Kerrich who visited Didlington in 1795. He was mainly interested in portraits and at Didlington he found 'a vast number which came from Ashwellthorpe'. His description of the subject of this paper is unmistakeable.

Drawing Room
An old picture of the Virgin of Sorrows well-painted. On one door Sir... Knevet kneeling in Armour and a Surcoat and St Christopher. On the other his Lady kneeling and St Catherine. Their Arms hang on a tree in each picture. His are Knevet quartering cheque O and G a band Ermine Clifton. Hers the same impaling O, a Fess S, over all a Saltire G. NB. in this the field of Knevet is O, and so is that of the Ermine bend of Clifton. NB. She has his Arms and her own on her Clothe or Mantle. He seems to have his only (i.e. Knevet quartering Clifton) on his surcoat. They seem to be of the time of

---

42 I am very grateful to David King for this document. Its reference is Norfolk Record Office (Norwich) Frere MSS Box K.1 (B). Depwade 100 (ii). It should be said that this note by Le Neve clearly formed the basis for a statement by Blomefield concerning stained glass in the east window of Ashwellthorpe church (vol. V p. 161). Blomefield's description of the window runs as follows: 'In the east window are the remains of a knight in armour, kneeling at an altar tomb, and Knyvett and Clifton quartered by him with a crescent; against him is a woman kneeling, in a dress of that age, with the said quarters in a lozenge, impaling or, a fess sab. surmounted by a saltire gul. and there was a picture of it at Ashwell-thorp which I take to have been erected either to the memory of ... Sir John Knevet ... or rather of Sir John his son and his wife Elizabeth, daughter of Sir Constantine Clifton..' Much of this is manifestly Le Neve's description of the painting. How the confusion occurred and what was visible in the church can now only be a matter for conjecture.

Edward 4 or Henry 7. NB By him is a helmet like those we now in Heraldry give to an Esquire but the Helmet over the Escutcheon of his arms which hangs on the tree is a Baron's Helmet.[43]

In the *Norfolk Tour* published in 1829, the picture was still apparently in the drawing-room at Didlington (called Dudlington). The writer however unhappily muddled his notes and failed to make anything of the subject matter of the central panel. His description is as follows:

An admirable family picture, of one of the Knyvets and his Wife, divided into three compartments – in the centre the man kneeling, (in armour) with uplifted hands; on the other side is his wife, in the same pious attittude – they have each their paternal arms, in a shield, supported over their heads on the branch of a tree; on the right compartment is a view of the interior (according to the artist's conception) of the Temple at Jerusalem; on the left, the Crucifixion of our Blessed Saviour, between Two Thieves, on Mount Calvery. The picture is by John de Mabuse, and is in the highest state of preservation.[44]

Finally, it seems likely that the Ashwellthorpe triptych was the painting referred to by Duleep Singh in 1908 in the preface to the publication of a seventeenth century Knyvett pedigree, and which he saw at Keythorpe, Leicestershire.

I am particularly anxious to discover one Marriage which would establish the identity of a kneeling (Knyett) King [*sic*: presumably 'Knight' is intended] in armour and his spouse who are on either side of the Virgin and Child in an exquisite old Triptych (at Keythorpe) by some Flemish Master,the Arms on the lady's shield having so far baffled the most learned Heralds![45]

Notwithstanding discrepancies in this history of descriptive writing (it is clear that only Kerrich understood or was interested in the central panel), one clear fact emerges. The sequence of places Ashwellthorpe – Weston – Didlington – Keythorpe contains within it both the history of the Knyvett inheritance and that of the descent of the barony of Berners.[46] There is no real reason to doubt that one is dealing with

---

43 Partially quoted by P. Tudor-Craig in *Richard III* Exhibition Catalogue (1973) p. 94. I am very grateful to her for the full references in the British Library. The general reference to the paintings is to be found in Add. MS 6391 fols. 138–9, letter from Thomas Kerrich apparently to William Musgrove of 19 Sept 1796. The description of the triptych is in Add. MS 5726 E(2) p. 3 one of Thomas Kerrich's notebooks dated 1795.

44 See *Norfolk Tour* (Norwich, 1829) p. 1343.

45 See F. Duleep Singh *Norfolk Antiquarian Miscellany* (1908) p. 80.

46 See *The Complete Peerage* under *Berners*.

the same object. The real break in its history came between 1908 and 1923 when the painting was sold out of the family to Lord Lee. But if it is possible to see *how* it survived, the reason 'why?' is less immediately obvious.

Two points seem worth making. The Knyvetts of Ashwellthorpe in some sense 'collected'. Edmund's grandson Sir Thomas (c.1539–1618) was a scholar and collector; and by the late seventeenth century the family had amassed a large picture collection, mentioned in the will of Sir John Knyvett (died 1673).[47] In 1795, Kerrich at Didlington was shown 'a vast number [of portraits] which came from Ashwellthorpe'. In such a setting, the survival of Christopher Knyvett's altarpiece is less surprising. The Ashwellthorpe emphasis on portraits and family pictures is however instructive. During the sixteenth century nobility and gentry became increasingly fascinated by the visible evidence of antiquity and status. In this process, portraits played an important role: and the Ashwellthorpe Triptych is a double portrait. It is clear that by the late seventeenth century, the identity of the donors had been forgotten. Le Neve was even told the man was a Clifton, though subsequent writers correct this to an unidentifiable Knyvett. To that extent, it sounds as if the painting survived as an object of family curiosity. There may, however, have been a slightly more positive side to it. The painting was also evidence for the Clifton inheritance and of the most permanently valuable marriage link in the earlier part of the family pedigree. Less chancey and problematic than the Stafford – Buckingham connection, it had opened genealogical doors to Cromwell, Cailly, Tattershall and – far beyond – the post-conquest Albini lords of Buckenham. It was the one connection which, asserted through doubtless almost ruinously expensive legal action and some dubious political tergiversations, finally gave the family by the end of the fifteenth century the passport to national and local, political and social importance of which before it had had no promise. It seems likely therefore that it was these resonances which helped to keep the painting in the family, long after it had been forgotten exactly which Knyvett was represented. It is in any case a very attractive painting; and to judge from its present state, the family looked after it reasonably carefully.

47 I am grateful to Dr Virgoe for drawing my attention to this ambient interest in pictures.

Windows in Early Tudor Country Houses*

RICHARD K. MORRIS

Recent publications on Tudor architecture have added considerably to our understanding of the buildings and their relationships to contemporary society, but they have generally neglected the examination of intricate architectural details such as mouldings.[1] So this paper is intended as a reminder of the fascinating and potentially valuable historical evidence which can be gleaned from a close formal analysis of such details in surviving Tudor country houses, and which could be more fully understood if a systematic national survey were undertaken.

Windows and their associated mouldings have been selected for this study because they constituted one of the few elaborate features of English secular architecture in the later middle ages and the sixteenth century. As with any stylistic examination, the conditions most appropriate for their analysis are periods with fairly rapid and definable changes of fashion, and in this respect the decades from the 1520s to the 1570s are ideal. Whereas in the fifteenth century, features such as mullion profiles are fairly standardised, the early Tudor period is renowned as a playground for stylistically-inclined art historians because 'Renaissance' motifs introduced from the continent are instantly recognisable alongside the indigenous Gothic repertory. In the process of transmission and selection of such features, the master mason as designer/builder continued to play a vital role, and the travel of craftsmen was often the way in which architectural ideas were disseminated, as in the later middle ages. It was not until the second half of the sixteenth century that the influence of the printing press began to erode this traditional procedure in England, with the arrival of extensively illustrated books of architecture such as those of Serlio and du Cerceau.[2]

* I am very grateful to the following for facilitating my research: Lord and Lady Saye and Sele at Broughton Castle; Mr J. D. Culverhouse and Dr E. C. Till at Burghley; Miss D. Hart at Hampton Court; and Mr C. Turner of Cluttons at Sutton Place. I am also particularly indebted to Dr Phillip Lindley of St Catherine's College, Cambridge, for his comments on the first draft of this paper.
1 Even Mark Girouard's excellent study, *Robert Smythson and the Elizabethan Country House* (Yale, 1983), tends to bypass this form of evidence in assessing Smythson's style.
2 The influence of woodcut illustrations in imported books such as Books of Hours has been demonstrated earlier in the century, e.g. at the de la Warr

The two case studies to be considered in this paper focus on two famous surviving houses: Sutton Place in Surrey and Lacock Abbey in Wiltshire. Both represent in their respective decades pioneering attempts at the design of a Renaissance window suitable for the Tudor context. This involved not so much wholesale changes to the form of the window as the modernisation of mullions and other details, and in this process lies a fascinating story.

As is well known, Sutton Place was built by one of Henry VIII's favoured courtiers, Sir Richard Weston, some time after he had been granted the estate in 1521.[3] Its windows are constructed entirely of terracotta and in this it resembles the main windows of Layer Marney in Essex, generally ascribed to c. 1520–5.[4] Such extensive use of terracotta for architectural features, as opposed to embellishments such as medallions, is almost unique amongst those Tudor courtier houses which survive. So it is not surprising that the authorship of each of these works (for they share little in common stylistically) has remained in doubt; except for a general but unsubstantiated assumption that they relate in some way to the best known extant example of terracotta in the period, at Wolsey's Hampton Court.[5]

In the case of Sutton Place, a firmer lead to its provenance appeared with the publication in 1977 of part of a terracotta window frame from an excavation on the site of the former Queen's Gallery at Hampton Court.[6] This demonstrated for the first time that terracotta had been used architecturally at Wolsey's palace, but of equal interest is the fact that the piece is in the same style as the window frames at Sutton Place, with a particularly distinctive mullion profile (pl. 1 A).[7] More terracotta

---

chantry at Boxgrove (see C. P. Cave, *Archaeologia*, LXXXV (1936), pp. 127–8), but their content is entirely decorative rather than specifically architectural.

3 For Sutton Place, see most recently *The Renaissance at Sutton Place*, The Sutton Place Heritage Trust (Sutton Place, 1983).

4 For drawings of the Layer Marney windows, see J. A. Gotch, *Early Renaissance Architecture in England* (London, 1901), pl. XIII.

5 Though Baggs wishes to link Layer Marney with Norwich and ultimately Flanders; see A. P. Baggs, 'Sixteenth-Century Terracotta Tombs in East Anglia', *Archaeological Journal*, CXXV (1968), pp. 296–301.

6 D. Batchelor, 'Excavations at Hampton Court Palace', *Post-Medieval Archaeology*, XI (1977), pp. 36–49.

7 Compare with Batchelor, *op cit.*, fig. 8, B. His report made the connexion with Wolsey's period of building at Hampton Court, but not the link with Sutton Place. It should be noted that the piece of window frame illustrated in his fig. 8, C, is stone, and not terracotta as the caption implies. I am grateful to David Batchelor for clarifying this and other matters relating to the report.

fragments from windows in a similar style were excavated at Hampton Court in June 1976, in the south range of the Clock Court, the second south range of the inner court of Wolsey's palace,[8] but these were not published (pls. 1, 3, 5). The latter pieces had been re-used as foundation material for a range which is generally considered to be amongst the later works carried out at Hampton Court during Wolsey's tenure. It must be assumed therefore that they formerly constituted windows in one of the original parts of his palace (erected c. 1520?), and which was demolished during his lifetime (i.e. before 1529): perhaps from the first south range of the inner court.[9]

The Clock Court terracottas are so close in design to the window components at Sutton Place that there can be no doubt that the same workshop was responsible. A similar combination of distinctive mouldings occurs in both works, of which the main mullion profile is particularly unusual. Instead of the hollow chamfer (quarter hollow) moulding so typical of Perpendicular mullions,[10] a flatter hollow is employed, flanked by canted fillets (pls. 1 B, 2, 3). A roughly comparable design of mullion with canted fillets is encountered in England, France and the Low Countries in the fourteenth century,[11] but there is no evidence that it continues in the late Gothic styles of any of these countries, and no other mullions of this profile – in any material – are known in the early Tudor period. Moreover, in the heads of the windows at Sutton Place, the mullions between the archlets have only one canted fillet per hollow, and exactly the same modification may be observed at Hampton Court in the two pieces which derive from a similar part of the window (pls. 1 C, 6, 7). As there is no obvious architectural reason for this variation, it serves to emphasise the very precise link between these two works, and this is substantiated by the similar designs used for the

8 See H. M. Colvin (ed.), *The History of the King's Works*, vol. IV (London, 1982), p. 130, fig. 12, for the plan.

9 I am extremely grateful to Daphne Hart for information about this and other matters relating to the Hampton Court excavations, and it is her numbering scheme which I have used to identify the terracottas. At least one of the excavated pieces, part of a mullion (no. 14), came from an excavation in 1972 on the site of the first south range of the Clock Court, though its exact location was not recorded. The terracottas published by Batchelor were also discards, re-used in the filling for a ditch on the site of the Queen's Gallery at some time before work started in 1534 (Batchelor, *op cit.*, p. 46).

10 For late Gothic mullions, see R. K. Morris, 'The Development of Later Gothic Mouldings in England, 1250–1400, Part II', *Architectural History*, 22 (1979), fig. 11, B.

11 See Morris, *op cit.*, p. 3 and fig. 11, F and N; and M Viollet-le-Duc, *Dictionnaire Raisonne de l'Architecture Française du XIe au XVIe Siècle*, vol. VI (Paris, 1868), pp. 333 and 335.

profiles of the window frames (pl. 1 A)[12] and the transoms (pl. 1 D). In fact, the only major difference is that the mullions at Hampton Court appear to have terminated in moulded bases (pls. 1 J and 3), whereas at Sutton Place they die directly into the sill (pl. 4). The use of bases is a feature which the Hampton Court windows share with those of the gatehouse at Layer Marney, and by analogy it is likely that decorated sills (and capitals?) were also part of the arrangement at Hampton Court, though none were recovered in the excavation.[13] However, none of the profiles or decorations used in the Layer Marney windows bear any detailed resemblance to the group under discussion,[14] and this sets in perspective the intimate connexion between the production of the terracottas at Sutton Place and Hampton Court.

It is therefore surprising to discover that the same wooden moulds were not re-used for these two commissions, as might have been anticipated.[15] Amongst the profiles, this shows most clearly in the mullions, which are consistently wider at Hampton Court (pl. 1 B), and it also applies to the other comparable components, the window frames and the sills (pl. 1 A, F, G). As the archlets of the windows at Hampton Court are plain whereas they are cusped at Sutton Place, different moulds would obviously be required for these components as well (pls. 5, 6). Even the 'antique' decoration running in the hollows of the mullions, and which is one of the most compelling similarities, reveals differences of detail and combination on close inspection, even though the overall vocabulary of trophies of arms, four-petalled flowers and ribbons is closely related. For example, a pair of bellows is depicted on each of the lengths of mullion at Sutton Place and appears on one of the pieces from Hampton Court, but the modelling of detail varies on close inspection (pls. 2, 3). Also, a consistent motif at Sutton Place is a lozenge

12 The pieces from Hampton Court (nos. 5 A–C and 7 A–B) are fragmentary, but comparison with the complete window frames at Sutton Place leaves little doubt that this is how they were used at Hampton Court (pl. 1A).

13 For Layer Marney, see Gotch, *op cit.*, pl. XIII. A simpler form of component for a sill was excavated at Hampton Court (nos. 5 A–C), and this is similar in general design to the lower undecorated sill component at Sutton Place (*cf.* pl. 1 F and G). These components clearly belonged to the lower register of the sill, because traces are visible on them of the double ogee moulding of the outer order of the window frame, as at Sutton Place (pl. 4).

14 One exception may be the small ornamental fragments, nos. 3 A and B from Hampton Court, which appear to be parts of the lowest order of a cornice decorated with a sort of foliate version of egg-and-dart pattern, as seen at Layer Marney (Gotch, *op cit.*, pl. XIII, bottom right, 'panelling'); though this is no more than a general resemblance.

15 For example, see M. Howard in *Renaissance at Sutton Place, op cit.*, p. 26, where it is suggested 'that moulds ... were passed from one building workshop to another'.

with a bead at each corner (pl. 2), but this is not found on any of the pieces from Clock Court; and though it appears on the section of window frame excavated from the Queen's Gallery site, its position in the sequence of ornament is changed in comparison with the window frame components at Sutton Place.[16]

One can only surmise why different moulds occur in two such similar works, but it may be that wooden moulds which were used over and over again for mass production had a limited life before they had to be replaced. Aesthetic predilection seems unlikely to have been a factor because the differences are so relatively slight and apparently inconsequential. What is significant, however, is that the fact that new moulds were employed for Sutton Place tends to argue against the suggestion that Sir Richard Weston may have acquired a 'job lot' of windows discarded from Hampton Court during the 1520s, and makes it more probable that they were specifically commissioned from the same workshop. Hampton Court would appear to be the earlier work, for it was well advanced when the famous Giovanni de Maiano terracotta medallions were made for Wolsey in or before 1521, whereas the Sutton Place estate was acquired by Weston only in the same year.

Clearly the architectural terracottas under consideration are not as refined in their decoration as individual works of art like the da Maiano medallions, though the Hampton Court fragments in particular are not without a certain delicacy of detail (pl. 3).[17] It is tempting to assign their production to a workshop directed by one of the lesser Italian craftsmen in England during the time of da Maiano and Torrigiano, on the grounds that the modelling of ornate detail in this particular material is indigenous to parts of Lombardy and Tuscany. However, what militates against this conclusion is that almost all the moulding profiles are entirely in the English Perpendicular idiom: the window frames have double ogee and casement mouldings, and the associated door frames at Sutton Place have ogees, hollow chamfer and casement mouldings (pl. 1 A, E). Only the mullion profile diverges from the Perpendicular norm, but this is best explained as an adaptation to display the novel 'antique' decoration to good advantage, by widening the angles of the

16 For illustration, see Batchelor, *op cit.*, fig. 8, B. I should stress that my article has concentrated on the Clock Court terracottas because at the time of writing it has not been possible to locate the terracottas from the Queen's Gallery site for inspection; and the illustration in the published excavation report is without a scale, which prevents any exact comparisons being made with Sutton Place.
17 They are considerably more polished than the plaques at Sutton Place decorated with putti and Weston's initials and rebus, but which are not part of the subject of this paper.

mullion and reducing the projection of the axial moulding. The addition of canted fillets to the mullion also relates to the introduction of relief decoration, which on continental examples (notably on pilasters) is almost invariably bordered by fillet mouldings of some sort. In contrast, almost all the mouldings of the terracotta windows at Layer Marney are much closer to continental Renaissance usage, and these may indeed be the work of a foreign craftsman, whilst serving to emphasise the familiarity of the Hampton Court/Sutton Place designer with indigenous Perpendicular forms.[18]

If this analysis is correct and an Englishman was responsible, then it demonstrates how far the ability to produce decorative terracotta had progressed in England by c.1520, in association with the development of moulded brickwork.[19] As for the 'antique' decorations of the mullions, they may be copied from the work of foreigners in England such as da Maiano, or from imported goods such as books and hangings, as other authors have suggested.[20] However, the evidence presented above about the profiles, which are the main concern of this paper, makes it quite clear that the employment of the same craftsman as designer was responsible for the transmission of the similar architectural forms from Hampton Court to Sutton Place.

The second case study concerns Lacock Abbey and a certain type of window executed in stone and dubbed 'Sharingtonian' after Sir William Sharington, the purchaser of this former nunnery.[21] Conversion work was carried out at some time between 1540 and 1553, and the windows are amongst the best surviving examples of architectural detail in a courtier house of these particular years, with the loss of the fabric of so many buildings from the later part of Henry VIII's reign and the so-called 'Somerset circle' period.[22] The windows are well known for their

18 It is interesting that the appearance of bases on the mullions at Hampton Court is not in accord with normal Perpendicular usage, and could have been influenced by a work such as Layer Marney, which may quite conceivably pre-date the works under discussion at Hampton Court and Sutton Place; in other words, the work of a foreign craftsman in England has affected the detail, but not the whole character, of a work in the same medium by an Englishman, perhaps trained originally as a brickmaker.

19 In fact, the opportunity provided by broken pieces from Hampton Court reveals how surprisingly coarse is the earth or clay employed in their manufacture; possibly a further sign that the makers were English, and not continental craftsmen with more experience in the processing of materials.

20 See for example, M. Howard, *Early Tudor Country Houses* (London, 1987), pp. 130–1.

21 See W. G. Clark-Maxwell, 'Sir William Sharington's Work at Lacock, Sudeley and Dudley', *Archaeological Journal*, LXX (1913), pp. 175–82.

22 For a further discussion of this group of windows, see Clark-Maxwell, *op cit.*, pp. 176-9: a date in the later 1540s, but before 1549, is implied.

use of scrolled brackets (consoles) beneath the sills, and in the heads of the lights, instead of the more usual cusped or uncusped archlets of earlier Tudor buildings like Sutton Place and Hampton Court. Authorities have compared the brackets in the window heads with the use of scrolls for the same purpose at Layer Marney, but the handling is more discreet at Lacock, where the omission of 'antique' decoration helps to emphasise the linear quality which was to become a feature of Elizabethan windows (pl. 9). The transom shares the same profile as the main mullion and does not cut across it, in contrast to Layer Marney, imparting a grid-like form to the window which is probably derived from French examples, as an examination of the detail confirms.

The mullions incorporate three features which are all highly unusual in windows of this date in England. First, the front surface of the main mullion and the transom is flat and square, and edged by parallel fillets to produce what I shall term a 'tramline' pattern (pls. 8 C ii and 9). This contrasts with the sharp, angular appearance of mullions in the Perpendicular tradition, with a single narrow fillet or an axial roll or roll-and-fillet moulding for the front termination. In fact, amongst earlier extant Tudor windows, only those at Layer Marney have this square profile, and its use there clearly indicates that the idea stems from pilasters decorated with low relief ornament, framed at the edge by fillets or comparable mouldings.[23] Given the wide occurrence of the pilaster in Renaissance architecture, it is not unlikely that the examples at Layer Marney and Lacock are independently derived from continental sources.

The second noteworthy feature at Lacock is the application of the sunk chamfer moulding to the diagonal faces of each mullion (pl. 8 C i). This moulding had enjoyed considerable popularity in much of the south of England in the Decorated period, but had gone out of fashion and disappeared by the end of the fourteenth century: it is unknown on the continent.[24] It is quite possible that the moulding was re-invented in England in the mid-sixteenth century without knowledge of its previous use, as a natural way of treating the diagonal faces of a mullion to compliment the tramline effect on the front surface (pl. 8 C). However, as Lacock appears to be the earliest extant example and as the house is converted from medieval buildings which formerly included a Lady Chapel of c. 1315, it is conceivable that Sharington's masons were looking back at models from the Decorated period.[25] As we shall see,

23 See Gotch, op cit., pl. XIII.
24 See R. K. Morris, 'The Devlopment of Later Gothic Mouldings in England, 1250–1400, Part I', Architectural History, 21 (1978), pp. 29–31.
25 As far as I am aware there are no medieval examples of sunk chamfer mouldings to be seen at Lacock now; but Sharington demolished the church which included the fourteenth-century Lady Chapel, and the possibility should

the sunk chamfer mullion is frequently encountered in early Elizabethan houses and therefore the building in which it first appears is of more than local significance. Though one must accept gaps in our knowledge caused by the loss of such important contemporary works as Old Somerset House, a feasible case can be made on present evidence that the renewed popularity of the moulding in the sixteenth century stems from its rediscovery at Lacock.[26]

The third characteristic of the windows is unique in the English context. At the intersection of the transom and the main mullion, a circle is carved, and there are semi-circles where these elements meet the window frame (pl. 9).[27] The motif of the circle can be traced back to medallions used fairly widely for architectonic decoration in the second half of the fifteenth century in northern and central Italy, as in some of Alberti's churches (*e.g.* S. Francesco at Rimini and S. Andrea at Mantua) and also in works of Codussi and others in Venice.[28] Pilasters were frequently decorated with circles and semi-circles, and it was particularly in this form that the motif spread to France, in châteaux of the Loire associated with the court of Francis I, such as Chambord and Azay-le-Rideau.[29] It was here, specifically in the courtyard elevation of the Francis I wing at Blois (usually dated 1515–24), that the motif was apparently first applied to window tracery (pl. 10),[30] for this step does not seem to have been taken in Italy. In England, the one surviving instance of the motif before Lacock is in the wooden panelling of the

---

be checked as to whether any of the lesser mullions of the 'Sharingtonian' windows (*i.e.* the mullions without a tramline) could be re-used medieval material.

26 None of the drawings of Old Somerset House are detailed enough to indicate the moulding profile of the sixteenth-century mullions.

27 For Brakspear's drawing of this window type, see Clark-Maxwell, *op cit.*, fig. 1.

28 Works from the second half of the fifteenth century which employ the motif in Venice include – S. Michele in Isola, the Palazzo Zorzi, Sta. Maria dei Miracoli, the Scuola di S. Marco, the Doge's Palace (courtyard), and the Scuola Grande di S. Giovanni Evangelista. Elsewhere in this period, the motif may be seen, for example, in Pienza (Cathedral), Fiesole (Badia), Rome (Sta. Maria della Pace) and Florence (Sto. Spirito), and clearly it occurs widely in northern Italy before 1500.

29 The motif seems to have lost popularity in the most fashionable works of the later part of Francis I's reign, judging by its absence from the contemporary parts of Fontainebleau and the Louvre; though du Cerceau records a fireplace decorated with the motif at the lost Château de Madrid (reproduced in A. Blunt, *Art and Architecture in France 1500–1700* (2nd edn., London, 1970), fig. 29.

30 Also cited in passing by Clarke-Maxwell, *op cit.*, p. 181, n. 1.

lower parts of the choir screen of King's College Chapel, Cambridge, dating to the 1530s.[31] The form of the panelling is a feasible design source for the window tracery at Lacock,[32] in which case a possible intermediary would be a carver with experience of the royal works, such as John Chapman, who is known to have worked at Lacock. If this hypothesis is pursued, perhaps more importance should be placed on the relevance of other earlier works in the home counties which could relate to Lacock, such as Layer Marney.

However, the solutions to window design at Blois and Lacock are sufficiently similar that it is tempting to argue that there could be a direct link between them, provided by the travel of foreign masons to England. Certainly there were French masons in Wiltshire in the summer of 1549, to work on Protector Somerset's new house at Bedwyn Broil, as recorded in a colourful letter from Somerset's steward to Sir John Thynne:[33]

> Further ye sent us downe such a lewde company of Frenchmen masons as I never saw the lyke. I assure you they be the worst condicyoned people that I ever saw and the dronkest; for they wyll drynke more in one day than three days wages wyll come to and then lye lyke beasts on the flore not able to stande. I have geven them dyvers warnyngs me selve and yet never the better. And now I perceive by Bryan they be departid and stolen away ... I think they make their repayr to London.

This group of masons sounds hardly suitable for our purpose! Nonetheless, the implication seems to be that French masons were not unknown in England in these years, apparently hired by the major figures at court like Protector Somerset to embellish their houses with Renaissance style carvings which the indigenous work force could not supply in sufficient quality or quantity. In such a situation, a courtier like Sharington was well placed to take advantage of their presence. A striking parallel is to be seen in the case of a group of the Howard tombs at Framlingham, c. 1536 and 1554–65, where the stylistic evidence points strongly to the presence of French stone carvers.[34] It is not

31 Illustrated in *e.g.* J. Lees-Milne, *The Tudor Renaissance*, (London, 1951), pls. 36 and 37.
32 I am grateful to Dr Christopher Wilson for drawing this parallel to my attention at the Symposium; it is also noted in passing by Lees Milne, *op cit.*, p. 52, n. 3.
33 Cited in full in M. Girouard, 'The Development of Longleat House between 1546 and 1572', *Archaeological Journal*, CXVI (1959), p. 210.
34 L. Stone and H. Colvin, 'The Howard Tombs at Framlingham, Suffolk', *Archaeological Journal*, CXXII (1965), pp. 159–71; and R. Marks, 'The Howard Tombs at Thetford and Framlingham: New Discoveries', *Archaeological Journal*, 141 (1984), pp. 252–68. The best known examples of named craftsmen with

recorded from what part of France came the group of masons sent to Bedwyn Broil. However, as they were presumably on a short contract, one may surmise that an area close to the Channel is likely, such as Normandy with its traditional links with southern England through the Caen stone quarries; and this is borne out by the case of the Howard tombs.[35] This suggests that in general their experience would have been on lesser buildings in the style of the older Loire school which continued to be influential in the provinces,[36] rather than abreast of the latest developments around Paris.[37] Exactly the same observations are made by Stone and Colvin about the Howard tombs – a commission executed in England in the 1550s, but deriving from works in the earlier French court style of the 1520s and 1530s, and with Francis I wing at Blois singled out as a source. In all, the art historical arguments are so similar to those put forward here for Lacock that further research is needed to see whether we are not dealing with connected workshops; but this lies outside the scope of this paper.

The use of circles to decorate window mullions has no known following in England after Lacock, though it is interesting to speculate on related works of this period which are lost without record, such as the pre-fire Longleat. The shortness of the episode tends to lend weight to the argument that a brief sojourn by foreign masons was responsible for introducing the motif. However, the other two features of the Sharingtonian mullions were to enjoy considerable vogue over the

---

French experience working in England in this general period are Nicholas Bellin and Allen Maynard: see respectively M. Biddle, 'Nicholas Bellin of Modena, an Italian Artificer at the Courts of Francis I and Henry VIII', *British Archaeological Association Journal*, 3rd ser., XXIX (1966), pp. 106–21; and Girouard (1959), *op cit.*, p. 216 *sqq*. For French craftsmen in the south of England, see also M. Whinney, *Sculpture in Britain 1530–1830* (Harmondsworth, 1964), ch. 2; and A. Blunt, 'L'influence française sur l'architecture et la sculpture décorative en Angleterre pendant la première moitié du XVIe siècle', *Revue de l'Art*, 4 (1979), pp. 17–29.

35 This supposition finds confirmation in the locations cited for the French sources for the Framlingham tombs, which are mainly provincial, and include sites in Normandy (Chanteloup and Rouen) and the north of France (Villers-Cotterets); Stone and Colvin, *op cit.*, pp. 168–9.

36 Later examples of the application of the circle motif include Chambord (the roofline architecture, after 1537), the Hôtel Pincé at Angers (1523–33), and the church of St Pierre in Caen. None of these apply the design to tracery, but a more thorough survey is needed.

37 Of course, there are obvious exceptions to this generalisation, notably the centrepiece of the Strand facade of Old Somerset House, the form of which implies a knowledge of Ecouen or Anet.

following decades. Both the sunk chamfer and tramline mouldings are to be seen at two other major sites associated with the Somerset circle, Dudley Castle and Sudeley Castle,[38] and at the latter the sunk chamfer also appears in the context of door frames and the fireplace surrounds. Some if not all of this fabric at Dudley belongs to the Duke of Northumberland's tenure up to 1553. At Sudeley the buildings of the outer court which contain these features are commonly attributed to c.1570 rather than to Thomas Seymour's time (1547–49) which, if correct, would suggest that their style is at least influenced by works undertaken there before 1549.

Examples of houses from the first half of Elizabeth's reign which employ sunk chamfer mullions are Old Gorhambury (porch, c.1568) and Burghley (parts of the west, south and east ranges, mainly 1570s?), both executed for patrons linked to the Somerset circle.[39] The sunk chamfer is less frequently encountered in the later part of Elizabeth's reign, when the ovolo moulding had become predominant for mullions, but it appears to have continued in use more in western areas and a rare Jacobean example is Charlton Park House, Wiltshire (c.1607 or later).[40] On the other hand, the tramline motif continued to be so widely used for large windows in Elizabethan and Jacobean great houses, such as Burghley, Kenilworth and Hatfield – usually in combination with the ovolo moulding – that listing all the examples would be a major task. It was to be the most influential of all the Sharingtonian features.

By way of conclusion it will be helpful to examine briefly the windows of two houses closely related to Lacock – Broughton Castle and Longleat – as they shed some light on the dissemination of the style. The relevant works at Broughton Castle, Oxfordshire, are associated with a curiously inconspicuous date of 1554 incised on one of the chimney-stacks, and have been described in detail by Harry Gordon Slade.[41] The

38 For Dudley and Sudeley, see Clark-Maxwell, *op cit.*; H. Brakspear, 'Dudley Castle', *Archaeological Journal*, LXXI (1914), pp. 1–24; and W. D. Simpson, 'Dudley Castle, the Renaissance Buildings', *Archaeological Journal*, CI (1944), pp. 119–25
39 William Cecil (Lord Burghley) entered Protector Somerset's household in 1547, and rose to be Principal Secretary to the Crown by 1550; Sir Nicholas Bacon was Cecil's brother-in-law.
40 Other Elizabethan examples used for mullions and known to the author are Condover, Shropshire, and Old Beaupre and St Fagan's castles, Glamorgan. Narrow sunk chamfers are used for the arches of doors and fireplaces in some buildings in Warwickshire (*e.g.* Charlecote Park, gatehouse; Kenilworth Castle, Leicester's new building; Baddesley Clinton), and this usage may be much more widespread geographically (*e.g.* it has already been noted in the work at Sudeley Castle of c. 1570).
41 H. G. Slade, 'Broughton Castle, Oxfordshire', *Archaeological Journal*, 135 (1978), pp. 158 *sqq.*

connexions with the Sharingtonian style have been known for some time[42] so there is no need to reiterate them here, except to note the characteristic scrolled brackets still visible at sill level in the north window of the Queen Anne Bedroom (pl. 7).[43] What has not been made explicit before, however, is that the appearance of the sunk chamfer moulding for the exterior profile of the mullions in this window, and in the north window of the Oak Room, corroborates the link with Lacock; though on the basis of Brakspear's drawing they are not so alike as to have been cut from the same template (cf pl. 8 A and C).[44] The interior profile of the Broughton mullions is quite different, consisting of delicate ogee and hollow chamfer mouldings, and seems to be without parallel in any of the contemporary works of the Somerset circle (pl. 8 B). Large ogee mouldings used on their own are not uncommon in Elizabethan and Jacobean mullions, but the combination with hollow chamfers and their employment on a smaller scale are more unusual. In this respect, both mouldings are met with in parts of Kirby Hall in Northamptonshire, where the work of c. 1570–5 is attributed to Thomas Thorpe; and also in the opening pages of the book of drawings of his son, John Thorpe, in the template profiles, some of which have some affinity with Kirby.[45]

Overall, the impression left by Broughton is that the architectural features of the 1550s are the work of one or more craftsmen (probably English) from what may be termed for present purposes a 'Thames valley school', familiar with the new classical (Sharingtonian) style of mainly French inspiration, and engaged in commissions in the home counties, south midlands and further south;[46] of which Lacock is an early and perhaps seminal example. On the evidence of comparative

---

42 E.g., Lees-Milne, op cit., ch. IV.

43 The scrolled brackets actually support octagonal shafts which terminate the window splays, rather than the sill proper; and the mouldings of the latter are much heavier than those of the sills at Lacock (pls. 7 and 8 D); for Lacock, see Clarke-Maxwell, op cit., fig. 1. These differences may be explained by the fact that the window in the Queen Anne Bedroom is converted from the medieval solar window, set in a thick wall; and this is probably the reason for the rather Gothic octagonal shafts of the splays (pl. 8 E), presumably re-used or adapted from the earlier window. On the other hand, the pendant bracket in the centre of the sill (pl. 7) relates in a general way to the use of pendant bosses in the miniature vault over the strong room in Sharington's tower at Lacock.

44 At the time of writing, I have not measured the mullions at Lacock: pl. 8 C is an enlargement to quarter-scale of Brakspear's drawing in Clark-Maxwell, op cit., fig. 1.

45 Reproduced in J. Summerson, 'The Book of Architecture of John Thorpe', Walpole Society, XL (1966), pls. 2 and 3.

46 E.g. Bishop Gardiner's chantry in Winchester Cathedral, c. 1555; see further Whinney, op cit., pp. 6–10.

architectural detail, it also looks as if a craftsman with experience of south midland works such as Broughton moved north-east along the limestone belt to the area of the Weldon and Barnack quarries, to be involved in important early Elizabethan houses there such as Kirby Hall, Burghley and Deene Park.[47]

An interesting footnote about the mullions at Broughton concerns the two projecting bays in the centre of the north elevation, the porch and the hall bay window. If indeed their extant fabric belongs with the 1550s remodelling, as Slade suggests, then the tracery provides the earliest dateable use of the ovolo moulding for mullion profiles.[48] Subsequently this became the norm for Elizabethan windows, but examples are surprisingly rare before the great houses of the 1570s, such as Kirby Hall and Leicester's buildings at Kenilworth.

Longleat is a slightly different case to Broughton because of its geographical proximity to Lacock, which makes it more likely that some architectural details at Longleat were part of the current local style of the area which had developed since the 1540s. Thus one finds the sunk chamfer moulding used for the window apertures of the basement and the roof turrets, even though the design of the present elevation was apparently not finalised until 1572.[49] Some of these apertures are thought to be survivals from the pre-fire house of the 1550s and 1560s, but others almost certainly were cut for the new work. Turning to the main windows of the elevation, their tramline grids are reminiscent of Lacock but developed into a fully coherent design which makes Sharington's pioneering work look academic and awkward by comparison (cf. pls. 9 and 11). Presumably we owe this sense of continuity to Sir John Thynne and craftsmen like Allen Maynard who had worked on the pre-fire house, and it is very likely that the tramline effect was a feature of some of the earlier windows. A contributory factor to the elegance of the present design is the introduction of a small chamfer moulding flanking the tramlines instead of the sunk hollow chamfer, which

47 For these works, see J. Summerson, 'John Thorpe and the Thorpes of King's Cliffe' *Architectural Review*, CVI (1949), pp. 291–300. With regard to Thomas Thorpe, the mason to whom the 1570s work at Kirby Hall is attributed, the evidence of the family monument in King's Cliffe church implies that he hailed from a local Northamptonshire family which went back at least two generations; though it is possible that he had worked further south earlier in his career.

48 The ovolo is also used for the bottom moulding of the sill in the Queen Anne Bedroom (pl. 8 D). Examples of the ovolo are found earlier in the sixteenth century but not for mullions, and they tend to be in materials other than stone, e.g. in wood, for the miniature ribs of the screen and choir stalls at King's College Chapel, Cambridge, 1530s.

49 For fuller detail see Girouard (1983), *op cit.*, ch. 1.

reduces the bulk of the mullion profile whilst adding to its linear quality (pl. 11). This may have been a modification introduced by Robert Smythson, and certainly he repeated exactly the same profile when he moved to work at Wollaton Hall, Nottingham, in the 1580s.

The overall design of the window itself is fully Elizabethan. In comparison with Lacock, the fussy brackets in the heads have gone, as at Broughton,[50] whilst the appearance of double transoms and a pronounced vertical emphasis has encouraged the suggestion that they represent a return to English Perpendicular tradition. In fact, it should not be forgotten that the form of the window is predominantly French in origin, as a comparison with the main windows at Blois demonstrates (*cf.* pls. 10 and 11),[51] and this adds weight to the thesis of strong French influence in the details of Sharingtonian buildings and their successors. The difference, however, is that the form of the 1572 windows at Longleat (but not their detail) could be the result of a fresh influx of French influence by way of printed architectural treatises, such as J.–A. du Cerceau's *First Book of Architecture* (1559).[52] For the application of the printing press to copiously illustrated books of architecture between the 1540s and the 1570s ultimately signified the end of the medieval tradition of the master mason as designer/builder and the customary transmission of architectural detail through itinerant craftsmen.

50 The heads of the windows of the Strand facade of Old Somerset House (1547–52) were also plain, but the windows were smaller.
51 Windows with double transoms and plain rectangular heads had developed in French domestic architecture during the fifteenth century, *e.g.* the Palace of Jacques Coeur at Bourges, courtyard elevation.
52 See *e.g.* Project XXIII for similar windows.

The Denzill Holles Commonplace Book: Memoranda of a Country Gentleman, c. 1558 Nottingham University Lib. MS PV I

ELIZABETH PORGES WATSON

The Commonplace Book of Denzill Holles is now in the manuscript collection of Nottingham University Library, being part of the Portland Collection deposited with the University by the late Duke of Portland in 1949. It is a representative example of its genre, eclectic and unsystematic. A large number of the entries are traceable to printed sources or to manuscript analogues, giving an indication of what was available to a young man of an exploratory turn of mind, belonging to the landed gentry and living in the Midlands in the 1550s. The manuscript deserves publication in that its compiler has provided an informal insight into the reading and reflective habits of his time and class as well as into his own formative enthusiasms. More specifically, a considerable amount of his material, especially in the fields of magical theory and medicine, can be paralleled elsewhere, but is often difficult of access. To have it available with full annotation would be useful to many different specialists in the period.

It is a small quarto volume, bound in parchment. Within the binding, which is of much later date than the manuscript itself, the folios are enclosed by vellum sheets cut down from a Gradual, probably of the fifteenth century. The first of these has a few scribbles, now illegible, probably of the period of the manuscript itself: similar scribbles appear also on the final vellum leaf, together with the words 'proclamation for the liuing of of' in what seems to be Denzill Holles's hand. From the cut-back strips of vellum left at the openings between ff. vii.v–viii.r and liii.v–liv.r it would seem that the manuscript was originally in sections kept in 'folders' cut down from the Gradual and that later these were clipped back, except for the first and last, and the whole bound together: Dr Backhouse has suggested that probably it was bought ready-made. My foliation does not include these vellum sheets.

The manuscript itself consists of 55 folios, paper, with hand and flower watermark, cuffed, with the initials IB, very close to example

11381 as given by C.M.Briquet.[1] F.1r of the manuscript is headed Liber Densilli hollis, with the note, iiii.d. *dimidium libri*, apparently referring to the purchase of the paper for his purpose: dimidium libri = a quire (24 sheets) or score (20 sheets) of paper. 'Densell Hollys' is then written again, between lines, in careful italic, and the rest of the side is taken up with the drawing of an escutcheon, heavily hatched, bracketed by the letters DH, elaborately decorated, the whole enclosed in a decorative circle. F.1v has the bookplate of the First Duke of Newcastle, the descendant of Denzill's eldest son, John Holles first Earl of Clare.

The first entries as such occur on f.2r: they continue, with blanks at 6v, 16r and v, to f.19r. Holles seems to have abandoned the manuscript at this point: the only later entries are at f.33r, where his 'secret alphabet' (see below) is set out and partly transliterated, possibly by another hand, and one entry, f.57v, again possibly in another hand. The contents, in Latin and English, are diverse. The considerable emphasis on astrology and especially natural magic, in which subjects Holles seems to have been an enthusiastic if unscholarly amateur, is notable, as is the range of various kinds of medicinal and household recipes. There are a number of general entries in prose and verse, including an acrostic poem on Denzill Holles's own name, f.14r. It is possible that some of the other verses that I have not traced are also by him.

The hand, with a few italic exceptions which I have noted, is secretary, and, with some possible exceptions mentioned in the footnotes, appears to be the same throughout. The inconsistency in the use of contractions and superscript letters has dissuaded me from supplying a diplomatic text, even in the transcription of the folio reproduced in appendix III. The expansion of contractions and the re-alignment of superscript letters is indicated in the text by underlining. Punctuation has been kept as in the manuscript, as have alignments, by which punctuation is frequently affected. Cancellations are indicated, and interlinear corrections printed as such. Lacunae and conjectural emendations are enclosed in pointed brackets.

From time to time Holles makes use of a 'secret alphabet' for details of magical experiments, especially those of a licentious nature. It is often used for single words or part of words, which makes it fairly easy to decipher even without the aid of the key at f.33r. It must have been very clumsy to use. It appears to be related to two of the alphabets

---

1 *Les Filigranes*, vol.IV, (Amsterdam, 1968), there dated 1552. Briquet states (vol.II, p.573) that this general type of watermark first appears in 1526, that it was common, with minor variations, to the end of the sixteenth century, and that the variety of initials, where these occur, indicate its use by a great number of manufacturers.

given by Gian Baptista Porta,[2] though the differences in form of some of the signs as well as the date of the manuscript itself suggest an earlier source. The key is given below, p. 152: its occurrence in the text is indicated by a point below the letters concerned e.g., angelos, f.8.v, the sample chosen.

The main source for a life of Denzill Holles is Cap. 8, *Memorials of the Holles Family 1493–1656* by Gervase Holles (1607–75).[3]

For the date of Denzill's birth, Gervase refers to 'the yeare of his age which is upon the picture I have of him at Grymesby, and upon that at Houghton'. The latter, later in the Welbeck Abbey Collection, is inscribed '*anno Domino* 1586, Aetat. suae 48'. Supposing the inscription to be correct, this would place his birth in or around 1538, and would indicate that the commonplace book was compiled when he was about 20: the date 1558 appears f. 2v. In 1559 or 1560 he married Elianor, daughter of Edmund Lord Sheffield of Butterwick, by whom he was to have nine children, of whom the eldest, John Holles, became First Earl of Clare in 1625. In a Deed of the 17 September, 1559, Denzill's father, Sir William Holles, settled upon the couple the manor of Irby, where Denzill subsequently spent most of life, and other lands in Lincolnshire. This change in his circumstances, with additional responsibility, may have been one reason for Denzill's abandoning his commonplace book: if so, he kept it apparently for little more than a year.

For some years he expanded and consolidated his estates. According to Gervase the land was good, prosperous and well managed, and his concern for its management and for his tenants is reflected in the provisions of his will, made in 1589. He was Commissioner of the Peace for Lincoln and also Member of Parliament for East Retford 1584–5 and 1596–7. Gervase says that he 'had something of martial employment' in the rebellion of 1569, as Captain of 252 foot-soldiers, though the rebellion was quelled before he could have engaged in combat. He also held the office of captain of musters in his county at the time of the Armada.

Towards the end of his life he was 'very much afflicted with the stone and gout, which certainly hastened his death much sooner than in reason might be expected.' He died on the 22 April, 1590, about nine months before his father, his wife having predeceased him.

At a later date his descendant and biographer would most likely have left only the detailed record of a public and substantial figure from which this account is condensed. In view of the nature of certain entries in the commonplace book, however, the two short paragraphs immediately preceding Gervase's account of Denzill's death and burial are worth quoting:

2 *De Furtivis Literarum Notis*, (Naples, 1563), pp. 85, 90.
3 Ed. A. C. Wood, Camden Third Series, vol. LV, (1939).

Theis were his virtues, and with theis he had his weaknes too, wh*ich* was an immoderate love to women, and from wh*ich* neither the virtues nor fertility of a noble wife could reclaim him. In a Pasquill made in those dayes of the Lincolnshire gentlemen I found theis rythmes of him —

> 'Hollys hits in every hole
> And Denzell drives through all their dintes.
> He gets his neighbours wives with fole
> And yet they say the man but mintes.'

And I remember that walking once in Irby groundes with the Earl of Clare he shewed me a good hansome farme house, telling me that that house his father built to please a foolish woman: the truth is he was seldome without one or other in it, for his private use and pleasure.

A. C. Wood refers here in a note to the commonplace book as 'A curious note-book of his (Denzill's) ... preserved in the library at Welbeck Abbey ... ' and cites the opening of the first entry f. 8v, an aphrodisiac recipe or charm, one of several examples in the manuscript. In so far as an apparently casual series of notes and jottings, máde in early life, can be taken as in any way indicative of the mature character of the compiler such entries would seem to support Gervase's account. Similarly, and more importantly, the wide range of entries concerned with household and medical recipes may relate to Denzill's good reputation as landlord and landowner. His youthful predilections, as indicated sketchily in the manuscript, seem not to have been abandoned, at least in these directions, with the manuscript itself.

As I have indicated earlier, Holles seems to have kept his Commonplace Book precisely at the cusp of adulthood, when full independence and responsibility were imminently foreseeable. His own awareness of the forthcoming transition may itself be indicated by his undertaking the project in the first place: his abandonment of it, apparently not much more than a year later, that it had served its purpose, or not. However unsystematic the entries themselves, the preparation and outlay were evidently not casual. He bought suitable paper: perhaps looked out or obtained parchment sheets to be cut down as folders. This last would have been all too easy at the period, when liturgical manuscripts in particular were common jumble. His pragmatic vandalism in this respect would accord with some of the verse epigrams of which he made note, whether or not he composed them himself:

> Christum sci (*sic*) bene sis(*sic*)
> Satis est sci(*sic*) setera (*sis*) nescis for example
>
> (f. 2v)

(If you know Christ truly it suffices even if
you are ignorant of the rest.)

The entries themselves can in such a context be taken as doubly revealing, regardless of their subject matter. Many can be seen as relating
directly to a public self, to an image active, Protestant, fashionably
caustic, eminently practical, with a wary, perhaps opportunist eye to
social and historical structuring. This image defines itself theoretically
and is expressed practically, in the first instance through epigram and
satire, moral and theological, verse and prose, as well as by historical
and heraldic notations: in the second by the attention given to medical
and household receipts and by careful lists made of military terms
(mot*tes* darmour, f. 2r) and of a traveller's requisites (f. 14v). This last is
I believe the only section of the manuscript yet to have been printed. It
is given in a slightly modernised form in Dorothy Hartley's *The Land of
England*, London 1979, pp. 246–7. I give it here in my own transcription,
by way of illustration and for its own interest:

> Purse dager kerchefe shoinghorne boget[4] *and* shois. Sper male[5]
> hood hal*ter* sadilclothe sporres *with the* horse combe. Bow arrowes
> sword bocler horne leshe[6] gloues string *and the* bracer[7]. pen paper
> *per*chance redwax pomis[8] looke *you* remember. penknife combe
> thimble nedel thrid point lest the gerthe breke. Bodking knife
> lingell[9] geve *your* horse meat see he be shod well. make mery singe
> if *you* cane take hed to the geare *that you* lose none

There are also small touches of perhaps rather self-conscious humanism. The longest entry (ff. 12r–13r), (God Counsell for a Com*mon*er
in the Court) is ironic in a similar register to that of some of Erasmus'
Colloquies, though with nothing of their subtlety. He has made a note of
11.161–5 of Horace's *Ars Poetica* (f. 2v) with textual abberations which
may be his own copying errors, and he makes at least one fairly ambitious poetic essay of his own, the acrostic poem on his own name
(f. 14r) professional love and constancy to an un-named lady. It is not a
very good poem: grammar, syntax and metre are all strained unbearably.It

---

4 Obs, form of Budget, purse. NED. Budget 1. Here possibly 'leather water
   bottle.'
5 Spear, Mail. Obs. forms, NED.
6 Leash. Obs, form, NED.
7 Either the Enarme, or strap for holding the buckler on the arm, NED. Bracer
   [1]2, or armour for covering the arm: armguard used in archery, fencing etc.
   NED. Bracer[2].
8 Pumice. Obs. form, NED. Used for smoothing parchment etc
9 Either shoemakers' waxed thread, NED. Lingel, sb.[1]., or coll. sing. the leather
   straps of a horse's harness. NED. Lingel sb.[2]1.

belongs very much to the age C. S. Lewis called 'drab'. That he made the attempt at all seems to me however to be interesting in itself, and I quote it accordingly, for your better judgement:

D Dreadfully I doubte lest that disdayne
E Enlarginge your ensence[10] *and* encrease my payne
N Not naked but nedye of *your* good grace
S Seinge *the* semelines of *your* sweete face
E Especially *and* eftsones engrafte in my harte
L Like one *that* longe hath lyen *and* ca*n* not starte

H Have not I harde happe if ye be not bet*ter*
O Only on you O love I haue the greater
L Let me not Languyshe wh*ich* love y*ou* Liberally
L Lende me y*our* Love Likewise devoide of Lecherye
I I am instely[11] ioyned to y*ou* in perfecte Love
S So that I shall son*er* sinke rather than once remove

I incline to think that some of the other verse pieces may also be Holles's own, especially those in English, for example entries c, d, e, f. 2v. Overall, the image of Renaissance competance and versatility is recognisable, however crudely sketched, and a number of these entries have their own interest, context apart.

The same is true of those entries that relate to a very different though essentially complementary frame of reference. Holles's interest in the occult, in *mysteriosa* and *mirabilia* is as typical of his time – and not only his time – as his landowner's sense of status, skills responsibilities. It has no bearing at all on the public image defined by that sense however, nor does it suggest an alternative. Holles had not the learning, capacity or ambition of a Doctor Dee. This is a private self-dimension, at times shamefaced, not without reason.

Entries of this kind show eclecticism typical of the Commonplace Book generally, but which may here be in itself more specifically indicative. There are a number of extracts from the *Secreta*, or *Secretes*, attributed to Albertus Magnus. Holles has drawn both on the Latin version (probably in the Venice edition of 1509) and the English (probably that of London, 1525) (e.g. ff. 8r, 9v, 23v): he clearly knew both well. His quotations range from a receipt for invisible ink, to *experimenta* 'ut homines videan*tur* esse sine capiti*bus*' (that men may seem to be headless), f. 9v, or 'to make eue*ry* mote in the sun seme a nedd*er* (adder)', f. 10r, as well as to others of more dubious intention: 'ut mulier te nimis deligat sume capillis ei*us et* dormeas cu*m* ea *et* tacta

10 From 'insense': anger.
11 Either from 'instellatio': placing among the stars, so 'firmly'; or from 'instealing': entering stealthily. Presumably coined for the alliterative effect.

pulv*er*em super ventr*em* suu*m* *et* habeas re*m* cu*m* ea et aliu*m* non diligit' (that a woman may be infatuated with you, take some of her hairs, reduce them to ash, then sleep with her and place the ashes on her belly, and you will enjoy her, and she will love no other), f. 9v. This would seem to put effect before cause. *Secreta* suggests that the ashes be sprinkled on the lady's sleeping place (*super feretrum*), this first being smeared with honey. Holles's version is perhaps more likely to arise from confusion than intentional humour.

This kind of gallimaufry seems to me at least to suggest a hangover from adolescence: an indiscriminating appetite for the curious, the forbidden, the sexually titillating. There are a number of other entries that suggest that Holles may have been attempting, more or less consciously, to dignify this range of preoccupation, if only in his own eyes, giving it some context of arcane learning. He draws up a table of the planetary dominations of the hours, as for purposes of magical working (f. 3r), and copies out, from any one of a number of what would have been easily accessible sources, tables of the planets, their metals, signs, houses, correspondencies (ff. 3r, 7r, 13v, 14r, 15v) and attempts a diagram for casting a nativity (f. 8r). He transcribes two magical texts of some length; the first citing the relation of the moon to the signs of the Zodiac appropriate to different kind of magical working, benificent and malific (ff. 4r–6v), occurs also with variations in BM MS 3850, which may be of a somewhat later date. The second, also in English, is the so-called *Liber Lunae* mentioned by Lynn Thorndike, *History of Magic and Experimental Science*, Columbia 1923, vol. II p. 223, as being widely circulated at least from the fourteenth century. It occurs also, in English in BM MS Harl. 89, 75 ff, sixteenth century, and in Latin, Bodley MS CCC ff. 162–8 probably late fourteenth century, for example. Both these texts have a certain, perhaps reassuringly cloudy grandeur of expression. Very different in kind is the entry on f. 11r: a very elaborate magical formula for obtaining and controlling a magical horse, in Latin. The idea is familiar in folklore, (e.g. the evidence given by Isobel Goudie at her trial for witchcraft in 1662), but I have been unable to find a source as such for Holles's version, which is packed with detail.

This entry is of quite a different type from any other in the manuscript. It is not popular, like many of the entries on f. 8v, nor learned like the *Liber Lunae* (f. 4v) nor even spiritually harmless like the *Secreta*. Its references to the *sigillum salomonis* link it with a learned tradition of a kind: the use of a *hostia* (consecrated Host) on which Names are to be written in bat's blood make this link far more dubious than may have occurred to the Protestant (cf. f. 2v) perception of Holles. This detail, and the protective use of the names of the Saints and of the *virtutes*

matris domini, suggest a pre-Reformation source. It was probably a manuscript, since spells of this kind rarely found their way into print, for
obvious reasons: also the copying is fuller of corrections and mis-
spellings than is usual for Holles: he may have had difficulty in reading
it. It is very heavily (and inconsistently) contracted: Holles's own habits
may here have combined with those of his source.

The only other indications of magic having any kind of practical
application occur in formulae such as those given in the sample folio,
f. 8v: love spells, spells to discover a woman's secret thoughts and so
forth: the next stage on it might be said from the analogous suggestion
copied from *Secreta*. They belong in form and detail to a manuscript
continuum. Analogues are not hard to find: indeed some of these
charms certainly have a common source with Bodley MS E Mus.243, 'A
booke of experiments taken out of dyvers authors', 1622. In general
they are a commonplace of human and predominantly masculine folly,
being found at all periods. Details of the charms given by Holles can be
paralleled with examples found in Greek magical papyri (*Papyri Magicae
Graecae*, ed. K. Preisendanz, Stuttgart, 1973), as well as in modern
folklore. That Holles's own interest in such material was something less
than impersonal can be seen as well as deduced from his use of a 'secret
alphabet' and by his careful overwriting of 'secrete tangat' (that she may
touch you privily) with the innocuous 'sapienter diligat' (that she may
love you wisely), f. 8v. Whether these charms were ever more than an
aid to fantasy is unlikely. To take the first example given on f. 8v:

> Ut mulier denudet se recipe panu*m* lineu*m* etingtu*m* in sanguine
> leporis et de illo fac lichnu*m* et candela*m*, et quando vis ut denudet
> se accede candela*m*, et si vis ut cessant extingue illam.

> (In order that a woman should undress herself take linen thread
> dipped in the blood of a rabbit and make of it a wick and a candle,
> and when you desire that she should undress herself bring the
> candle, and if you wish they should stop put it out.)

What the reaction of any comely serving wench might have been to such
an experiment I cannot imagine, and suspect regretfully that Holles
himself never put it to the embarrassment of proof.

Holles's acquisition of information admittedly useful and admirable
shows a similar eclecticism. His medical notes in particular generally
agree in their herbal prescriptions with those of Turner, Gerard and
Culpeper, but the lack of astrological and other learned detail suggests
Holles may have drawn on popular rather than professional sources.
He has made a note of three verses dealing with diet and general health
which are largely parallel in content, substance and some phrasing to

the much longer *Diatorie* in the Lambeth MS 853 p. 182 (*Dietarium* Sloane MS p. 1, printed in both versions, English and Latin, EETS OS 32, 1868, ed. Furnivall, pp. 54 ff: *The Babees Book*). There is a curious passage, f. 7v, 'qualiter puer crescit in ventro matris sue..' (in what way a child grows in its mother's belly). The details of the development of the bones, teeth and internal organs differ completely from those given by the classically based medical theory of Holles's own time. A version of what must be a common source exists in Anglo-Saxon (BM MS Cotton Tiberius A.III ff. 40r–41r, formerly ff. 38.v–39.r, translated by W. Bonser, *The Medical Background of Anglo-Saxon England*, London, Wellcombe Historical Medical Library, 1963, p. 265). I have so far been unable to trace it further.

The most elaborate of the medical entries occurs at f. 17r:

> The copye how to make the souerayne wather *that* doctor steuenes phisicion *and* a great cunnynge man of long experience did use *and* ther*with* did many cures *and* always kept it secret tyll a lytel before his deth *that* the archbishop of canterbury gat it of him in wryting':

English; an elaborate and detailed recipe, with an account of its effects. The Archbishop was most probably William of Warham, ?1450–1532, as being the only Primate of about this date of whom it could be said, as here, that he 'lyved tyll he was not able to drynke of a cupp, but sucked his drynke out of a holowe thynge of silver and gylt...

This seems to have been a famous tonic. It occurs in a slightly simpler form in Culpeper's *London Dispensatorie*, 1653, as 'Dr Stephen's Water'. Elaborate (usually highly alcoholic) 'waters' of this kind were very popular. Like this one, they were often extremely costly. The wealth of circumstantial detail, as well as the full version of the recipe itself, make this one of the most interesting entries.

The manuscript concludes with two medical recipes 'for the hardness of the splene..' (f. 19r). Holles says 'Thes medsens were geven me by doctor perpont...' and they make an interesting contrast. (a) is in English, and of the same type as other folk and popular herbal remedies given earlier in the manuscript, e.g. f. 17r, (b) is in Latin, and highly technical in its vocabulary.

They conclude the Commonplace Book aptly enough. Holles was essentially a practical young man, facing adult life and the world of his time on practical terms and in the event doing so with fair success, whether or not he retained other of his interests as they appear here. He was a gentleman, upwardly mobile in his own society. He was not a mage, still less a scholar or a poet, but it is not irrelevant to the man or to the world as he saw it to state the fact.

Contents of the manuscript, itemised

f. 2r (a) list of items of armour, military terms and equipment: of considerable linguistic interest. English.

         (b) two epigrammatic couplets, English (the second with Latin motto), possibly by Holles.

         (c) list of the Officers at the Coronation of Anne Boleyn, condensed from Hall.

f. 2v (a) Horace, *Ars Poetica*, 161–5 with some textual oddities.

         (b) Quatrain, lampooning the Doctrine of Transubstantiation. Latin.

         (c) two couplets, epigrammatic and moral. English. Possibly by Holles.

         (d) quatrain, English. As (c).

         (e) moral couplet. English. As (c) and (d).

         (f) couplet. Theological. Latin.

         (g) tag from Pliny? (Epist 627–4).

f. 3r (a) table for determining the planetary domination of the hours, for magical purposes.

         (b) list of the planets with their proper metals.

f. 3v (a) three verses on diet and the management of health, English. These are parallel in content and some phrasing to the much longer *Diatorie*, Lambeth MS 853; of EETS OS 32, 1868, ed. Furnivall, *The Babes Book*, pp. 54 ff.

         (b) a date: 1558.

         (c)–(e) moral verses, English, possibly by Holles.

f. 4r (a) Magical text, English, citing the relation of the Moon to the Zodiacal signs appropriate for different kinds of magical operation. The same text, with minor variations occurs in BM MS B.3850, which may be of a slightly later date. I have met no version of it in print.

f. 4v (a) as f. 4r. (a) concluded.

         (b) '*The bouke of hermes de Imaginibus*': the so-called *Liber Lunae* (cf. Thorndike, History of *Magic and Experimental Science*, Columbia 1923, vol. II p. 223). English: either copy of a translation or a running translation of a Latin text. This work is of widespread occurrence, with some variation in the names of the hours given: e.g., BM MS Harl. 89, ff. 75 et seq.: (English), MS CCC. 125, ff. 62–8 (Latin) but again I have met no version of it in print.

f. 5v (a) as f. 4v (b) continued.

f. 6r (a) as f. 4v continued: the headings for the last two hours of the night are omitted.

f. 6v blank

f. 7r (a) rough diagram for casting a nativity, with errors and corrections.

         (b) table of the planets, their houses, metals and temperatures.

f. 7v (a) 'qualiter puer crescit in ventro matris sue ...': source as yet unidentified. There is a possible analogue, of very much earlier date, in BM MS Cotton Tiberius A.

f. 8r   (a)   'of *the* art of workings of experimen*tes* or co*n*clusions': the planetary dominances suited to different kinds of magical operation. The main source is Albertus, *Secretes*, possibly in the English translation of ?1525, though there are interesting discrepancies.

f. 8v   (a)–(j)   magical recipes, mostly aphrodisiac, in English and Latin. Analogues for most of these can be found without difficulty, e.g. in Bodley, MSS E Mus. 173, E Mus. 243, but the details, and some of the vocabulary in both English and Latin, are of considerable interest. Partly in the 'secret alphabet'.

f. 9r   (a)–(j)   various recipes and charms, English and Latin. The principle source for the latter is Albertus Magnus, *Secreta*, probably in the edition of 1509. Partly in the 'secret alphabet'.

f. 9v   (a)–(j)   various recipes and charms, Latin. The principle source is again Albertus, *ut supra*. Holles may also have made use of *Magiae Naturalis* Lugduni, 1526.

f. 10r   (a)–(j)   recipes in Latin and English: the former as f. 9r and v *supra*; the latter household and medicinal, for which many analogues can be found.

f. 10v   (a)–(i)   as f. 9r above.

f. 11r   (a)   an extremely elaborate magical formula for obtaining and controlling a magical horse: Latin.

f. 11v   (a)   recipe to make a red ruby white, etc. Latin. In *Magiae Naturalis, vide* f. 9v *supra*.

f. 12r   (a)   'God Counsell for a Com*m*oner in the Court'. This piece has something in common as to tone with some of the *Colloquies* of Erasmus, though it is more clumsily cynical. I have as yet been unable to find a source as such.

f. 12v   (a)   as f. 12r (a) continued.

f. 13r   (a)   f. 12r (a) concluded.
         (b)–(e)   recipes, English and Latin, mainly concerned with the preparation of parchment for writing, paint, sizes, etc. Most can be paralleled elsewhere.

f. 13v   (a)   *de gradibus siccitatis et caliditatis etc.*
         (b)   *de etate lune* etc.
         (c)   *de 12 signis*
         (d)   *de 7 planetis* these sections are taken and condensed from Albertus Magnus *Secreta, vide* f. 8r and v *supra*.
         (e)   a recipe for gunpowder, English.
         (f)   a recipe for varnish, English.

f. 14r   (a)   an acrostic poem, English, on the name Densel Hollis (*sic*) professing love and constancy.
         (b)   table of correspondencies, relating complexion, temperature, age, colour and season. Latin.
         (c)   couplet giving corrective medicine for the different bodily organs. Latin.
         (d)   epigrammatic summary of the four complexions. Latin.
         (e)   *a playe of the cards*, which are then listed, in Latin.

f. 14v (a) a full and very practical list of requirements for travelling, possibly on campaign. English.

(b) recipe for catching fish, versions of which are fairly common. English. Apparently in another hand.

(c) *Isti sunt abusiones mundi*: a corrupt version of the chapter headings of the *Tractatus de Duodecim Abusionibus Mundi* sometimes attributed to St Augustine or St Cyprian. Semi-proverbial: it occurs in Berchorius, *Dictionarium Morale*, under *Abuti*.

f. 15r (a) a list of heraldic devices, with the titles associated with them. This is a very curious entry. Some heads (e.g. Red Dragon: Rex Angelie, referring to the dexter supporter of the Arms of Henry VII or the sinister of Henry VIII) are straightforward. Others, referring to the personal badges of particular holders, of the titles given, are more obscure. Some appear to be simply inaccurate, but others I have not as yet been able to trace at all. The College of Arms has been most helpful in directing me to possible source-material. English: (devices); Latin: (titles).

f. 15v (a) table of correspondencies: *Elements, Complexions, Tempora anni, partes mundi, 4 partes of man*: English and Latin.

(b) table of correspondencies: *4 partes lune, 4 ages of man*. English.

ff. 16r and v (blank).

f. 17r (a)–(j) recipes, cosmetic and medicinal. English. Analogies exist for most of these.

f. 17v (a)–(j) as f. 16r *supra*.

f. 18r (a) 'The copye how to make the souerayne wather *that* doctor steuenes phisicion *and* a great cunnynge man of long experience did use *and* ther*with* did many cures *and* always kept it secret tyll a lytel before his deth *that* the archbishop of canterbury gat it of him in wryting': English.

f. 18v (a) conclusion of f. 18r (a) *supra*.

(b)–(c) simple and compound herbal remedies. English and Latin.

f. 19r (a)–(b) two medical recipes 'for the hardnes of the splene ... geven me by doctor perpont'. English and Latin.

The following ff., to the end, are blank except for f. 33r which has the 'secret alphabet' written out, with transcription into secretary hand above, faintly and not certainly in Holles's hand.

Transcription of the 'secret alphabet' used by Denzill Holles

A — ✛

M — 𝟴𝟴

B — ϑ

N — ℘

C — ∀

O — ℧

D — ※

P — ⌽

E — ∅

Q — ↓

F — ‡

R — ↑

G — ↑

S(Z) — ⊹

H — ↓

T — ‡

IJ — ✳

UVW — ⅄

K — ⬦

X — ⚹

L — ⬦

Y — ⊶ , ⬦

the/thee/ye — ⬦

Vt mulier ✱✱✱✱ se recipe parui linea et in tn̄
in sanguine leporis et de illo fac lichium et candela, et
quando vis vt ✱✱✱✱ se accede candela, et s vis vt
cessent extingue candela illam ⁊

᷐᷒᷑᷈ ✱✱᷐᷈᷑ ⁊

Si vis a muliere diligi scribe hec noia sequentia in ⚬✝᷐᷑ⁿ
Abdon, Abea, Abrita, ✝᷐᷑᷈, ✝᷑✝ ✱ ✝᷑᷈, phales, et dic ⟨⟩
V᷈᷑✝I᷐ ✝✝᷐᷐᷑ sequente ✝᷑hin᷐᷈ te ⚬᷐᷑᷈nū per⟨⟩
quatuor milliaria X hi nocentū, qui passi sunt amare in
christi: ⁊ per ✱martires, ✝o gelos, confessores, a✱ostolos, ⁊
✱ang᷑elistas: q̄ illa ⚬✝✱✱᷐ q̄ de te comederit: aut in
te aspicit statim in ✝᷐᷑᷈᷑ ardesut! Si vis vt te ✱✱✱
✱✱✱at da illi parte ma᷑x comes✱re ⁊ i ostenderis illi ⟨⟩
✱o᷑m ⁊ cōtemplatur sine dubio i. a✱bit! hec noia tribi
debent ante om̄ solis, si nō credideris pha cune ⁊ te in
sequatur ⁊

Secreta ✱✱✱ ō✝⚬ cognoscere
Recipe harba brone vel celidonia et si ponis sub
aure eius dextra et ✱✱cet tibi ōnia que fecit et est
verū et expertā ⁊

flou ✝⚬✝✝⚬ a ᷐᷈✝᷑ fell
lys✝✱᷑✝ ō✱o ws᷈✝✝✱
✝✝fs ✱o᷑o

Noru✝ fe✝⚬ Io✱des⚬✝ ᷐✝o ma✝✱oy, ma✝✱aus
in ✝o ✝✝lus g. ✝✝✝᷐ ⁊ ca✝᷑᷑ hand
✱ou✝e✝ ua✝⚬ ⚬✝✝᷑᷑ ✝o᷑oy✝⚬✝᷑ i6 u
✝✝o✝᷑

                  t

Ut mulier dednudet[1] se recipe panu*m* lineu*m* etingtu*m*[2]
in sangine[3] leporis et de illo fac lichnu*m*[4] et candela*m*, et
quando vis ut denudet se accede candela*m*, et si vis ut
cessent extingue illa*m*//

           pro/ amore

Si vis a muliere deligi scribi hec no*min*a sequentia in maro[5]
Abadon, Abea, Abrita, Caon, Sds, pholles, et dic . . .
coniuratione sequente/ coniuro te maru*m* per . . .[8]
quatuor milliaria innocentiu*m*, qui passi sunt amore . . .[9]
Christi: et per martires, angelos, confessores, apostolos *et*
euangelistas: *quod* illa mulier que de te comederit: aut in
te aspicat statim in amore ardescat./ Si vis ut te sequatur
tange illam infra pectus cu*m* maro/ *et* si vis ut te <sapie*nter*
diligat>[10] da illi parte*m* mare comedere/ *et* si ostenderis illi . . .
pomu*m* et contemplatur sine dubio te amabit/ hec no*min*a scribi
debent ante ortu*m* solis, si no*n* credideris *pro*ba cane et te . . .
sequatur)____[11]

         Secreta mulierum cognoscere/

Recipe harbam brone[12] vel celledonia[13] et si ponis sub
aure eius dextra/ et dicet tibi om*n*ia que fecit et est
veru*m* et expertu*m*)____/

          For to make a woman tell
          in her/slepe what she
          hath done

Wryt thes wordes mago, magyon, magrone*m*,
in the palme of *the* hand *and* laye *the* hand
upon her naked papes when she is a
slepe[14]

f. 8v: Translation

In order that a woman should undress[1] herself take linen thread dipped[2] in the blood[3] of a rabbit and make of it a wick[4] and a candle, and when you desire that she should undress herself bring the candle, and if you wish that they should stop put it out/ /

for love

If you desire to be loved by a woman write these names following in cat-mint[5] Abadon, Abea, Abrita, Caon, Sds,[6] pholles, and speak[7] ... with the following conjuration/ I conjure you O cat-mint by[8] ... the four thousands of innocents, who have suffered through the love[9] ... of Christ: that the woman who shall eat of you: or look upon you may at once burn with love./ If you desire that she follow you touch her beneath the breast with the cat-mint/ and if you desire that she should/ love you wisely[10] give her part of the cat-mint to eat/ and if you show to her an apple and she looks at it without doubt she will love you/ these names should be written before sunrise, and if you have not believed this try it with a dog and it will follow you)__[11]

To know the secrets of women/

Take the herb bryony(?)[12] or celendine[13] and if you place it below her right ear she will also tell you everything she has done and this is true and proven)__

Notes

1. 't' has been written in above in clear, possibly in a later hand.
2. Apparently from ML *extinguo*: to slake or quench.
3. For *sanguine*. Bodley MS E Mus.243 has a love-spell using a candle with a wick of red thread: f. 51.v.
4. *lichnus*: wick.
5. *marum*: cat-mint or cat-thyme. The attraction of cats to this herb and their ecstatic manifestations of pleasure at its scent might suggest its use as an aphrodisiac, though *maro* may here be a slip for or conflation with *malo* or *pomo*, apple. Cf. n. 11 infra.
6. Apparently for Sadas: cf. n. 11 infra.
7. Decorative penstrokes to fill out the line.
8. As 7 above.
9. As 7 and 8 above.
10 'secrete(?) tangat' 'that she may touch you secretly) has been overwritten 'sapienter(?) diligat' (that she may love you wisely) apparently in the same hand.
11. A version of this spell occurs in Bodley MS E Mus.243 f. 49v:

A booke of experiments taken out of dyvers authors. 1622.

Wryte on an Apple these names following Abdengbea, Abrata, Caon, Urion, Sadas, pholles, and say this coniuration followinge coniuro te

154

pomu*m* per quadraginta quatuor millia innocentiu*m* qui *pro Christi nomine* passi sunt et per martires et per Angelos et per Archangelos ut qua mulier te comedit vel te vidit in amore meo stati*m* acce*n*sa sit *et* geue her a pece of *the*Apple to eat.

Here there is no mention of cat-mint, but Holles's source may have intended that its juice should be used for writing the words of power on the apple. An inscribed apple is one of the commonest of love charms, though the names and details vary, and charms in this general category, where the use of names of power, herbal and animal ingredients are the varying but common denominators are ubiquitous and persistent. Early examples may be found in *Papyri Graecae Magicae*, K. Preisendanz (rev. A. Henrichs) Stuttgart, 1973, and the tradition lasts well through the Renaissance period.

The writing here, where the 'secret alphabet' is not used, is italic up to this point, reverting to secretary for the final entry.

12. Possibly either a form of *bryonia*, bryony, or for *branca*: *ursina*, bearsfoot, a popular name for various species of hellebore.

13. For *chelidonia*, celendine.

14. Charms to this end are again extremely common, the details varying in elaboration and unpleasantness. Here in the first charm the magical agent in herbal; in the second the effect apparently depends only on the use of the magical names.

Skelton and Heresy

JOHN SCATTERGOOD

On 4 May 1528 Thomas Bowgas, a fuller of St Leonard's Colchester, appeared before Cuthbert Tunstall, Bishop of London to abjure the heresy he was accused of – seemingly without much argument. Bowgas's confession covered heretical views of a mainly Lollard sort: he objected to pilgrimages and to the worship of images. And though he agreed to abjure he had enough spirit to express himself in homely and colourful terms. He said that a man need not go on pilgrimage to Sir Thomas of Canterbury or to Our Lady of Grace, that he wished he had Our Lady of Grace in his bakehouse, that to set a candle before the sepulchre was like lighting a candle to the devil, and that 'if he had the crucifix, the image of Our Lady and other saints, and crosses in a ship, he would drown them all in the sea'. Two of his beliefs were apparently of a more radical tenor: he held that there was no other church of God but man's conscience, and that he would as soon be buried in his own house as in church. After Bowgas had read his abjuration he received absolution from the bishop on condition that he should go in procession on Sunday 10 May to his local church, bearing a faggot on his shoulder, and afterwards hear mass on bended knees on the steps of the choir. The penance was evidently performed satisfactorily and Bowgas disappears from the records.[1] As heresy trials went, this was not a particularly important one: the faith was preserved and no life was lost. What gives it some significance for students of literature, however, is that John Skelton appeared among the witnesses, and this fact helps to provide a context for his last known poem, *A Replycacion Agaynst Certayne Yong Scolers Abjured of Late*, published by Pynson probably in 1528.[2]

This was not the first occasion on which Skelton had adverted to the question of heresy in his poems. In 1512–13 Henry VIII was heavily

---

1 For accounts of Thomas Bowgas see J. Strype, *Ecclesiastical Memorials*, (Oxford, 1822), I (ii) p. 58; *Letters and Papers, Foreign and Domestic of the Reign of Henry VIII*, eds. J. S. Brewer, J. Gairdner, and R. H. Brodie, (22 vols., London: HMSO 1862–1932), IV (ii) 4242; and for a modern account John F. Davis, *Heresy and Reformation in the South-East of England, 1520–1559*, (London: Royal Historical Society 1983), p. 62.

2 Skelton is quoted from *John Skelton: The Complete English Poems*, ed. John Scattergood, (New Haven and London, 1983).

engaged in the Holy League against France and was fearful, rightly as it
turned out, of invasion by the Scots, who had an 'auld alliance' with the
French, while he was out of the country. In order to dissuade James IV
from attacking England, Nicholas West, Dean of Windsor, went to
Scotland in March 1513 with a monitory brief from the pope and a copy
of a 'bull executorial', and again on 9 August 1513 apostolic censures
were pronounced against the Scottish king.[3] But two days later he wrote
to Henry VIII, then in France, that unless he gave up his attempt to
conquer France he could expect war with Scotland. Henry VIII wrote to
James IV on 12 August accusing him of being one of a group of
'.. scysmatyques and their adherentes beynge by the generall connsayll
expressely excommunicate and interdicted',[4] and after James IV's death
at Flodden on 9 September Skelton reiterates this point, among others,
in an addendum to *Agaynst the Scottes* (1513):

> He was a recrayed knyght,
> A subtyll sysmatyke,
> Ryght nere an heretyke,
> Of grace out of the state
> And dyed excomunycate.   (XII Add. 26–30)

The wording of this makes it clear that Skelton, who knew what heresy
was and what it was not, regarded James IV as an enemy of the church
in that he disobeyed papal injunctions and divided the Church, not that
he was a questioner of its doctrines. However, in *Collyn Clout* (late 1522
or 1523) he speaks more precisely of the ways in which the laity question
the doctrines of the Church, in a passage full of self-consciously chosen
learned language:

> Some make epylogacyon
> Of hygh predestynacyon;
> And of resydevacyon
> They make enterpretacyon
> Of auquarde facyon,
> And of the prescyence
> Of divyne assence
> And what ipostacis
> Of Chrystes manhode is.   (XIX 519–27)

Elsewhere he mentions the arguments made 'Agaynst the sacramentes'
(517–8) and the disdain manifested towards 'preestly dygnytes' (538).

---

3 *Letters and Papers*, I(i) 791 and 809; see also 806 and 810.
4 Quoted from Edward Halle's *Chronicle*, (1809), pp. 547–8. Copies of the letter
   also appear in BL MS Harley 787 fol. 58r, and in BL MS Harley 2252
   fols. 42r–43r.

These arguments, says Skelton, are made by the laity (496) against the Church and he identifies them with heresy:

> ... some have a smacke
> Of Luthers sacke,
> And a brennynge sparke
> Of Luthers warke,
> And are somewhat suspecte
> In Luthers secte.
> And some of them barke
> Clatter and carpe
> Of that heresy arte
> Called Wytclyftista,
> The devylyshe dagmatista.
> And some be Hussians,
> And some be Arryans,
> And some be Pollegyans,
> And make moche varyans
> Bytwene the clergye
> And the temporalyte.   (540–56)

And he continues by instancing some of the criticisms made against the clergy. The growth of a literate and an educated laity was one of the features of the fifteenth and early sixteenth centuries and, as one historian puts it: 'In the long run it was bound to involve not merely critical attitudes toward the Church but also more constructive intellectual and religious ambitions which could not be excluded from the sphere of religion.'[5]

In 1528, however, when Skelton was writing the *Replycacion*, the threat came not from the laity so much as from heretical elements within the Church itself. The 'yong scolers' mentioned in the title, though they are not named, appear almost certainly to be Thomas Arthur and Thomas Bilney, two Cambridge trained theologians,[6] but Skelton generalises his poem out to make it a more comprehensive attack on particular aspects of heresy.

5 A. G. Dickens, *The English Reformation* (rev. edn. London, 1967), p. 24.
6 The identification of the 'yong scolers' with Arthur and Bilney was first made by J. B. Mullinger, *The University of Cambridge from the Earliest Times to the Royal Injunctions of 1535*, (Cambridge University Press, 1873), I 607–8. For accounts of Arthur and Bilney, see James Gairdner, *Lollardy and the Reformation*, (4 vols., London, 1908–13), I 393–406, 544–5, 567–9; Arthur Ogle, *The Tragedy of the Lollard's Tower*, (Oxford, 1949), pp. 266–77; William A. Clebsch, *England's Earliest Protestants*, (New Haven and London, 1964), pp. 206–7, 278–80; Dickens *op cit.*, pp. 101–3, 117–20; J. A. Guy, *The Public Career of Sir Thomas More*, (Brighton, 1980), pp. 167–71; Jasper Ridley, *The Statesman and the Fanatic: Thomas Wolsey and Thomas More*, (London, 1982), pp. 191–2; Davis *op cit.*, pp. 30–5, 46–53, 66–8.

Both Arthur and Bilney were perhaps from Norfolk and both were at Trinity Hall. Arthur took an MA there and was admitted to a fellowship at St John's in February 1518 before becoming principal of St Mary's Hospital. He was charged with heresy, along with Bilney, in 1526 and both appeared before Wolsey in late November 1527. Arthur recanted and did his penance: whether he changed his views or not is not known, but after his trial he at least kept them to himself and disappeared from heretical circles. He became a tutor and wrote plays, but died at Walsingham in 1532.

Bilney, however, was a much less amenable figure: though in appearance insignificant and in demeanour meek, in matters of belief he was tough-minded and ultimately intransigent. He was ordained priest in the title of the Priory of St Bartholomew in Smithfield in 1519 and was active in spreading heterodox views: Robert Barnes, John Lambert, Matthew Parker, and Hugh Latimer amongst others were all influenced by him. He was a well respected and charismatic figure. He obtained licence to preach throughout the bishopric of Ely on 23 July 1525 and it was largely the views he set forth in his sermons after this that brought him into conflict with the authorities. As soon as dissent was taken outside the universities it became a dangerous matter. He appeared before Wolsey in 1526 and undertook on oath not to preach further the doctrines of Luther. Whether, in a technical sense, Bilney could be said to have kept his oath is debatable; but he continued to preach heterodoxy, Lutheran or otherwise, and it was his sermons against the worship of saints, against the veneration of relics and images, and against the spiritual value of pilgrimages, preached in and around London at Whitsuntide 1527, which brought him before Wolsey again in November. After much argument and delay he made an abjuration, which was controversial at the time and is still argued about, and performed his penance. Like Arthur he was imprisoned for about a year, and when he was released in 1529 he returned to Cambridge. Accounts of his life say that for two years he was despondent, feeling he had betrayed what he really believed in, and that by deciding to resume preaching in 1531 he was consciously courting martyrdom: he told his friends when he left Cambridge that he would 'go to Jerusalem'. Inevitably, he was arrested, tried as a relapsed heretic, and burned on 19 August 1531.

Skelton's reasons for involving himself in anti-heretical propaganda in 1527–8 were probably both personal and more generally political. By temperament he was an authoritarian in religious matters (as well as in others) and had an almost uncomprehending antipathy to heterodoxy. No doubt it irritated him also that the university of Cambridge, where he had been a student, should have become the centre of the English reform movement. It was also the case that the threat of heresy had increased a good deal since 1522–3. On 2 December 1525 Edward Lee could write to Henry VIII, 'hitherto, blessed be God, your realm is safe from infection of Luther's sect'.[7] But Tyndale's New Testament began to circulate in 1526 and heretical books and pamphlets in English, though printed abroad, began to be imported in larger numbers. The threat carried by means of the printed word had to be answered in literary terms. On 7 March 1528 Bishop Tunstall gave Sir Thomas More a special licence to possess Lutheran books so that he might write to refute them. It seems entirely reasonable, similarly, that Skelton, who took much pride in his role as *orator regius*, would have regarded polemics against heresy as an appropriate subject for his literary attention. As is clear from the fulsome dedication, Skelton wrote the *Replycacion* at Wolsey's suggestion ('presentis opusculi fautore excellentisimo') and since More wrote his *Dialogue Concerning Heresies* (published 1529 but written in 1528) at Tunstall's request,[8] it may be, as William Nelson says, '... that the *Dialogue* and the *Replicacion* form part of an officially inspired concerted attempt to destroy the heretical movement in England with the weapon of eloquence'.[9]

There are major differences between the works. More's is set out in the form of a Socratic dialogue, written in leisurely, spacious prose, where the arguments move backwards and forwards with an appearance of rationality (an appearance only, of course, because More controls both sides of the dialogue), as the author seeks, with simulated patience and temperance, to educate his opponent back into the right way of truth. Skelton's poem, on the other hand, is a piece of direct invective, written in a mixture of alliterating and rhyming prose and racing Skeltonic verse. However, this should not obscure what is basically a similarity of approach which manifests itself in a number of features both of a precise and a general sort, suggesting that there may have been some attempt to combat heresy from a centrally organised point of view.

Perhaps the most immediately apparent similarity between the two works is the fact that neither mentions Bilney by name, though both address the issues raised by his case. In his *Dialogue* More mentions many

---

7 Quoted by James Gairdner, *op cit.*, I 509, from BL MS Cotton Vespasian C iii fols. 211–12.

8 More's *Dialogue Concerning Heresies* is quoted from the edition by Thomas M.C. Lawler, Germain Marc' Hadour, and Richard C. Marius, (New Haven and London, 1981). (This is vol. 6 of *The Complete Works of St Thomas More*.)

9 *John Skelton, Laureate*, (New York, 1939), p. 216. See also H. L. R. Edwards, *Skelton: The Life and Times of an Early Tudor Poet*, (London, 1949), pp. 248–9. But neither scholar develops the comparison very far.

names, including those of Richard Hunne, Jerome Barlowe, William Roye, and William Tyndale, but not Bilney: instead he uses some variation of the formula 'the man that ye write of'.[10] Perhaps this is because he is unwilling to defame Bilney in print – 'to preserve the mannys estymacyon among the people' (417.22) – while there was a chance that he might repent. Or perhaps he may have wished to preserve a certain detachment and depersonalise the arguments. Or he may have simply reasoned that by omitting Bilney's name he was denying him publicity. Any or all of these ideas may have been in Skelton's mind too. Like More, in some places in his work he uses names in the context of criticism, in others he supresses them (VI 38, XIX 1037) and frequently manifests some sensitivity about defaming his enemies. In the *Replycacion* his address to Arthur and Bilney is direct and he naturally uses the second person plural pronoun: when he wishes to be more specific he uses phrases such as 'some of you...' or 'One of you..' (XXIV 146, 186). More and Skelton had to come to terms with both a general movement and particular cases within it, and it is interesting that they sought to solve their difficulties in much the same way.

The arguments they seek to make are as much about intellectual authority as about doctrine and both More and Skelton seek to disparage the opponents of orthodoxy as well as to defeat them in argument. Both criticise them for their youthfulness and lack of experience. More writes as follows to his friend about his initial misgivings about the Messenger and his representation of theological opinions: 'Upon these wordes and other lyke/ whan I consydered that your frende was studyous of scrypture/ and all thoughe I now have a very good oppynyon of hym/ nor at that tyme had not all the contrary/ yet to be playne with you and hym bothe/ by reason that he set the matter so well and lustely forwarde/ he put me somwhat in doubte whether he were (as yonge scolers be somtyme prone to newe fantasyes) fallen in to Luthers secte.' (34.24–30) And the youth of the reformers in contrast with the experience of More is constantly held before the reader. Skelton likewise refers constantly to 'Yong Scolers' or 'rechless yonge heretykes' or 'friscajoly yonkerkyns' or 'devyllsshe pages' (271). In fact the reform movement in England was essentially a young man's movement: both Arthur and Bilney were probably in their early thirties by 1528 and many other adherents were of about that age or younger.[11]

10 On More's use of names see *Dialogue Concerning Heresies ed cit.*, pp. 472–81.
11 On the youthfulness of the reformers see particularly H. Maynard Smith, *Henry VIII and the Reformation*, (London, 1962), pp. 252–3 where the ages of the Cambridge group are calculated for the year 1518.

Both More and Skelton are also anxious to denigrate the intellectual status of the reformers, who were for the most part from the university of Cambridge. In the *Dialogue* the Messenger is at one point described as having 'new comen from the unyversyte/ where he was as ye wote at lernynge' (247.11) and at others he affirms that 'in the unyversyte where he had bene/ there were that had none evyll oppynyon of Luther/ but thought that his bokys were by the clergye forboden of malyce and evyll wyll' (345.10–13). More's case is that the committed reformers corrupt those at the university who are too gullible to resist them. In one place he refers to somebody who is probably to be identified with Dr Robert Forman, rector of All Souls, Honey Lane, London, who had 'not only taught and wryten and covertly corrupted dyvers lyght and lewd persons/ but also had bought grete nomber of the bokys of Luther/ and Wyclyfe/ Husse/ and Zuynglyus/ and such other heretyques/ and of many one sorte dyvers bokys/ to be delyvered as he coud fynd occasyon unto yonge scolers of the universytees/ such as he thought of youth and lyghtnes most lykely to be sone corrupted' (379.11–17). More does not specify which universities, but Forman was a book agent to Cambridge.[12] Skelton is more explicit: he addresses a 'Eulogium consolationis' to the university of Cambridge to remind the institution which nurtured him that not all her sons were unworthy and, characteristically, offers himself as an example of somebody who has turned out well. And he furthers disparages the young reformers by conferring on them a comic status as bar-room intellectuals:

> Drowned in dregges of divinite,
> ... they juge themselfe able to be
> Doctours of the chayre in the Vyntre
> At the Thre Cranes... (XXIV 6–10)

Skelton refers to a London tavern which was, according to Ben Jonson, a meeting place for 'pretenders to wit', yet it had no reputation as a place where reformers assembled; they seem to have met more often at the White Horse in Cambridge.[13] However, accuracy may not be the main point here. To associate criticism of the church with drinking in order to discredit the critics is something Skelton had already done in *Collyn Clout* where he says that reformist talk takes place:

> Whan the good ale soppe
> Dothe daunce in theyr foretoppe. (XIX 530–1)

---

12 Forman had been examined and suspended by Tunstall on 19 March 1528. See Davis *op cit.*, pp. 56, 59.

13 For Jonson's reference to the Three Cranes see *Bartholomew Fair* I i.33. For some speculation about the group of reformers who met at the White Horse Tavern see Clebsch *op cit*, p. 42, and for a broader survey Maynard Smith *op cit.*, pp. 251–62.

More uses a similar slur against Bilney who, he says, '...under pretexte of love and lyberty waxed so dronke of the new must of lewd lyghtnes of mynd and vayn gladnesse of harte/whyche he toke for spyrytuall consolacyon/that what so ever hym self lysted to take for good/that thought he forthwith approved by god' (257.31–5) - though from what may be deduced about Bilney's puritanical lifestyle his drunkeness is likely to have been metaphorical.

These accusations, of course, are personally derogatory but they do, nevertheless, bear some relation to more serious issues. According to More and Skelton, by trusting to a knowledge which is imperfect the reformers are prejudicing their own salvation and the salvation of those who believe their sermons. As Skelton puts it '...they were but febly enforced in maister Porphiris problemes, and have waded but weakly in his thre maner of clerkly workes, analeticall, topicall, and logycall; howbeit they were puffed so full of vaynglorious pompe and surcudant elacyon, that popholy and pevysshe presumpcion provoked them to publysshe and to preche to people imprudent perilously...' And both More and Skelton embark on what is in part a refutation of the reformers' positions and in part a process of educating them.

Their case is not that the reformers are unintelligent, but that they are perversely dedicated to a deliberately restricted idea of what constitutes the proper idea of study.[14] The Messenger in More's *Dialogue* has effectively set aside all branches of learning except scripture: 'I understode hym to have gyven dylygence to the latyn tonge/As for other facultyes he rought not of. For he told me meryly/that Logycke he rekened but bablynge/Musyke to serve for syngers/Arythmetrycke mete for marchauntes/Geometry for masons/Astronomy good for no man/ And as for phylosophy/the most vanyte of all/And that it and Logycke had lost all good dyvynte/with the subteltyes of theyr questyons/and babelynge of theyr dyspycyons/buyldynge all uppon reason/which rather gyveth blyndesse than any lyght/For man he sayd hathe noo lyght/but of holy scrypture' (33.24–34). This, he said, was 'lernynge ynoughe for a crysten man' (33.36). And it was the text alone which he studied, for he found that was sufficient for him: 'as for interpretatours/he tolde me that neyther his tyme wolde well serve hym to rede/and also he founde so grete swetnes in the texte selfe/that he coulde not fynde in his harte to lese any tyme in the gloses' (34.4–7). Any difficulties he tried to resolve himself, with the help of God, by comparing texts: 'the best and surest interpretacyon was to lay and conferre one texte with another/whiche fayle not amonge hem well and suffycyently to declare themselfe' (34.8–12). Skelton's 'yonge scolers' are

14 See *Dialogue Concerning Heresies ed cit.*, pp. 448–50.

also believers in something approaching a *sola scriptura* position in that they pay scant attention to other branches of learning:

> whan they have delectably lycked a lytell of the lycorous electuary of lusty lernyng, in the moche studious scolehous of scrupolous philology, countyng them selfe clerkes excellently enformed and transcendingly sped in moche high connyng, and when they have ones superciliusly caught

> > A lytell ragge of rethorike,
> > A lesse lumpe of logyke,
> > A pece or a patche of philosophy,
> > Than forthwith by and by
> > They tumble so in theology... (XXIV 1–5)

They are so bad at logical thinking, says Skelton (92–113, 234), that what they affirm is 'farther than their wytte wyll reche' (13). Thus they treat scripture in a clumsy and inappropriate way: 'Ye cobble and ye clout...' (222) to the detriment of everything.

The object of both More and Skelton is to inculcate in the young reformers a proper respect for the accumulated wisdom and authority of the church, as it is set forth in the writings of the fathers, and as it forms part of the traditional teaching and doctrine of the Christian religion. As More demonstrates again and again, the meaning of scripture is frequently obscure and surprising, and that the individual, relying on nothing but the text and his own interpretation of it may easily go astray: 'Harde it were quod I to fynde any thynge so playne that it shold nede no glose at all' (168.19–20). It is more reliable to accept the collective established wisdom of the church which, inspired as it is by the holy spirit, cannot err: 'yf the chyrche of Cryste entendynge well/do all agree upon any one thyng concernyng goddes honour or mannys soule/it can not be but that thynge must nedys be true. For goddes holy spyryte that anymateth his chyrche and gyveth it lyfc/wyll never suffer it all consent and agre togyther upon any dampnable errour' (224.11–17). More's touchstone for the truth of doctrine is always the *consensus fidelium*, 'the hole consente and agrement of all crysten people this fyften hundred yere' (346.30–1), and in this 'the consent and comen agrement of the olde holy fathers..' is especially important (169.30). In order to substantiate and lend authority to points he is making, More frequently in the *Dialogue* draws up lists of the fathers,[15] and this fairly common polemical method commended itself to Skelton (who was rarely slow to display his learning):

> Saynt Gregorie and saynt Ambrose,
> Ye have reed them, I suppose,
> Saynt Jerome and saynt Austen,

15 On More's lists see *Ibid.*, pp. 528–9.

With other many holy men,
Saynt Thomas de Aquyno
With other doctours many mo...   (275–80)

By arguing the reformers into submitting to the authority of the church
and the fathers both More and Skelton hope to re-educate them into a
right-thinking acceptance of correct doctrines. And the one most
centrally at issue has to do with worship, particularly the worship of
saints and images of saints. After citing his list of authorities Skelton
refers the reformers to their views – orthodox and authoritative – on
three categories of worship, *latria*, *hyperdulia*, and *dulia*:

> They saye howe *latria* is an honour grete,
> Belongyng to the Deite.
> To this ye nedes must agre.
>   But, I trowe, your selfe ye overse
> What longeth to Christes humanyte.
> If ye have reed *de hyperdulia*,
> Than ye know what betokeneth *dulia*:
> Than shall ye fynde it fyrme and stable,
> And to our faithe moche agreable,
> To worshyppe ymages of sayntes.   (282–91)

More also has a version of the same teaching (97.23–33) and refers to it
frequently elsewhere. The only way the individual can be sure of the
safety of his beliefs, says Skelton, is to submit to the authority of
orthodoxy, for that is what is 'fyrme and stable'.

And both he and More are good examples of their own teaching, or
at least present themselves in that way, because each makes a point of
stressing that he has submitted his own work to the church authorities
so that he can be sure that it is doctrinally correct and acceptable. More,
in the opening of his first book, gives a long account of his fears of
being misrepresented by the reformers, which caused him, he says, to
publish the *Dialogue*, and of his scrupulous care in having his book read
over by others: '...to make and put forth any boke (wherin were treated
any suche thynges as touche our fayth) wolde I not presume/but yf
better lerned than myself/sholde thynke it eyther profytable/or at the
lestwyse harmlesse. To whose examynacyon and iudgment I dyd the
more studyously submyt thys worke/for two thynges in specyall/among
dyvers other...' (23.6–11) – and he instances the long and detailed
account he had given of the Messenger's heterodox views which some
might find offensive, and 'certayne tales and mery wordes' which he had
used which might not be thought appropriate to the subject matter.
Skelton also makes the point that his 'lytell pamphilet' will always be
'humbly submytted unto the ryght discrete reformacyon of the

166

reverende prelates and moche noble doctours of our mother Holy
Churche..' By the shrewd employment of what is little more than a
modesty formula,[16] both More and Skelton demonstrate themselves to
be what they urge the young reformers to become – humble, compliant
with authority, and respectful of the traditional teachings of the church.
And when Skelton defends poetry against his reformist detractors as a
fitting medium for treating doctrinal matters[17] he does so on the
impeccable authority of Jerome who, in his letter to Paulinus prefacing
the Vulgate, had praised the poetry of the Psalms of David:

> ... if this noble kyng,
> Thus can harpe and syng
> With his harpe of prophecy
> And spyrituall poetry,
> And saynt Jerome saythe,
> To whom we must gyve faythe,
> Warblynge with his strynges,
> Of suche theologicall thynges,
> Why have ye than disdayne
> At poetes, and complayne
> Howe poetes do but fayne.   (343–53)

The same manner of argument which is used to substantiate doctrinal
points – a reliance on the comfort of patristic authority – serves to
justify Skelton's use of poetry to defend the faith.

   In general terms, therefore, both More and Skelton attack the
reformers on similar issues, and on more specific levels also both attack
Bilney – though without naming him – in relation to similar shortcomings. There is a difference in that Skelton confines himself to
reformist views on the worship of saints and images while More also
attacks Bilney for what he takes to be Lutheran views of a broader sort,
but their more personal attacks concentrate on similar matters – Bilney's
bad faith and evasiveness, and the suspicion that his abjuration was not
wholly sincere. More refers to Bilney's appearance before Wolsey in
1526 where he was treated with great generosity: 'This man had also
bene before that accused unto the gretest prelate in this realme/ who for

16 For examples of this sort of dedication see K.J.Holzknecht, *Literary Patronage
   in the Middle Ages*, (London, 1966), pp.90–155. But both More and Skelton
   use their dedications as a sort of protective device, because they know that
   they are handling theologically sensitive material.
17 For the background to this problem see Ernst Robert Curtius, *European
   Literature and the Latin Middle Ages*, trans. by Willard R.Trask, (London, 1953),
   pp.214–27. For the sixteenth-century development of some of these ideas
   see John N.King, *English Reformation Literature: The Tudor Origins of the Protestant
   Tradition*, (Princeton University Press, 1982), pp.14–19, 209–31.

hys tender favour borne to the unyversyte/dyd not procede far in the matter agaynst hym. But acceptyng his denyall with a corporall othe that he sholde from that tyme forth be no setter forth of heresyes/ but in his prechyngys and redyngys impugne them/dysmyssed hym very benygnely/ and of his lyberall bounte gave hym also money for his costys' (268.16–22). And this is what Skelton apparently refers to in the following lines:

> Some of you had ten pounde,
> Therwith for to be founde
> At the unyversyte,
> Employed whiche myght have be
> Moche better other wayes.　(146–50)

Both also refer to Bilney's odd abjuration in 1527 where he was allowed to abjure heretical beliefs and proceed to penance without any confession of his fault. More calls it 'perjury' and says: 'I wyll not say that his iudgys dyd wrong. But surely me thynketh I may well say that they shewed hym great favour in that they receyved hym to penaunce without the confessyon of his faute. And I thynke verely it was a favorable fassyon of abiuracyon/ and so straunge that the lyke hath bene very seldome sene yf ever it were sene before' (279.7–13). Skelton had similar doubts and suggested a more public withdrawal by Bilney:

> Some juged in this case
> Your penaunce toke no place,
> Your penaunce was to lyght;
> And thought, if ye had right,
> Ye shulde take further payne
> To resorte agayne
> To places where ye have preched,
> And your lollardy lernyng teched,
> And there to make relacion
> In open predycacion,
> And knowledge your offence
> Before open audyence...　(197–208)

Neither had very much faith that Bilney had actually given up his reformist opinions. More thought that Bilney's pride would prevent his acceptance of the authority of the church: 'I never can conceyve good hope of his amendment/ all the whyle that I se that pryde abyde styll in hys harte/ that can not suffer hym for shame to confesse his faute' (279.15–18). And Skelton had similar suspicions:

> And yet some men say,
> How ye are this day,
> And be now as yll,
> And so ye wyll be styll,
> As ye were before.　(176–80)

Both, in Bilney's case, turned out to be correct.

It ought to be clear from what has been said above that the approaches that More and Skelton took in 1528 to countering heresy by literary means were very similar in both the general arguments deployed and in the particulars of Bilney's case on which they concentrate. A detailed comparison of the *Dialogue* and the *Replycacion* strengthens the sense that there was some general organisation in the way in which the traditionalists sought to defend the church against the reform movement. Perhaps Skelton's poem was meant to be a fairly instant response to the threat of Arthur and Bilney (that he was capable of working quickly on political invectives is shown by *A Ballade of the Scottyshe Kynge* which was written in 1513 within days of the Battle of Flodden) while More's prose was intended as a more considered piece of intellectual refutation.

But the similarity between the two pieces also throws an interesting sidelight on a particular aspect of the history of the period which has caused some controversy in recent years. It has become almost customary for a contrast to be drawn between the firm but relatively kindly adminstration of policy against heresy under Wolsey and its harsh and severe administration under More. William A. Clebsch, after remarking that 'persecution and execution of English Protestants became commonplace after More replaced Wolsey in the chancellorship', goes on to contrast the two men as follows: 'the Protestants who rejoiced that the house was swept clean by the downfall of Wolsey, soon knew that seven devils had rushed in with More's elevation. More reserved his tender spirit for family and friends. No Protestant ever glimpsed it.'[18] Or, as Jasper Ridley, contrasting Wolsey 'the statesman' with More 'the fanatic', puts it: 'More was a far more zealous persecutor than Wolsey.'[19] John Guy, more subtly, explains that in fact Wolsey used his powers to mitigate the severity of others besides More: 'More was bitter ... that his predecessor had neglected to exploit fully his investigative and other responsibilities, having a unique opportunity as legate *a latere* and lord chancellor. Rigidly orthodox and never tolerant of heresy, Wolsey had, nevertheless, been no irrational or vindictive bigot, showing kindness to both Hugh Latimer and Robert Barnes, and tending to impede the efforts of the zealots on the episcopal bench. Wolsey was not a persecutor: he burned heretical books not men, and his legative powers, far from launching an English Inquisition, were used to override the bishops' jurisdiction, enforcing the cardinal's preference for the perpetual imprisonment of convicted heretics, rather

18 *Op cit.*, p. 270.
19 *Op cit.*, p. 253.

than for burnings.'[20] Even before he became chancellor, More took a harsh line with heretics: Book IV Chapter xiii of the *Dialogue* is headed 'The authour sheweth his oppynyon concernyge the burnynge of heretykes/ and that it is lawfull/ necessary and well done' (405.34–406.1).[21] And Skelton also threatens heretics with burning if they do not repent: '...ye shalbe blased/ And be brent at a stake' (294–5). How this squares with Wolsey's views, to whom Skelton dedicates the *Replycacion*, is difficult to imagine. Perhaps Wolsey's interest in Skelton's diatribe was more formal than actual, or perhaps he did not mind heretics being threatened with the fire but preferred that the threat be not carried out. However, it may be worth considering the possibility that in 1528 there was more of an official consensus, though an uneasy one, on the combatting of heresy than has been supposed and that Skelton saw no essential incompatibility in writing a poem which took an almost identical line to that of More's *Dialogue* but which at the same time was dedicated to Wolsey. However, if there was a consensus it was a very temporary one, and with Wolsey's fall from power the threat of burning became rapidly the fact.

20 *Op cit.*, pp. 104–5.
21 The extermination of heresy had been one of More's aims when he took office; see Roper's *Lyfe of Sir Thomas More*, ed. E. V. Hitchcock, EETS pp. 24–5.

The Te Deum Altarpiece and the Iconography of Praise

PAMELA SHEINGORN

The hymn known as the *Te Deum* praises God with the voices of earthly singers and through its text joins these voices to those of choirs of angels, prophets and patriarchs, apostles and martyrs, who in heaven eternally sing, 'Sanctus, sanctus, sanctus.' The *Te Deum* was frequently sung during the Middle Ages, for example, at the close of Matins in the daily recitation of the Divine Office. This paper discusses works of art that represent the eternal praise of God both enacted and described in the *Te Deum*.

Art historians have assigned the term *Te Deum* to a group of fifteenth and early sixteenth century English alabaster panels whose subjects suggest that they once belonged to altarpieces with this theme. No *Te Deum* altarpiece survives due to the widespread dismantling and even destruction of alabaster altarpieces during the Reformation, although three or possibly four panels in Genoa probably once belonged to the same altarpiece. It is not possible to assemble a *Te Deum* altarpiece from the other existing panels because they are not of uniform size. Nonetheless the compositions of the individual panels indicate that they were probably part of a larger whole.

It is not the purpose of this paper to re-define the corpus of *Te Deum* panels as established by Philip Nelson[1] and, more recently, by Francis Cheetham.[2] Rather its goal is to place these altarpieces both in their physical context, the choir of the late medieval church, and in their ritual context, the celebration of the Christian liturgy at the close of the Middle Ages. It is suggested here that the name assigned to these altarpieces, though not incorrect, nonetheless obscures both their iconographic position in the history of the visual arts and their central role in liturgical celebration. This obscurity is a result of a methodology that describes and studies the pictorial arts of the Middle Ages without sufficient consideration of their purpose in relation to Christian ritual. Art historians study medieval art in terms of its subject matter, whereas medieval Christians frequently experienced these subjects in terms of

1 Philip Nelson, 'Some Further Examples of English Medieval Alabaster Tables', *Archaeological Journal*, 74 (1917), 113–19.
2 Francis Cheetham, *English Medieval Alabasters* (Oxford: Phaidon. Christies, 1984).

their appearance in the liturgy. This paper attempts to reconstruct that experience.

The opening lines of the *Te Deum* create an image of a vast multitude united in adoration of the triune God:[3]

> We praise you, O God; we acknowledge you the Lord.
> All the earth worships you, the Father everlasting.
> To you all angels, the heaven, and the powers of the universe cry out unceasingly:
> Holy, holy, holy, Lord God of hosts;
> Heaven and earth are full of the majesty of your glory.
> The glorious company of the Apostles,
> The praiseworthy fellowship of the Prophets,
> The white-robed throng of Martyrs,
> All praise you.
> The holy Church throughout the whole world acknowledges you,
> The Father of infinite majesty;
> Your worshipful, true, and only Son;
> And the Holy Spirit, the Comforter.

A reconstructed *Te Deum* altarpiece would replicate the image implicit in these lines. A tall panel, most probably of the Throne of Grace Trinity surrounded by angels, some censing and some holding chalices for the blood of the crucified Christ, would occupy the central position. Flanking the Trinity would be panels filled with figures all facing the same direction, the centre. Each panel accommodates one group – the apostles, the nine orders of angels, the prophets led by John the Baptist, female saints led by the Virgin Mary, male saints and martyrs, and clergy representing the hierarchy of the church.[4] In addition, there might have been narrow end panels with single figures of saints.

Many panels of the Throne of God Trinity survive, for this subject could form the centre for altarpieces with a variety of themes. Of the other subjects there are relatively few. There is only one each of the apostles[5] and of the nine orders of angels,[6] both in Norwich. Because the panel of the apostles is damaged, only Peter, Paul, Andrew, and

3 Translated by Joanna Dutka from the *Liber Usualis* and included as item 49 in the section 'Latin Songs' in her monograph, *Music in the English Mystery Plays*, Early Drama, Art and Music Reference Series 2 (Kalamazoo: The Medieval Institute, 1980).

4 For the presumed constituents of the *Te Deum* altarpiece see E. S. Prior and A. Gardner, *An Account of Medieval Figure Sculpture in England* (Cambridge, 1912), 494–5.

5 Church of St Peter Mancroft, Norwich; illustrated in Nelson, (1917), pl. X, 2, and in P. Lasko and N. J. Morgan eds., *Medieval Art in East Anglia 1300–1520* (Norwich, 1973), 55.

6 Norwich Cathedral; illustrated in Nelson, (1917), pl. X, 1.

John the Evangelist can be identified; distinctive clothing and attributes assign each angel to a different order. Two panels of female saints are known, one in Norwich[7] and one in Amherst, Massachusetts.[8] Attributes identify many of the figures, including Barbara, Catherine, and Ursula. On the Amherst panel the Virgin Mary leads the group. There is another panel of nine saints and martyrs in the Burrell Collection in Glasgow.[9] Four panels of the prophets survive – one in the Victoria and Albert Museum,[10] one in Norwich,[11] one in Genoa,[12] and the fourth in the Fogg Art Museum.[13] Led by John the Baptist with his lamb, the prophets include Moses, Isaiah, and possibly Jeremiah and Gideon. Of the known panels of Holy Church, one survives in Genoa,[14] one in the Victoria and Albert Museum,[15] and one in the Nottingham Castle Museum.[16] The inclusion of Edward the Confessor, who holds a large ring, and possibly of Thomas Becket as archbishop makes this a specifically English grouping. In addition there is a Holy Church panel in the Burrell Collection in Glasgow[17] and another was sold at Sotheby's in 1983.[18] The figures appear in groups of nine frequently enough to suggest that this number was deliberately chosen to correlate with the

7 Vestry, Church of St Peter Mancroft, Norwich; illustrated in Nelson (1917), pl. XI, 2; Prior and Gardner, fig. 570b; Lasko and Morgan 56.
8 Mead Art Museum, Amherst College, Amherst, Massachusetts; illustrated pl. 1. See also Philip Nelson, 'Some Unpublished English Medieval Alabaster Carvings', *Archaeological Journal*, 82 (1925): 25–6 and pl. X, 1; entry on this panel by P. Sheingorn in *Gothic Sculpture in America*, vol. I, The Northeast, ed. Dorothy Gillerman (New York: Garland, forthcoming 1988).
9 Burrell Collection, Glasgow, inv. 41.
10 Victoria and Albert Museum A188–1946; illustrated in W. L. Hildburgh, 'Further Miscellaneous Notes on Medieval English Alabaster Carvings', *Antiquaries' Journal*, 17 (1937): pl. LIII, 1; Cheetham, (1984), 312.
11 Vestry, St Stephen's Church, Norwich; illustrated in Nelson (1917), pl. XI, 1.
12 Palazzo Bianco, Genoa; illustrated in R. Papini, 'Polittici d'Alabastro', *L'Arte*, 13 (1910), fig. 1; Nelson (1917), pl. XII.
13 Fogg Art Museum, Harvard University, Cambridge, Massachusetts; illustrated pl. 2; see also entry by P. Sheingorn in Gillerman, forthcoming.
14 Palazzo Bianco, Genoa; illustrated in Papini (1910), fig. 1; Nelson (1917), pl. XII.
15 Victoria and Albert Museum A11–1946; illustrated in Cheetham, (1984), 311.
16 Nottingham Castle Museum; illustrated in *Illustrated Catalogue of the Exhibition of English Medieval Alabaster Work, Held in the Rooms of the Society of Antiquaries, 26th May–30th June, 1910* (London, 1912) pl. XVII; Papini (1910), fig. 5; Nelson (1917), fig. 1; Prior and Gardner (1912), fig. 570a; Francis Cheetham, *Medieval English Alabaster Carvings in the Castle Museum, Nottingham* revd. edn., (1973), 41.
17 Burrell Collection, Glasgow, illustrated in *Antique Collector* (June, 1955).
18 Illustrated in Sotheby's *Sale Catalogue, The Hever Castle Collection*, (6 May 1983), lot 255.

nine orders of angels. In fact, a panel with nine figures formerly in the Lambert Collection in Audenarde combines representatives of several choirs – it includes Peter, Paul, Andrew, a martyr, a pope, a bishop, two clerics, and a king.[19] Possibly this panel belonged to an abbreviated *Te Deum* altarpiece in the form of a triptych and was balanced by a panel with the nine orders of angels.

Although the alabaster industry flourished in the area around Nottingham from about 1340 to about 1540, almost all of these panels have been dated to the fifteenth century, and a number of them to the second half of that century. At the 1986 Harlaxton symposium Linda Rollison pointed out that the accepted periodisation of alabasters did not sufficiently take into account the fact that records confirm continued production of alabasters until the Reformation.[20] During the Marian period some churches purchased alabaster altarpieces to replace those that had been discarded or destroyed a few years earlier. Thus it seems reasonable to conclude that alabaster altarpieces of the *Te Deum* were produced during the Early Tudor period and certainly that they were visible components of church interiors until the Reformation.

According to a tradition that arose at least as early as the eighth century, the *Te Deum* came into being as a spontaneous composition on the night of St Augustine's baptism in 387. Ambrose, who baptised Augustine, and Augustine himself extemporaneously sang alternate verses and were thus considered co-authors of the hymn.[21] There is a reference to the *Te Deum* in the Rule of St Benedict and, with some exceptions as noted in rubrics, it was recited in the Divine Office at the close of Matins and followed immediately by Lauds. Although daily recitation must have resulted in quick memorisation and little need to refer to the written word, the text of the *Te Deum* was included with the other canticles at the end of the Psalter at least as early as the Utrecht Psalter.

The canticles receive an unusually expansive treatment in the Utrecht Psalter, each being accompanied by the full-width illustration characteristic of the handling of each of the Psalms. For the *Te Deum*, entitled 'Hymnum ad Matutinis', the artist followed his usual practice of providing

19 The Lambert Collection was dispersed in 1926. See Jean Squilbeck, 'Quelques Sculptures anglaises d'Albâtre conservées en Belgiques', *Antiquaries Journal*, 18 (1938), 62 and pl. XXIV, 2.

20 Linda Rollison, 'English Alabasters in the Fifteenth Century', *England in the Fifteenth Century: Proceedings of the 1986 Harlaxton Symposium*, ed. Daniel Williams (Woodbridge, Suffolk: The Boydell Press, 1987), 245–54. For her suggestions regarding the periodisation of English alabasters see 'Notes on a Late Medieval Art Industry', *Art History*, 9 (1986), 86–94.

21 M. Huglo, 'Te Deum', *New Catholic Encyclopedia*, (1967–79), 13, 954–5.

a literal interpretation of the text.[22] Thus the composition centres on the Trinity, made up of the hand of God, the cross-nimbed figure of Christ, and the dove. Seraphs and angels surround the Trinity and directly below stands the author, probably Ambrose. The middle register is given over to heavenly worshippers of the Trinity, the martyrs, prophets, and apostles, with the martyrs identified by their palms, while below the Church on earth joins in praise of the Trinity. Each of these groups is specifically mentioned in the text of the *Te Deum* and each corresponds to one of the types of alabaster panel described above.

In spite of this important model, the expansive literal method of illustrating the *Te Deum* did not continue in manuscripts. As other visual material such as a life of Christ or a passion sequence was added to the Psalter, illustrations to the Canticles were correspondingly de-emphasised. For example, in the St Alban's Psalter of the early twelfth century the *Te Deum* received only a historiated initial.[23] The stem of the historiated T encloses figures who must be SS Ambrose and Augustine. They look up at Christ, who is flanked by angels. This sharply curtailed treatment includes only angels out of the groups that the text describes as singing their praises to the Trinity.

In an English manuscript from the beginning of the thirteenth century, the Munich Psalter, the composition suffers further reduction, with only the figure of St Ambrose being shown.[24] And even this much pictorial treatment is unusual, for Nigel Morgan observes that by this time historiated initials illustrating the Canticles are 'rarely found'.[25] The common pattern was to use the historiated initial to demarcate sections of the manuscript, so that only the first canticle received an initial. Rare examples of *Te Deum* illustration demonstrate a move away from the subject of the hymn and toward the historical circumstances of its composition. Thus the figure of a bishop with an asperging brush in the *Te Deum* initial in the fourteenth century Queen Mary Psalter must refer to Ambrose's baptism of Augustine,[26] and the scene is definitely one of baptism in a Bohun manuscript, a psalter of about 1360–73 now in Vienna.[27]

22 Ernest T. de Wald, *The Illustrations of the Utrecht Psalter* (Princeton: Princeton UP, 1932), pl. CXXXVIII (fol. 88r).
23 Fol. 193v; Otto Pächt, C. R. Dodwell, and Francis Wormald, *The St Albans Psalter* (London: The Warburg Institute, 1960), 269 and pl. 93b.
24 Fol. 155v; Bayr. Staatsbibl. MS Clm. 835. Nigel Morgan, *Early Gothic Manuscripts I 1190–1250* (London: Harvey Miller, 1982), 68–72.
25 Morgan 70.
26 Fol. 292v; British Library MS Royal 2 B. VII. George Warner, *Queen Mary's Psalter* (London, 1912), pl. 285.
27 Fol. 136r; Vienna, Oesterreichische Nationalbibliothek MS 1826*. M. R. James and E. G. Millar, *The Bohun Manuscripts* (Roxburghe Club, 1936) 44 and

Since illustration of the text of the *Te Deum* yields neither the direct source for *Te Deum* altarpieces nor information as to how these altarpieces were understood, let us turn now to uses of this text other than as part of the Divine Office. Another important context for the *Te Deum* is the drama. In the English mystery cycles, which enjoyed public performance annually until they were suppressed as part of the Reformation, the *Te Deum* is sung several times. The first of these occasions is during the Creation. Clifford Davidson describes the circumstances in which the *Te Deum* is sung in the York play of the Creation: 'The first act of ... God is to create the heavens and the nine orders of angels who are to give him everlasting praise, honor, and reverence (I.23–24). Surely the actors representing angels were somehow hidden at the beginning of the scene, and, when God declared his thought at lines 22–24, they rose up as if newly created and sang the *Te Deum*.'[28] 'After the completion of the *Te Deum*, God, with a gesture which indicates the playing area or *place (locus)* below, creates earth...'[29] That is, the singing of the *Te Deum* takes place before the beginning of time, outside of and indifferent to the created universe. In the N-Town Creation God mentions twice that he creates the angels to worship him with song (11.32–9):[30]

> In hevyn I bylde Angelles fful bryth
> my servauntys to be and for my sake
> with merth and melody worchepe my myth
> I belde them in my blysse
> Aungelles in hevyn evyr more xal be
> In lyth ful clere bryth as ble
> With myrth and song to worchip me
> Of joye thei may not mys.

At this moment a rubric instructs the angels in heaven to sing and the text gives a portion of the *Te Deum*:

> Tibi omnes angeli tibi celi et vniuerse potestates. Tibi cherubyn et seraphyn incessabili voce proclamant. Sanctus. Sanctus. Sanctus. Dominus deus saboath.

---

pl. LIII (f); Lucy Freeman Sandler, *Gothic Manuscripts 1285–1385* (London: Harvey Miller, 1986), 2: 147–9.

28 Clifford Davidson, *From Creation to Doom: The York Cycle of Mystery Plays* (New York: AMS Press, 1984), 23.

29 Davidson 24.

30 For an edition of this text see K.S.Block, *Ludus Coventriae or The Plaie called Corpus Christi*, EETS ES 120 (London, 1922).

Saved souls sing the entire hymn in the Harrowing of Hell plays in both the Chester and the Towneley cycles and at the close of the Last Judgement in the Towneley cycle. In every appearance this hymn is sung by a group, a chorus, never by an individual, and its every appearance is outside of earthly time and place.[31] Those who sing God's praises are not human beings living on earth; angels and saved souls exist rather in eternity and in heaven. The repetitions of this hymn suggests that it is *always* being sung, though usually outside of the hearing of mortals. When we hear it, we experience a vision of the eternal worship or praise of God that takes place without reference to time. This is, of course, consistent with the biblical sources of the *Te Deum*, and it is to these sources that we now turn.

Two biblical writers report visions that include the singing of 'Sanctus, sanctus, sanctus': Isaiah in his book of prophecy and John in the Apocalypse. In Isaiah 6:1–3 we read: 'In the year that King Ozias died, I saw the Lord sitting upon a throne high & elevated: and his train filled the temple. Upon it stood the seraphims: the one had six wings, and the other had six wings; with two they covered his face, and with two they covered his feet, and with two they flew. And they cried one to another, and said: Holy, holy, holy, the Lord God of hosts, all the earth is full of his glory.' Artists represented this vision in illustrations both of the book of Isaiah and of commentaries on it.

In Apocalypse 4:8 John records his vision of the throne surrounded by the four living creatures: 'And the four living creatures had each of them six wings; and round about and within they are full of eyes. And they rested not day and night, saying: Holy, holy, holy, Lord God Almighty, who was, and who is, and who is to come.' During the early Christian period the four living creatures came to be understood as symbols or emblems of the four evangelists. In illustrations of this vision artists represented the four living creatures joining in the Adoration of Christ and the lamb.

From these biblical sources, artists drew inspiration for a major subject, one that art historians call 'Christ in Majesty'. In her monograph on the decoration of the apse from the fourth to the eighth centuries Christa Ihm establishes the early association of this subject with liturgical space.[32] According to Caiger-Smith, 'The traditional decoration of the apse was a picture of Christ surrounded by the emblems of the Evangelists, which is found in many churches on the

---

31 For citations of each use of the *Te Deum* in the English cycle plays see Dutka 42–3.
32 Christa Ihm, *Die Programme der Christlichen Apsismalerei vom vierten Jahrhundert bis zur Mitte des achten Jahrhunderts* (Wiesbaden: Steiner, 1960), 42–51.

Continent. It is possible, in fact, that apses were specially constructed in order to hold paintings of this kind, so that the image of Christ should seem to float over the altar.'[33] An especially well-preserved English example dating to the early twelfth century adorns the chancel vault at Kempley, Gloucestershire.[34] Surrounding the enthroned Christ are seraphim, the symbols of the evangelists, the Virgin Mary, and St Peter. At the sides sit the apostles and the heavenly Jerusalem may be seen above the window recesses.[35] Similar representations survive at St Gabriel's Chapel, Canterbury, at Coombes, Sussex, at the Hospital of St Thomas, Canterbury, and in Westminster Chapter House.

Such images of Christ in Majesty appeared frequently enough in English churches that John Mirk, in a sermon for St Luke's day included in his book of exemplary sermons called the *Festial*, felt that he had to correct possible misinterpretations: 'Then for thes foure euangelystys ben lyknet to fowre dyuerse bestys, and soo byn paynted yn fowre partyes of Cryst, that ys: for Marke a lyon, for Mathew a man, for Luke a calfe, and for Ion an eron. Wherfor mony lewde men wenen that thay wern suche bestys and not men.'[36]

With changes in architectural style in England, 'apses were seldom constructed after the later part of the thirteenth century'.[37] Thus fields for large fresco paintings like those at Kempley were no longer available. This does not mean, however, that the subject of God in Majesty adored by the choirs of heaven disappeared. Rather, it adapted quite effectively, taking thorough advantage of new media. The stained glass and carved mullions and jambs in the large windows now dominating the east ends of chancels could represent this subject. An excellent example is the Beauchamp Chapel in Warwick, where the building accounts run from 1442–63. As Philip B. Chatwin observes, 'The decoration of the chapel was undoubtedly a united scheme.'[38] At the point of the arch over the great east window sits God enthroned and surrounded by a large aureole. Thirty figures carved on the jambs and mouldings represent the nine orders of angels. Saints occupy the lower part of the stone carving, and in the glass were angels, saints, apostles, prophets, and martyrs.

---

33 A. Caiger-Smith, *English Medieval Mural Paintings* (Oxford: Clarendon, 1963), 2.
34 Illustrated pl. 3. See also Margaret Rickert, *Painting in Britain: The Middle Ages* (Harmondsworth: Penguin, 1954), 76–7.
35 Caiger-Smith 4.
36 John Mirk, *Mirk's Festial: A Collection of Homilies*, ed. Theodor Erbe, *EETS ES*, 96 (London, 1905), 261.
37 Caiger-Smith 2.
38 Philip B. Chatwin, 'The Decoration of the Beauchamp Chapel, Warwick, with Special Reference to the Sculptures', *Archaeologia*, 77 (1927), 331.

We have moved from a biblical text, the Sanctus, to its illustration, the adoration of God in Majesty. But we have also moved into a very specific context, the liturgical space in which the Mass was celebrated. As Barbara Lane comments, 'The intimate connection between religious art and the liturgical ceremonies it illustrates ought to be self-evident.'[39] It is now time to examine the 'intimate connection' between representations of the adoration of God in Majesty and their liturgical context. In fact there is a direct textual link: the *Sanctus* sung by the choirs of heaven is also part of the ordinary of the Mass. This relationship was clearly understood by the artist who provided a two-page illustration to the *Sanctus* in a Carolingian manuscript, the Metz Sacramentary from about 870 illuminated in the court school of Charles the Bald.[40] On the left page of the opening, choirs of angels, apostles, martyrs, confessors and virgins gesture in adoration. All turn toward the large figure of Christ on the facing page, the words of the 'Sanctus' of the Mass written beneath him.

Such an illustration provides more than a biblical reference for the 'Sanctus' in the form of a pictorial citation. As Joseph Jungmann observes, '[the Sanctus] ... is intended to do more than recall to our mind that the seraphim sang this hymn, ... [it] is rather a reminder that the earthly church should take part in the heavenly singing'.[41] In fact, in early Christian times, and from then into the twelfth century, the *Sanctus* was sung by all the people. Through their singing, they dissolved not only the boundaries separating heaven and earth, but also those separating time and eternity, for they participated in the 'Eternal Mass in the Heavenly Jerusalem'. Medieval commentators, such as Rupert of Deutz, explained the liturgy in this way. For them, according to Jungmann, '[p]art of the value of the Church's liturgy is that it is already a participation in the never-ending song of praise of the City of God'.[42]

That is surely the understanding expressed by a page devoted to the Sacrament of the Holy Mass from a fifteenth century German *Biblia Pauperum*.[43] In this complex and highly didactic miniature, both the

39 Barbara G. Lane, *The Altar and the Altarpiece. Sacramental Themes in Early Netherlandish Painting* (New York: Harper and Row, 1984), 1.

40 Fols. 5v and 6; Paris, BN MS lat. 1141. F. Mütherich, *Sakramentar von Metz*, Codices selecti phototypice impressi, xxviii (Graz, 1972), fols. 5v, 6.

41 Joseph A. Jungmann, *The Mass of the Roman Rite: Its Origins and Development* (New York: Benziger, 1955), 2: 128.

42 Jungmann 135.

43 Illustrated pl. 4. Munich, Bayr. Staatsbibl. Clm 826. For an extensive discussion of this miniature see Lotte Brand Philip, *The Ghent Altarpiece and the Art of Jan van Eyck* (Princeton: Princeton UP, 1971), 63–4, 79–81.

church on earth, as represented by the kneeling figures surrounding the altar, and the church in heaven, as represented by the nine choirs of angels above the band of clouds, are present at the moment of Transubstantiation. As the priest raises up the Host, Christ appears above the altar. From one of his feet blood streams into the chalice and the other touches the Host in literal confirmation of the words on his scroll, 'For this is my body.' This is Christ as the Man of Sorrows, here accompanied by the dove of the Holy Spirit, who transmits a message from God enthroned above: 'You are my beloved Son in whom I am well pleased.' Thus all three persons of the Trinity are present. None of the mortal beings see the immortal company, for all eyes are fixed on the priest, but that company is nonetheless present, and their presence eliminates the barrier between 'temporal' and 'eternal'. As Lotte Brand Philip comments, 'The miniature, as a representation which explains the meaning of the Eucharistic rite, depicts the normally invisible Eucharistic truth together with the earthly performance of the Sacrament. This results in an interesting fusion of the heavenly with the earthly event.'[44] The conscious experience of such a fusion was the prerogative of the saints. In his life of St Venantius, an abbot who lived in the fifth century, Gregory the Great describes an episode in which Venantius heard the music of the Eternal Mass:[45]

> The same Venantius, indeed, was returning one Sunday from the basilicas of the saints, after completing his prayers, supported on his stick, and he stopped still in the middle of the forecourt of the church of the holy confessor, listening carefully, his eyes turned for a long time towards heaven. Then, stepping forward a few paces, he began to groan and to sigh. Asked by those who accompanied him what it was, and to tell them if he had seen some divine thing, he replied 'Woe on us apathetic and idle creatures! I see that in heaven the solemnity of Mass is far advanced, while we are so dilatory that we have not even started to celebrate this mystery. I tell you in truth that I have heard the voices of the angels in heaven, singing "Sanctus!" and proclaiming the praises of the Lord.' Then he ordered Mass to be said immediately in the monastery.

With this idea of the Eternal Mass in mind, let us turn to a text which exists in manuscripts contemporary with our *Te Deum* altarpieces, the *Lay Folks' Mass Book*. This text in English describes the actions of the priest during the mass and instructs the literate laity as to what

44 Philip 66.
45 Gregory of Tours, *Life of the Fathers*, trans. Edward James (Liverpool: Liverpool UP, 1985), 110–11.

they should do while the priest enacts the ritual:[46]

> At tho ende [he] sayes sanctus thryese,
> In excelsis he neuens twyese.
> Als fast als euer that he has done,
> loke that thou be redy sone,
> and saye these wordis with stille steuen
> priuely to god of heuen.
> In world of worlds with outen endyng
> thanked be ihesu, my kyng.
> Al my hert I gyue hit the,
> grete right hit is that hit so be;
> with al my wille I worship the,
> Ihesu, blessid mot thou be.
> with al my hert I thank hit the,
> tho gode that thou has don to me;
> swete ihesu, graunt me now this,
> that I may come vn-to thi blis,
> there with aungels for to syng
> this swete song of thi louyng,
> sanctus: sanctus: sanctus.
> Ihesu graunt that hit be thus. Amen.

That is, during the Sanctus, the laity were to pray that they might one day join the heavenly host in the eternal chanting of Sanctus. Nor would they have missed this part of the Mass, for at the beginning of the *Sanctus*, they heard the ringing of the *Sanctus*, or 'saunce' bell so frequently encountered in the inventories of Edward VI's commissioners.

Members of the laity repeating this prayer: 'with angels for to sing', might well have looked up and found themselves surrounded by angels. Angels carved in stone occupy the spandrels of the transepts of Westminster Abbey, completed in the thirteenth century. They dominate the Angel Choir of Lincoln Cathedral, where many hold musical instruments. But it is the fifteenth century that has been called 'the century of angels'. In a paper on the iconography of angels in English wooden roofs given at the Twenty-second International Congress on Medieval Studies at Kalamazoo, Michigan, Lynn Courtenay observed that angels were ubiquitous on these roofs. Bishop Reginald Pecock might well have been thinking of such interiors when, in his *Book of Faith*, he called the church in heaven 'the chirche of aungels'. In a number of cases, as at Ewelme, Oxfordshire, angels hold scrolls for phrases from the *Te Deum*.

46 Thomas Frederick Simmons, ed. *The Lay Folks' Mass Book. EETS OS*, 71 (London: Trübner, 1879), 28. The quotation is lines 308–27 of Simmons text B: BL Royal MS 17 B xvii, dated about 1375.

In presenting her intepretation of the subject of the Ghent Altarpiece as the Eternal Mass in the heavenly Jerusalem, Lotte Brand Philip suggests, 'In any case, it is quite obvious that the blessed must sing the heavenly songs which are sung to the Lamb in the Apocalypse.'[47] We have already noted that one of those songs is the 'Sanctus'. What, then, is the relationship between these representations of the Eternal Mass in which the *Sanctus* was sung, and the *Te Deum* altarpiece? It has been the goal of this paper to demonstrate that the subjects are actually the same. The text of the *Te Deum* describes the singing of the 'Sanctus'. It tells us who sings it and where – it provides the context. And this context is, in fact, the Eternal Mass. Since the *Te Deum* describes the singing of the 'Sanctus', and the 'Sanctus' is sung at the Eternal Mass, we may conclude that what the so-called 'Te Deum' altarpiece actually represents is 'The Celebration of the Eternal Mass'.[48] Further, many of the works of art called 'Christ in Majesty' actually represent this same subject, as is clear from their architectural, liturgical context. If these works of art were known by this title we would understand them as indicative of the transformation of sacred space into the infinite reaches of heavenly space. We would, with medieval worshippers, perceive the direct link between the earthly mass and the eternal mass, between the church on earth and the heavenly Jerusalem.

47 Philip 65.
48 For a group of representations of Christ in Majesty found largely in Egyptian churches and clearly influenced by the liturgy, Christa Ihm suggests the term, 'liturgical *Maestas*' (Ihm 48).

Henry VIII and King David

PAMELA TUDOR-CRAIG

'If the highest spiritual power go astray, it cannot be judged by man but by God alone' (Pope Boniface VIII, of the Papacy, Bull 'Unam Sanctam' 1302).

'Though the law of every man's conscience be but a private court, yet it is the highest and supreme court for judgement or justice' Henry VIII of himself (*Letters*, ed. M. St Clare Byrne, London 1968, p. 68)

'You alone know every thing? But what if you were wrong...?' Martin Luther (E. Erickson, *Young Man Luther*, London 1959, p. 241).

Ever since he came to the throne, Henry VIII's Kingship had carried an Imperial dimension.[1] In the development of his total image, the Imperial aspect reached its apogee in 1527, eight years after Henry had accepted defeat on the pragmatic issue of actually becoming Holy Roman Emperor. In 1519 Henry had listened to Cuthbert Tunstall's advice that 'his own islands were an Empire worth more than the barren Imperial Crown'.[2] Tunstall's high boast was no more than a translation of the adage, then three centuries old, 'Rex in regno suo est imperator ...'[3] It represented the high point of authority for Henry VIII while under the guidance of Cardinal Wolsey, and as such was illustrated in the

---

1 For the Imperial significance of the hooped crown see my chapter in the forthcoming book on *The Round Table in Winchester Castle* edited by Martin Biddle. The topic of Imperialism in Henry VIII's reign has received much scholarly attention in recent years. Alistair Fox and John Guy (ed.), *Reassessing the Henrician Age: Humanism, Politics & Reform*, Oxford 1986, provides a key to the field. Walter Ullmann, 'This Realm of England is an Empire' *Journal of Ecclesiastical History*, vol. 30, no. 2, April 1979, pp. 176–203, is a foundation document. R. Koebner, 'The Imperial Crown of this Realm: Henry VIII, Constantine the Great and Polydore Vergil' *Bulletin of the Institute of Historical Research* XXVI, No. 73, May 1953, pp. 29–52 discusses Henrician Imperial terminology going back to 1513, but in 1509 John Wynattes was paid for heraldic carving of the 'Crowne Imperial', no doubt a part of the trappings of the Coronation itself (PRO L.C.9/50 FD.152). There is also an unpublished Cambridge Ph.D thesis of 1977 that I have not consulted. I am grateful to John Guy for putting me in touch with this material.
2 Ullmann, 'This Realm of England ...' p. 176.
3 Ullmann, *loc. cit*, quoting the Code of Justinian.

Golden Bulla,[4] a remarkable seal marking the year 1527, the giddy peak of Wolsey's ascendency. In this one image Henry VIII appears in the full Italianate paraphanalia of the Renaissance, in a pose derived from recent seated figures by Michelangelo – his Moses and his Medicean Princes in San Lorenzo, Florence. Here, and here alone, Henry is invested with the artistic trappings with which Wolsey surrounded himself, of which we catch an echo from the Cardinal's Patent Rolls;[5] from the Inventory of his plate[6] and from his surviving tapestries at Hampton Court. The difference between the talent at Wolsey's behest and the service the King himself could command after Wolsey's demise is demonstrated by a comparison between the Golden Bulla and the Great Seal of 1532, a quaintly traditional almost 'Gothick' piece. In the 1542 seal there is Renaissance sound and fury, but the panache of the Golden Bulla has been lost in an overloading of Italianate detail. In the Golden Bulla Henry VIII's Imperial Crown is so startlingly emphasised that I have conjectured that an actual crown made at that time may be represented, an Imperial Crown too heavy for the head of any of Henry's children.[7] Of Henry's personal interest in the symbolic import of Crowns we have striking evidence. The only one of his later queens to be honoured with Coronation was Anne Boleyn, and she was allowed to use the Crown of St Edward, never otherwise offered to a Queen not regnant. St Edward's Crown, I believe, was of ancient, solid, domical form. The bowed hoops over soft caps-of-maintenance of more up to date Imperial Crowns were represented in the embellishment of the Triumphal Arch of Apollo and the Muses which Holbein designed for Anne's wedding.[8] Henry VIII's sense of the sacred grew, rather than diminishing, with the fall of Cardinal Wolsey – he replaced him after all with one of the only two English Saints to hold such a position. Anne Bolyn's first public appearance was on Easter Sunday. Her coronation was on Whitsunday. Such a choice of dates argues royal initiative.

4 All these seals were illustrated by A. Wyon, *The Great Seals of England*, London 1887, pls. 101 *et seq.*
5 In the Public Record Office. A number were illustrated by Erna Auerbach, *Tudor Artists*, London 1954. They merit full and carefully reproduced publication. The penmanship is faint but exquisite.
6 For Wolsey's Plate see the forthcoming study by Phillipa Glanville.
7 King Arthur's Round Table, my forthcoming article. For the three crowns used at the Coronations of Henry VIII's children, and the documents showing that the Imperial Crown was too heavy (and surely too large) for Edward or Elizabeth to wear see Janet Arnold, 'The Coronation Portrait of Queen Elizabeth', *Burlington Magazine* 120, 1978, pp. 729–35, esp. p. 732. The whole issue of our ancient crowns was addressed by Martin Holmes in two magisterial articles, 'The Crowns of England', *Archaeologia* 86, 1936, pp. 73–90, and 'New Light on St Edward's Crown', *Archaeologia* 97, 1959, pp. 214–223.
8 Illustrated *inter alia*, by Neville Williams, *Henry VIII and his Court*, London 1971.

Imperial power, however, could not take Henry VIII far enough. In 1521, in his 'Assertio septem Sacramentorum' Henry himself had conceded primacy to the Holy See – though Thomas More had begged him at the time, 'either to leve owt that point, or ellys to towche it more slenderly', but Henry 'wold in no wise eny thing minishe'.[9] Imperial power was not enough for Henry VIII because, in his eyes, it was dependent upon papal power. It had been proved in 1440 by Valla[10] that the Donation of Constantine, the gift by that Emperor of spiritual supremacy and temporal dominion over Rome, Italy and the Western Regions to Pope Sylvester, was a fabrication of the eighth century. There had been plenty of earlier critics of the Donation,[11] yet it was still officially supported in the pageantry associated with Charles V's crowning as Holy Roman Emperor in 1529. As Charles made his triumphal entry into Bologna on 5 November, the scene of the Emperor Constantine presenting the Imperial Crown and Sceptre to Pope Sylvester was staged.[12] But by 1529 Henry VIII had found his own way out of the secular subservience to a spiritual ruler which Charles V was prepared to acknowledge. Henry's escape he owed to Martin Luther, the adversary for whom he had sharpened his quill in 1521: it was his own conscience.

Henry certainly knew and studied the medieval arguments in favour of Papal Supremacy. His copy of Triumphus' *Summa de Potestate Ecclesiastica* is annotated in his own hand.[13] There is no direct indication of the date at which Henry studied this text, but his characteristic marks of reference – marginal lines ending with three dots to suggest arrows, and pointing hands, occur in places

9 J. B. Trapp and H. S. Herbrüggen, *The King's Good Servant: Sir Thomas More 1477/8–1535* London 1977, no.117, p.64, quoting E. F. Rogers *The Correspondence of Sir Thomas More*, Princeton 1947, p.199.

10 Laurentius Valla, 'De Falso Eredita et Eminentita Constantini Donatione Declamatio'. Peacock made the same point. See Ullmann 'This Realm ...' pp.191–94.

11 For example the English 13th century canonist Alan: 'quod dictum habeatur de quodlibet rege vel principe qui nulli subest' or his Bolognese contemporary Azo: 'quilibet rex hodie videter eandem potestatem habere in terra sua quam imperator ergo potuit facere quod sibi placet'. See Ullmann, 'This Realm ...' pp.176 et seq.

12 See Roy Strong, *Splendour at Court: Renaissance Spectacle and Illusion*, London 1973, pp.86–91, esp. 91.

13 Augustinus Triumphus, *Summa de potestate ecclesiastica* 1326, British Library I.B. 3131. The title page is missing but it is of the 2nd edition, printed in Cologne in 1475. The seven editions printed before 1500, two of them from Lyons, centre of the French court, are a measure of the ferment of interest in its subject at the end of the Middle Ages. Despite his critical MS annotations, Henry VIII's copy of this text is still catalogued in the British Library as a printed book, and the same applies to his copy of *the Bokes of Salomon with the Psalter* to which I shall return. Where the importance of the annotations in a particular copy outweighs that of the printed text, should it not be found in the manuscript department?

suggesting that he was deeply engaged in Papal and Imperial Power.[14] These were abiding interests. However, a pointer to the issue of Indulgencies[15] suggests the 1520s, and the most famous of his injections ('neither is it in our's'[16] beside the passage declaring that it was not considered unnatural in antiquity to have several wives) – puts his study not earlier than the arrival on the scene of Anne Boleyn. Henry's last annotations are on ff.284 and 300, so his thorough reading of this key text of Papal supremacy is as well attested as his eventual, if rather belated, involvement in the Bishop's Book of 1537, and the King's Book of 1543.[17] Through Augustinus Triumphus Henry VIII would have assimilated at second hand the principles of Roman law. Augustinus quoted from Justinian's Codex.[18] By the simple expedient of referring the 'princeps' of Roman law books to the Pope, the Pope can become justice incarnate. The very attacks on the Papal position which Augustinus defends – like Dante's declaration that the powers of the priesthood came from the Emperor – could percolate beyond Augustinus' defence to the reader, anxious to seek out the weak spots in Papal claims. To Augustinus 'the declaration of anti-Papal theses will serve to bring out the true Glory of the Roman sovereignty'. They might, or they might not. The eagerness in later medieval circles erked by Roman supremacy to read this text suggests it was, at best, a two edged weapon, a defence which hinted at future lines of attack.

Henry VIII would have done even better with Bracton[19] who followed English pre-Conquest tradition. Bracton's 'In sede ipsius regis quasi throno Dei' would have been balm to Henry's ears. But did he know Bracton? That great jurist wrote in the reign of Henry III, the first English King to reach towards the Imperial Crown, for his brother, Richard, Earl of Cornwall. Henry III was also

14 On f.1 verso, Henry marks passages concerning the possibility of Papal resignation. Against the phrase 'Utrum a papa possit appellat ad deum' he writes 'de appellatione'. On f.2a against the entry 'Si papa honoris exhibitione', Henry writes 'de honore exhibenda per papa'. On f.3a he puts a pointing hand by 'Utrum papa in potestate claviium possit excedere vel errare', and on the same page he notes 'de restitutia scismaticorum'. On f.5a, he notes 'de imperatore legum institutione' and 'de regum correctione'.
15 f.126b 'de causa Indugencie', followed by on f.128a a pointed hand to the passage on the merits of the Saints.
16 f.193b–194a, 'ergo nec in nobis'.
17 For a lucid summary of Henry's personal participation in those works, see J.J. Scarisbrick, *Henry VIII*, London 1969, pp.520–543. The corpus of Henry VIII's marginalia which Scarisbrick drew up on pp.522–523 omits the three texts discussed in this article.
18 See Michael Wilks, *The Problem of Sovereignty in the later Middle Ages: the Papal Monarch with Augustinus Triumphus and the Publicists*, Cambridge 1963, pp.152 et seq. Triumphus was to the Avignon Schism what St Augustine was to the Fall of Rome – as temporal supremacy lay in ruins, spiritual supremacy was discerned by the scholars.
19 Henry Bracton (d.1268) author of *De Legibus et Consuetudinibus Angliae 1235–59)*, first pub. 1569. See Wilks, *The Problem of Sovereignty*, p.166 n.ii.

the first English King to ask the question Charlemagne had asked 'what does the Sacrament of Coronation make me?' only to receive the same ecclesiastical snub: no more than a deacon. Could the thinking of Henry III, Edward I and their advisors have been available to Henry VIII and his advisors on that same question: what does Coronation make me? That Henry VIII did consider these issues in thirteenth century terms, there are three pieces of evidence, two direct, the other oblique. The first evidence lies in his revision of the Coronation Oath.[20] I cannot agree with Ullmann that these revisions are the work of 'an eighteen year old precocious, highly receptive and intelligent young man'.[21] If Henry VIII had made these revisions upon ascending the throne, why were they not used at his own Coronation?[22] He was crowned according to the Oath as devised in the reign of Edward I, and first used for Edward II in 1307 and still in use, enshrined in the late fourteenth century *Liber Regalis* at Westminster Abbey. If, on the other hand, Henry altered the service towards the end of his life, why were his revisions neglected at the Coronation of his son? They harmonised with English churchmanship as it had developed by 1547. They were not so used. It is my belief that Henry pored over the Coronation Oath during the years of crisis over his divorce; that he made these revisions before his son was born, and that they were put aside and forgotten before Edward VI came to the throne.

The text of Henry's revision is so hard of access that it is offered here as an appendix (Appendix I). Observe in the first paragraph the insertion of the phrase 'the holy chirche of ingland'. As Professor Robin Storey has pointed out,[23] the phrase 'Church of England' first appeared in the Statute of Carlisle of 1305. Its reemergence here is surely significant. A bill for the liberties of the English church was presented at Henry VIII first Parliament. Fourteen of the Episcopate, five Deans and Chapters, one hundred and fifty-eight lesser clergy and nearly two hundred religious houses took up general pardons offered four days after Henry's accession, while fines were paid by the Bishop of Salisbury and the Abbots of Gloucester and Cirencester.[24] Clearly the English Clergy had some way to go before their King could refer to them as the 'holy church of England'. But by the later 1520s Henry was anxious to carry his clergy with him. After that gesture of courteous acknowledgement, however, Henry inserted a new clause: 'nott preiudiciall to hys jurysdiccion and dignite ryall' which casts a long shadow upon the 'lawfull right and libertees' of the Holy Church of Eng-

20 For the full text of Henry VIII's revisions of the Coronation Oath, set in the context of other historic revisions, see L. G. Wickham Legg, *English Coronation Records*, London 1901, esp. chapter XXI, 'The Coronation Oath as revised by Henry VIII', pp. 240–241. The MS is BL Cotton. Tiberius E. VIII, f. 89.
21 Ullmann: 'This Realm of England ...' p.183. Ullmann is not aware of any authority later than Legg who deals with these revisions.
22 See Archbishop Dene's register at Lambeth, f.177, quoted by Wickham Legg, p. 240.
23 In a lecture given to the 1987 Harlaxton Symposium.
24 Further material from Robin Storey's forthcoming paper.

land that he had just pledged to uphold. Henry was so keen on 'not prejudicing his jurisdiction and dignity royal' that he inserted the same clause into the safeguarding of the honours and dignities of the crown – until he observed the absurdity, and struck it out.

In the second paragraph he has extended the wording from 'And that he shall keepe the peax of the holie church and of the clergie and of the people with good accord ...' to 'And that he shall *Indevore hymselfe* to kepe unite in hys clerge and temporell subjects ... And then he added the critical phrase: '*according to hys consien[ce]*

In the fourth paragraph he slipped in 'approved' before 'customs' and added 'not preiudiciale to hys croune or Imperiall Juris (diction)' to qualify his promise to uphold the laws and (*approved*) customs. A tyrannical note creeps in at the end of that paragraph of the laws which the nobles and people have chosen *wt hys consent*. A further qualification '*in that whych honour and equite do require*' rounds off his promise to keep a stable peace.

This document surely bears the stamp of Henry at full flood, the Henry VIII who was described by the Dukes of Suffolk and Norfolk to the papal nuncio in September 1530 as 'Emperor *and Pope* in his own kingdom' (italics mine).[25] This is the Henry of the draft bill to Parliament of 1532 declaring the three Estates as one body politic presided over by the King. The Three Estates go back to the first Coronation Oath of St Dunstan's time.[26] Can we pinpoint the identification by Henry VIII of this essential factor, his conscience? The most ironic twist in the history of the English Reformation is the contrasts in attitudes to the divorce adopted by Pope Clement VII, by Cardinal Wolsey, and by the King.[27] In blunt terms, the Pope was prepared to countenance bigamy; the Cardinal stood by a subtle legal technicality, and the King quoted Biblical precedent, specifically Leviticus XVIII, 16. In the winter of 1528/29 Henry made a public announcement of his dread that he had lived nearly twenty years in sin 'these be the sores that vex my mind, *these be the pains that trouble my conscience*, and for these griefs I seek a remedy ...'[28] (italics mine).

As Baldwin Smith asked with his customary humour: 'that most thorny of all Henrican problems – the dating of the king's conscience',[29] and settled for the winter of 1526/7. To the Pope's suggestion that Henry commit bigamy, Henry's representative wrote home in September 1530 'that he did not know whether it would satisfy your Majesty's conscience'.[30] It is the papal role to be the con-

---

25 *Calendar of State Papers*, Spanish IV, 734, no. 445.
26 Wickham Legg intro. p. xxxi.
27 This material depends upon Chapter 7, 'The Canon Law of the Divorce' in J. Scarisbrick's *Henry VIII*, esp. pp. 256 et seq.
28 Quoted in Hall's Chronicle, 754 f. See Scarisbrick, *Henry VIII* p. 287. If Hall was inaccurate, Henry's statement to Charles V in 1529 came to the same thing; L. Baldwin-Smith, *Henry VIII, the Mask of Royalty*, London 1971, p. 111.
29 L. Baldwin-Smith, *Henry VIII*, p. 114

science of Kings, yet here we have a King unable to follow papal advice against the dictates of his conscience. What, indeed, has Coronation made of him? Ullmann points to the enthronement prayer where the King is styled 'typus Christi, Christus Domini, Mediator Dei et hominum ...'[31]

The second direct piece of evidence that Henry VIII was thinking of his status in terms of Coronation, and that in the light of his thirteenth century predecessors, lies in his commissioning of a great painting of his Coronation for the gallery of Whitehall Palace. This major undertaking occupied a significant number of the artists working for the court in 1531.[32] The historial precedent for such a picture was near to hand: the painting of the coronation of St Edward over the King's bed in the Painted Chamber of Westminster Palace, carried out for Henry III. As Paul Binski has pointed out, the iconography of the thirteenth century coronation is Solomonic[33] as was, of course, that of the actual King's throne supported by lions, commissioned by Henry III and Edward I. As Bracton vaunted 'in Sede ipsius regis quasi throno Dei'.[34] In confidence based on such a doctrine Henry VIII could claim he was right not because so many said it, but because 'he knoweth the matter to be right'.[35]

So to the oblique evidence of Henry's interest, or that of his advisors, in what Coronation had conferred upon him; I have discussed elsewhere the implications of Hans Holbein's Portrait of 'The Ambassadors' (pl.1), with its implied date of 11 April 1533, the day on which Archbishop Thomas Cranmer offered to take upon himself the dissolution of Henry's marriage to Catherine of Aragaon.[36] Richard Foster's work and mine depended heavily upon the pioneer researches of Mary Hervey,[37] but we did not discuss one of her identifications: the star of David in the middle of the Coronation floor in the painting. No such star of David occurs in the central roundel of that floor now, though the Star of David pattern occurs in the pavement, also thirteenth century, also original Cosmati work, around the shrine behind the High Altar of Westminster Abbey. The immediate question is whether the present central roundel is original. In its favour is the fifteenth century description[38] by the Westminster Monk John

30 Baldwin-Smith, p.112, quoting *Letters Patent*, IV, (3) 6627.
31 Ullmann, 'This Realm ...' p.182.
32 For the documentation of this lost painting, see Erna Auerback, *Tudor Artists*, pp. 150–192. She lists 42 named painters, including John Betts I, under Andrew Wright, soon to become Sergeant painter.
33 See Paul Binski, *The Painted Chamber at Westminster*, London 1986, pp. 42–43, pls I & XXXVI–XXXVII
34 For Bracton, see Wilks, *The Problem of Sovereignty*, p.166 and footnote ii, giving Bracton's pre-Conquest source. 'potestas enim regis potestas Dei est'.
35 *PRO State Papers I*, vol. 77, ff.175–176b.
36 R. Foster & P. Tudor-Craig, *The Secret Life of Paintings*, Woodbridge 1986, chapter six, pp. 75–107.
37 M. F. S. Hervey, *Holbein's Ambassadors, the Picture and the Men*, London 1900.
38 BL Cotton Claudius A. VIII.

Sporley, who said it was of four colours. It is certainly of a many-coloured marble. Sporley says nothing of a Star of David. We are left with the real possibility that the Star of David, which is discretely placed in shadow behind the skull and under the table, (pl. 2) is an addition by Holbein, part of the elaborate and esoteric programme to which every feature of the painting conforms.[39] It is my conviction that the central quincunx of the Coronation floor was intended to mark the place where the throne was placed for the Secret and Sacramental part of the Coronation ceremony, the Anointing. The throne stands over the central circle, which with its four colours representing the four elements, represents the British microcosm over which our Soverign here receives power to rule. The four subsidiary circles mark the stations for four prime officiants.[40]

The format of a quincunx, the central figure supported by four attendants, is equally suited to mark the stations of a processional route, where the celebrant might be flanked by four acolytes. For that reason it is commonly found in Cosmati pavements, like that in Anagni. A quincunx implies the four essences around the Quintessence. John Sporley described the central circle as of a four-coloured marble, and Holbein's painting applied the Star of David to it. The Star of David symbolises the union of the four elements, and thus again the quincunx.

The Star of David is a mysterious symbol, apparently first found in fragments of sculpture from the first-second century synagogue at Capernaum. Its cabalistic meaning is a shield. Perhaps it is in this sense that it is found carved on the fourteenth century Abbey Gateway at Bury St Edmunds, and in burnt bricks on the facade of Cardinal Morton's Episcopal Palace of the 1490s at Hatfield. However, in this central if secret position on Holbein's Coronation floor, it can only refer to King David himself, who was anointed by Samuel in the midst of his brethren 'and the spirit of the Lord came upon David from that day forward'.[41] The iconography of 'the Ambassadors' was not prompted by Henry VIII: Holbein did not enter Royal Service for several years after 1533, but it must have been worked out by persons well acquainted with the King's mind. Other than de Dinteville and de Selve, the most likely intermediary was the rising politician Thomas Cromwell,[42] or Stephen Gardiner. Gardiner had the legal background

---

39 On the whole issue of whether the floor in Holbein's painting is really intended to be the Abbey floor, see Richard Foster's forthcoming Ph.D. thesis. I believe it does refer to the Abbey floor, however inaccurately.

40 As shown so often in illuminations of the Coronation: see for example, Corpus Christi College, Cambridge, MS 20, f. 68. This MS was dated 1330–39? in the catalogue of *The Age of Chivalry*, Royal Academy, London 1987, cat. 11, p. 20. Two of the Bishops hold vessels containing the unction, two support the crown.

41 I Samuel, XVI, 13.

42 It would appear Thomas Cromwell had acquaintances, in particular one John Godsalve, among the merchants of the Steelyard, for whom Holbein was working until he had his major commission for The Ambassadors.

that would have included familiarity with Bracton. He had been Ambassador in France (1531–32). In 1533 he was acting secretary to Henry VIII, and his '*de Vera Obedientia*' of 1535 gave chapter and verse to the authoritative position adopted by the King.[43] Whether prompted by Gardiner or Cromwell, or on his own initiative, Henry VIII appears to have turned more and more as his reign progressed towards King David as his only satisfactory archetype. For a King who explored Leviticus and Deuteronomy, the 'discovery' of David was scarcely difficult and David provided what no Christian Emperor could offer – his authority was directly derived from God, with no Papal intermediary.

The dwindling of the royal interest in his Arthurian past can be observed. Geoffrey of Monmouth was in the ascendant when Henry came to the throne,[44] but Geoffrey's claims for Arthur were under attack from Polydore Vergil. It was to confute Polydore Vergil that Henry appointed Leland King's Antiquary in 1533, though Leland had featured in royal payments from 18 October, 1528.[45] Leland was closest to the Royal elbow in the critical first half of 1533, composing with Nicholas Udall the texts for the pageants arranged to adorn the Coronation procession of Queen Anne Boleyn on 31 May.[46] However, he did not produce his '*Assertio Inclytissimi Arturii*'[47] until 1543, and by then Henry VIII had virtually lost interest in the subject. David, and his equally glorious son, Solomon, were Henry's new mentors. By 1543, Henry, like David, but unlike Arthur, had his own young Solomon beside him.

It was no great feat of scholarship for Henry VIII to discover King David, who had played a large part in the fragmentary understanding of the Old Testament throughout the Middle Ages. Of the thirty four Old Testament Types in the windows of Kings College Chapel, Cambridge, carried out between 1515 and 1531, six concerned David or Solomon. Of the eighty Types flanking the New Testament scenes in the Biblia Pauperum of c.1460, thirteen are concerned with David or Solomon.[48] David was the patron of that independent city, Florence, and Michelangelo's sculpture of him had been standing in the Piazza della Signoria for five years when Henry came to the English throne. The Royal Inventories of 1649–51 reveal that Tudor Palaces had been clad in Davidic hangings.[49] It is hard to discern which of the tapestries were already in

---

43 For Stephen Gardiner as one of the inner circle of the Privy Council who steered the country under the King from 1529, see J. A. Guy, 'The Privy Council, Revolution or Evolution', pp. 59–69 of *Revolution Reassessed* ...

44 His *History of Britain* was first published in Paris in 1508.

45 *Letters and Papers Foreign and Domestic*, vol. VI, Henry VIII.

46 *Letters and Papers Foreign and Domestic*, vol. VI, Henry VIII, no. 564.

47 Translated by William E. Mead and published by the Early English Text Society, London 1925, vol. 165.

48 For the Biblia Pauperum see the definitive edition and fascimile by Avril Henry, Aldershot 1987.

49 See Oliver Millar, 'The Inventories and Valuations of the Kings Goods 1649–51', *Walpole Society* 43, 1972.

the Royal Collection in Henry VIII's time, except for the pair of David and Saul, and of Solomon, with Cardinal Wolsey's arms, in the Privy Gallery at White-hall. But the preponderance of David not only over other Old Testament scenes, but over virtually every other topic, is a striking aspect of the tapestry lists. Apart from Wolsey's pair, there were five pieces of King David in the Privy Gallery at Whitehall, plus four pieces of 'David' and six pieces more of 'the history' of King David, five pieces of Greenwich stuff with the 'history of Solomon'. At Windsor there were four tapestries of David, 'David and Nathan', 'Solomon giving Judgement' and 'David and Abigail'. These were much more highly valued than the rest, and immediately followed by 'Triumphs', surely Wolsey's 'Triumphs' still at Hampton Court. It would seem that Palace walls echoed with David and Solomon.

Apart from his exalted position as the Lord's Elect, David was honoured, wherever the Psalter was the chief instrument of Christian worship, as its reputed author. The Reformation brought familiarity with the Psalter not only to the Religious with their endless offices, not only to the educated folk with the *Books of Hours*, but to the entire nation through Cranmer's adaptation of Monastic Offices to Morning and Evening Prayer, the staple of Anglican wor-ship for 300 years. David slaying Goliath becomes an alternative subject for a side altarpiece in the Laudian decorations at Bratton Clovelly in Devonshire,[50] not only because it is the figure of little chap against big bully, but because, as the Anonymous Rex Pacificus of 1302 put it: '*The Goliath of Rome is to be confronted by the new King David*'.[51]

The association between English Coronation and King David, the Lord's Anointed, implied in Holbein's painting of 1533, is confirmed by the icon-ography of his title page for Miles Coverdale's publication of the Bible in English of 1535 (pl. 3). It marks the first introduction into this country of the Germanic compartmentalised border with its message as Corbett and Lightbown say 'patent to anyone familiar with the great controversies of the day'.[52] Their analysis of it, however, misses significant features. The page is crowned with the Tetragramaton, an alternative to the absurdities of anthropomorphic represen-tations of the Trinity seized upon by the Hebrew Scholars of the Reformation. The left margin pairs Moses receiving the tables of the Law (Exo. 21) with Christ sending out the disciples to preach the Gospel (Mark 16). From Moses' cloud there issue not only the Tables of the Law, but for good measure, the four trumpets of the Last Judgement. In the sending out of the disciples not only

---

50 Uncovered by Anna Hulbert and her team of conservators in 1987.

51 See Wilks, *The Problem of Sovreignty*, p. 234.

52 For the Miles Coverdale Bible of 1535 and the official 'Great' Bible by Thomas Cranmer of 1539, see, *inter alia*, Trapp and Herbrüggen *The King's Good Servant*, no. 144, p. 75 and Margery Corbett and Ronald Lightbown, *The Comely Frontispiece: the Emblematic Title Page in England 1550–1660*, London 1979. Introduction, p. 3, and pp. 39, 40 and 46. Corbett and Lightbown accept both title pages as Holbein's work.

Peter but all the Apostles carry keys. Below these groups are two preaching scenes, Esdra and Acts 2. Peter is at the forefront, but the other Apostles, each with a flame over his head, are only just behind. But the surprise is in the lower margin. To anyone familiar with one of the staples of Christian iconography, the 'Tolle Lege' would take a sharp breath here. In the ancient scene, known from the fourth century, Christ is flanked by Peter and Paul. To Peter he delivers the keys, to Paul the book. At first glance we have a Tolle Lege here, for the central figure is offering the book and Paul is at his accustomed station. But here the resemblance ends. The central figure is not Christ, but Henry VIII, Imperially enthroned. giving the Book to the clergy, who kneel on his right hand. As is customary with a Tolle Lege, his gesture crosses his body so he gives with his left hand to the Bishops on his right-hand side. On his left-hand side, there kneels a group of the laity, headed by two or more coroneted aristocrats. The final touch is the replacement of Peter, obviously out of favour on account of his association with the Papacy, not by Moses, the normal, but priestly, representative of the Old Law, but by David, playing his harp.

The 1535 Bible was not authorized by Henry VIII, but the publishers were confident enough of his approval to depict him distributing it on the Title Page. Here, then, by 1535, Holbein or his advisors have saught fit to put David in the position of Royal Supporter in chief. But when it came to the Great Bible four years later (pl. 4), Holbein's now official royal imagery had undergone a further apotheosis. The enthroned Henry has been translated to the top margin, ousting the Tetragramaton, which is replaced by a diminutive figure of God hovering in blessing over the royal head. This is the last human figure of God on an English Protestant title page. The lower border is now occupied by the grateful multitudes, listening to the word of God from the pulpit and ejaculating 'vivat rex' (with the exception of a pair of children, who, being behind in their Latin studies, can only manage 'God Save the King' – could that be for the first time?) So in the Great Bible David is subsumed into Henry, the Lord's Anointed.

In April 1533, as we have seen, Holbein was prompted to place the Star of David on the Coronation floor of the Ambassadors. Two years later, he replaced St Peter by King David on the Bible Title Page. By 1542 the king was virtually identified with David in his most intimate activity: his private prayer. The Book of Hours had been the staple prayer book of the laity since the fourteenth century, supplemented by a selection of Psalms, notably the Penitential ones, with a Calendar and collection of other devotional prayers. In returning to the full Psalter, once again Henry VIII was harking back to the thirteenth century, but with a difference. His purpose was not so much the repetitive recitation of the Psalms, but their careful study.

> Item delivered to the Kings highness the VI day of January [1541/42] a psalter in Englishe and Latyne covered wth crimoysyn satyne ij s
> Item delyvered the same tyme a psalter/provobes of Salomon & other smalle bookes bound together price xvj d

The identification of both these books has been established beyond question.[53] 'The Bokes of Salomon' are still in the Royal Collection of the British Library (c.25, B4[b]), and despite their critical marginalia, repose among the printed books. The Psalter is of course Henry VIII's famous Psalter, British Library Royal MS 2 AXVI.[54] These two books entered Henry's Library five years after he had commented on the Bishops Book, a work had undertaken during the months of desolation after the death of Jane Seymour. More immediately, they reached him two months after he had heard of Queen Catherine Howard's infidelities, and thirty-seven days before her execution. These weeks must have been the most bitter of his life. By way of distraction, he banqueted with twenty six ladies, and once more he threw himself into serious reading.

As Hattaway observed,[55] the 'Books of Solomon' are annotated in the same way as the Augustinus Triumphus, with Henry's characteristic marginal lines ending in three dot arrow heads and pointing hands. To examine the passages Henry has marked is to eavesdrop upon him during the weeks of Catherine Howard's trial. The annotations go only as far as Chapter V out of the thirty-one chapters, nor do they extend into the appended Ecclesiastes or the Book of Wisdom. In addition to the verses marked,[56] Henry has commented 'bene' by Chapter III, v.5, in his translation (Coverdale's) 'put thy truste in the Lorde with all thyne herte...', and ironically beside Chapter V, vv.3–5, which for him read 'for the lyppes of an harlot are a droppynge hony combe and hyr throate is softer than oyle. But at the last she is as bytter as wormwode and as sharpe as a tuo edged sword. Hyr fete go downe unto death and hyr steppes pearse thorowe unto hell'. In the same chapter he marked v.19 'Lovynge is the hynde and frendlye is the roo' 'for voyses' reminding us of Henry the composer. But the next verse 20 'My son why wylt thou have pleasure in an harlot?' he marked – and put the book aside apparently for ever. He had already scored in the first chapter v.28 'Then shall they call upon me but I wyl not heare...' Proverbs was proving a text too close to his condition. We have no evidence he used this printed text

53 Michael Hattaway, 'Marginalia of Henry VIII in his copy of the Bokes of Solomon etc' *Transactions of the Cambridge Bibliographical Society*, 1965, Cambridge 1968, pp. 166–170. 'The Bokes of Solomon', for instance, carries the Royal Library Press mark, no.1183, which runs only until April 1543. Hattaway's identifying text comes from Thomas Berthelet's priced account of books and bindings delivered to Henry VIII, reprinted in E. Arber's transcript of the Stationer's Register, vol.II, pp. 50–60.

54 G. F. Warner and J. P. Gilson, *The British Museum Catalogue* of *Western Manuscripts in the old Royal and Kings Collection*, London 1926.

55 Hattaway, *ibid*.

56 Henry emphasizes the following passages: Proverbs, Chapter I, v.8 28. Chapter II, v.10, 20–21. Chapter III, v.1, 3, v.8, 13–15, v.23, v.29. Chapter IV, v.3, v.13, v.25. Chapter V, v.3–5, v.20. Hattaway published his emendation of 'remember the wife of thy youth' to 'wives'.

again,[57] but it continues to be interlocked with his thinking. He handed the book over to a professional scribe to enter in red ink, and a fair hand, copies of the marginalia he had just made in his MS Psalter. The printed version is in English, but Henry's Latin notes are transcribed without translation. The collation of the two is not helped by the fact that the change in numeration of the Psalter occurs between the two books. We can establish that Henry took this initiative fairly soon after receiving the Psalters, for the transcriptions from the manuscript to the printed work are only partial. In the MS Psalter in Latin, which Henry annotated liberally throughout, his marginalia were inscribed with three different writing instruments: a quill, a lead stylus, and a soft orange chalky writing tool, perhaps easier to use but not so precise in application. Only those notes which are in ink have been transcribed into the printed book. We know, therefore, that Henry returned at least twice to his study of the Psalter, and the transcript copies only the earliest of his notations.

If we turn to Henry's marginalia in his actual psalter, Royal 2 A XVI, we find it consistently self-congratulatory. The King aligns himself with the author at every turn. It never occurs to him that he might be among the enemies against whom the Psalmist fulminates. (Henry's marginal emphases in the form of lines are too numerous to quote here.) The first stage of marking peters out at the end of our Psalm 109, so there are no more annotations beyond that point in the red transcription into the printed book. The orange crayon markings all occur between Psalm 67 and Psalm 103. The lead markings continue to Psalm 111, but like the ink ones, are more profuse in the earlier Psalms, where they frequently reaffirm the earlier notes. The places where Henry has been moved to add words in the margin are itemised in a second appendix (appendix II). Henry found here plentiful confirmation of his cruel reaction to Catherine Howard. Relentlessly throughout his notations he marks the evil end of the wicked. Certain emphases take on a different flavour if understood in terms of the translation he used. Psalm XXXI v.6 which he marked '*Those whom the Lord abhors*' in Coverdale's Psalter reads: 'I hated these vayne witches observyng inchauntements for I cleved and trusted to the Lorde'. Coverdale's translation of Psalm XLIX v.5, which Henry marks '*pulchra monituo*' reads: 'But man in his glistering fortune shall not abide'. Only in one place – Psalm XXXVIII, v.25, does Henry's comment strike a note foreign to that of the Psalmist. Against what Coverdale translates: 'I have been yong and am old, and yet sawe I never the righteous forsaken or his seed begging their bread', Henry VIII wrote (*dolens dictu.*[58])

---

57 The importance attached to the book of Proverbs in the education of his son, however, is amply attested in the oft-quoted report of Richard Fox, PRO, S.P., I, vol.195, ff. 213–14. Holbein made a drawing of Henry VIII as Solomon in a Judgement of Solomon.

58 There is a long list of books delivered to the King during the period of his grief over Catherine Howard – devotional works, Bibles, scholastic texts of the 12th and 13th

Henry's annotated Psalter is a remarkably revealing document. He points to every reference to sacrifices, to idols, to confession, to good works. Taken in conjunction with his annotations to the King's Book, which like the second Psalter annotations in lead, are probably among the fruit of his last marriage, they cast a strong light on Henry's religious stance during his later years. He emerges, if this be not a contradiction in terms, as a Psalter Christian – convinced of direct cause and effect between conduct and fate. God's enemies are his enemies – more, his enemies are God's. Coverdale's version of Psalm XI, v.6 reads: 'He wyl sende fyre upon the ungodly lyke rayne, brennynge, lyghtenynges, brymstone, and hote whirlwyndes for such part shall they drynke'. '*Bene*' say Henry VIII. Who was he thinking about? A covey of Cardinals? The French King, the Emperor? Or Catherine Howard awaiting execution? Psalm XXI: 'The king shall joy in thy strength...' is among the passages marked with special royal approval: '*pro rege oratio*'. If that piece of regal exaltation (Thou has made him most blessed for ever) seemed fitting to his taste the general production of his private Psalter can have done little to please the Royal eye. The text is written out in a not very distinguished Humanist script, with an effusive dedicatory letter by John Mallard, 'orator in the French tongue' in the household accounts for 1540–41[59] Mallard (naturally) address Henry as another David. The Psalms chosen for illustration are standard. After the Royal Arms on f.1b, there are pictures at the head of Psalms I, f.3; Psalm XXVII, f.30; Psalm XXXVII, f.48; Psalm LIII, f.63b; Psalm LXIX, f.79; Psalm LXXXI, f.98b; Psalm XCVII, f.118. The scenes chosen in each case are unexceptional. The novelty is that the figure of David is a convincing and unmistakeable portrait of Henry VIII himself. The image of Henry harping with his fool, Will Sommers,

centuries, Church Fathers. See *Letters and Papers Foreign and Domestic* XCIII, ii, 108–10. For a discussion of this especially devout phase of Henry's life, see C. Erikson, *Great Harry*, London 1980, p. 329.

59 Perhaps Mallard himself was author, not only of the script but of illuminations. Could anyone else have done them so badly? He was scribe and illuminator of a volume of his own poems in French of c.1530–40 (Oxford, Bodleian Library, Bodley 883, see: O. Pacht and J. J. G. Alexander *Illuminated MSS in the Bodleian Library*, Oxford 1973, vol.3, no.1330). Mallard was also responsible for Royal MS 7D. XIII and Royal 20B. XIII. This latter – a book of French cosmography with descriptions of ports and islands, would have been of practical advantage to Henry VIII in the invading days of the early 1540s. In the preface to that work, where he includes mathematics among his qualifications, Mallard asks Henry VIII to make him his poet as Morot is in France. Another copy, presumably slightly earlier (Paris Bibl. Nat. fonds franc. 1382), had been dedicated to Francois I. Mallard was happy to style both his royal patrons 'King of France' For the other Mallard works in the Royal Collection. See Warner and Gilson, *British Museum Catalogue*. In addition to his talents as historian, poet, cartographer, painter, linguist, calligrapher, orator, arch flatterer, Jean Mallard was probably a French spy.

for Psalm LIII ('The fool hath saith in his heart there is no God ...') is justly famous. The significance of the image of Henry 'seated reading in a bedroom' at the head of Psalm I (pl. 5) ('Blessed is the man that walketh not in the counsel of the ungodly, nor standeth in the way of sinners, nor sitteth in the seat of the scornful') has been much illustrated, but not discussed in the literature. This is not just a vignette of Henry VIII reading a book at bedtime in a pause between wives five and six. It illustrates, literally, verse 2 of the Psalm 'His delight is in the law of the Lord; and in his law doeth he meditate day and night'. 'The day' is suggested by the view into the garden; 'the night' by the bed. Henry is himself the Blessed Man.

Henry as the young David killing Goliath (pl. 6) (has flattery ever gone further?) reflects the prophecy of 1302 by the author of Rex Pacificus 'The Goliath of Rome is to be confronted by the new King David' (see above page). The stilted military gentleman posing for Goliath also appears on Henry VIII's painted reading desk in the Victoria and Albert Museum (pl. 0).[60] A marginal comment in Mallard's neatest hand expounds the illumination: 'Christi plena in Deum fiducia', the Psalm is XXVII. So Henry VIII stands in the shoes not only of David but of Christ, a Christ overcoming Papacy Supremacy.

The most significant of all these illuminations, and the least well known, is the 'Salvum me fac' picture, Psalm LXIX (pl. 8). For at least half a century before 1540, this psalm had been illustrated not by Jonah escaping from the whale as in the Middle Ages, but by David in Penitence.[61]

Jean Mallard surely knew the Book of Hours made for Francois I in which that King was twice represented, once kneeling before St Marcoul, but the other time in the guise of the penitent David.[62]

---

60 Henry VIII's Reading Desks in the Victoria and Albert Museum (W.29–1932). The outer lid carries the arms of Henry VIII with Catherine of Aragon, so it must have been made before c.1527. The inner lid is ornamented with Venus and Cupid confronting Mars. The falling flap has heads of Paris and Helen, and in the centre there is a head of Christ. Mars/Goliath is derived ultimately from an engraving of c.1510 by Hans Burkmaier. An inscription on applied parchment declares: HENRICI OCTAVO REGI ANGIAE DE RELIGIONES CHRISTIANAE MAXIME PROTECTOR TRIBUE SERVO.

61 I am grateful to Nicholas Rogers for pointing this out to me.

62 This MS which is closely dated 1539–40, was sold at Christie's 24th June, 1987, lot 265. I am grateful to Janet Backhouse for telling me of it, and leading me to her own article, 'Two Books of Hours of Francois I' British Museum Quarterly XXXI, 1966–7, pp. 90–96, pl. XXVIII. I am also grateful to Hans Fellner of Christie's for correspondence about it, and for sending me the catalogue at a moment's notice. Francois I was earlier represented as King David harping in Paris Bibl. Nat. Nou. Acq. Lat. M5.82, 2152, 2V. These Hours had belonged to him between 1514 and 1531. In the Psalter of Charles VIII of c.1490 (Paris, Bibl. Nat. Lat., 774, f.1) David harped and Charles knelt in prayer. So the fusion of David and King happened in France in the early 16th century.

So the idea of King David carrying a recognisable royal likeness was used in France a year or eighteen months before Henry VIII's Psalter was illuminated. There was a new dimension to the iconography of David in penance. Hans Holbein's famous print of c.1524[63] contrasted the traffic in Indulgences under a Medici Pope with King David, Manasseh and an 'open sinner' receiving forgiveness for their faults directly from God. Francois I, it would seem, was not averse to being depicted in a similar attitude of repentence, and David's reason for seven Penitential Psalms are represented. His first glimpse of Bathsheba in her bath appears in the background of the French King's kneeling portrait. No touch of Bathsheba was acceptable in Henry's miniature. On the contrary, another marginal annotation in Mallard's hand points to a different, but well-known gloss upon the Psalm 'save me O Lord for the waters are come in even unto my Soul' as referring to Christ's Agony in the garden. Mallard writes: 'Christus in Augustia mortis invocat Deus'. Faint echoes of Giovanni Bellini and Andrea Mantegna are resolved.[64]

So, by Christmas 1541, it was possible to over-trump the image of Henry enthroned on the Title Page of Cranmer's 1539 Bible. Mallard's Psalter offers the King a portrait of himself in the sandles of Christ in the Agony in the garden. Henry saw no reason to modify the language of the Medieval Coronation Order itself. There the King is described as 'Typus Christi'.

In his youth Henry had been interested in his historic role as descendent of King Lucius, of King Arthur, of Constantine's Mother. By the winter of 1541, the only prototype which fitted his expanded sense of Kingship was David. But David was flawed. It had to be David without Bathsheba: David as Type of Christ.

---

63 Engraved by Hans Lutzelburger, and first used in a calendar by Johann Capp, c.1527.
64 Giovanni Bellini's Agony in the garden is National Gallery 726; Andrea Mantegna's National Gallery 1417. Both were probably painted in the 1460s. The National Gallery also possesses an illuminated initial derived from the Mantegna (1417a).

APPENDIX I

As revised by Henry VIII

The Othe of the king*es* highnes at every coronation
The king shall then swere that he shall kepe and mayntene the lawfull right and
the lib*er*tees of old tyme gr*au*nted by the rightuous Cristen king*es* of Englond to
the holy chirche of ingland *nott preiudyciall to hys Jurysdiccion and dignite ryall* and
that he shall kepe all the lond*es* honours and dignytes rightuous [not preiudiciall
to hys Jurysdiction and dygnite ryall and fredommes of the crowne of Englond]*
in all man*er* hole w out any man*er* of mynyshement,
and the right*es* of the Crowne hurte decayed or lost to his power shall call again
into the auncyent astate, 'And that he shall *Indevore hymselfe to kepe vnite in hys
clergye and temporell subiec[ts]* And that he shall *according to hys con*sienc[e] in all his
iudgement*es* mynystere equytee right Justice shewyng wher is to be shewyd
mercy And that he shall gr*au*nte to holde lawes and *approvyd* customes of the
realme and lawfull *and not preiudiciall to hys crowne or Imperiall Juris[diction]* to his
power/kepe them and affirme them which the noblys and people haue made and
chosen *w hys con*sent,
And the evill Lawes and customes hollie to put out, and stedfaste and stable peax
to the people of his realme kepe and cause to be kept to his power *in that whych
honour and equite do require.*

* Deleted in Henry VIII's hand.

*Henry VIII's marginal notes in his Psalter, B.L. Royal 2A XVI,
following our current Psalter enumeration.*

Psalm I

v.1 'nota quis sit beatus'
v.4 'nota quid de impiis'
v.6 'et iusti et impii iudicium

Psalm II

vv. 2–7, 8, 10–12 'quia parvm prodest
fremere contra dominum id fremen-
tium munus'

Psalm IV

v.5 'nota de sacrificijs'

Psalm V

v.4 'nota bene de mendacibus'
v.7 'nota locum oracionis'

Psalm VIII

'Pro rege oratio'

Psalm XVIII (only in MS>)

v.20 'de operibus
v.22 'iusta dies mandata
v.23 de operibus'
vv.39–43 & 48–50 'de confortione'

Psalm XIX (only in MS)

'de gloria dei'

Psalm XXI 'Pro rege oratio'

v.7 'nota causam'
v.8 'nota quid ait de Christi inimicis'
v.12 'nota ca(usa)m'

Psalm XXIV

v.3 questio'
v.4 solutio'

Psalm XXVII

v.4 apta peticio'

Psalm XXVIII

v.2 'extollatione manuum'

Psalm XXIX

v. 'de domini potentia'

Psalm XXX 'de gratiarum actione'

v.5 'nota causam'
v.6 'quos odio habet dominus'

Psalm XXXVII

v.1 'pulchra monitio'
vv.18–22 'nota de inimicis dei quid ait'
'nota qui sunt qui debita non salvunt
et qui solvunt'
v.25 dolens dictum'
v.28 'de iniustis'
v.29 'de iustis'
v.35 'nota de impio'
vv.38–end de iustis et impiis/ de iustis'

Psalm XL

v.6 'de sacrificio'

Psalm XLI

v.11 'bene'

Psalm XLIV

v.20 'de idolatria'

Psalm XLIX

v.4 'nota laude psalterij'
v.12 pulchra monitio'
v.17 nota quid de vita ait'
v.20 specially ticked

Psalm L

v.14 'de sacrificiis et voto'
v.16 'nota quid peccatoribus ait Dominus'
v.16 'bene'

Psalm LII

v.1–5 'de Maliciosis'
v.5 'eor(um) remuneratio'
and in second annotation 'dissentoribus'
vv.6–7 'de iustorum opprobrio in maliciosis'

Psalm LVI

vv.10–13 'differentia verbi et sermonis'

Psalm LVIII

v.3 'de peccatoribus'
v.11 in second annotation 'de meritis'

Psalm LXII

v.10 'pulchra doctrina'
v.12 added in second annotation 'de operibus'

Psalm LXIII

v.11 'nota de rege'

Psalm LXIV

v.3 'de malignatibus'

Psalm LXV

v.1 'nota de votis'
vv.8–13 'nota de beneficiis nobis a deo concessis'

Psalm LXVI 'nota de laudibus deo dandis'

v.13 'de votis'

Psalm LXVIII

v.3 'de iustis'
v.26 'de assignatis locis'
v.30 'de volentibus bellum'

Psalm LXXII

In second notation v.4 'officium regis'

Psalm LXXIV

vv.8–17 'bene'

Psalm LXXVIII

v.5 'Mandatum patribus datum'
v.8–10 'acta veteris testamenti'
v.11 in second notation 'dei miracula'
v.22 added in second notation 'causam'

Psalm LXXIX

vv.10–11 added in second notation 'nota de nolentibus audire dominum'

Psalm LXXXIX

v.19–37 'promissio David facta'

Psalm XCII

v.10 in second notation 'de dono domini'

Psalm XCIV

In second notation v.10 'de confessione'
v.12 'quis sit beatus'

Psalm XCVII

In second notation v.7 'de sculptilibus'
In second notation v.11 'notabile dignum'

Psalm XCVIII

In orange notation v.5 'de adoratione'

Psalm XCIX

v.5–7 in orange notation 'bene'

Psalm CII

In second notation vv.9–10 'non in perpetuum irascetur/questione de ira domini'
vv.14–22 in second notation 'bene'

Psalm CIV

In second notation v.35 'nota bene'

Psalm CVI

In second notation v.31 'nota bene'
In second notation v.42 'nota bene'

Psalm CIX

vv.4 = 28 'de peccatore quid ait'
In second notation vv.8–9 'de peccatore'

There are no more annotations or marginal lines after Psalm 111.

For many corrections of my transcript of Henry VIII's handwriting and the translation I am greatly indebted to Linzee Colchester.

The numbering of the Psalms is in accordance with the Greek Septuagint version used in the Vulgate and later Roman Catholic versions. The numbers in brackets follow the Hebrew version, as in the Book of Common Prayer, the Authorised Version and more recent English translations.

I

1 N.B. who is blessed
4 N.B. what about/happens to the ungodly
6 The judgment (*iudicium*) of both the righteous and the ungodly

II

2–7, 8, 10–12 because there is no advantage in murmuring/grumbling against the Lord: such is the function of murmurers/grumblers.

IV

5 N.B./Mark of sacrifices

V

4 (? should be v.6) N.B./Mark well about liars

7 N.B./Mark: a place for prayer

VIII   A prayer for the King

XVII (XVIII)

20 of/concerning works

22 A proper/suitable day appointed. (This appears to have no relevance to XVII, 22)

23 concerning works

43 & 48–50 of encouragement

XVIII (XIX)   Of the glory of God

XX (XXI)   A prayer for the King.

7 N.B./Mark the reason

8 N.B./Mark what he says about Christ's enemies

12 N.B./Mark the reason

XXIII (XXIV)

3 The question

4 The answer

XXVI (XXVII)

4 A proper request/Petition

XXVII (XXVIII)

2 with raising of hands/hands raised (*manuum*)

XXVIII(XXIX)   Of the power of God

XXIX (XXX)   Concerning the giving of thanks/the act of thanksgiving

5 the reason

6 those whom the Lord hates

XXXVI (XXXVII)

1 Good advice (*monitio*)

18–22 N.B. what he says about the enemies of God

N.B. who they are who do not pay their debts and those who do. (*no Solvunt solvunt*)

25 a sad saying/lament

28 of the wicked (*iniustis*)

29 of the righteous

35 N.B. of the wicked man

38–end of the righteous and of the wicked (*impiis*) of the righteous

XXXIX (XL)

6 of sacrifice

XL (XLI)

11 good (lit: well)

XLIII (XLIV)

20 of Idolatry/worshipping idols

XLVIII (XLIX)

4 N.B. with praise upon the harp (or other stringed instrument, e.g. psaltery (*psalterij* – no 'y' in Latin)

12 good advice (*monitio*)

17 N.B. what he says about life

20 ticked

XLIX (L)

14 of sacrifices and prayer

16 N.B. what God says about sinners

16 (should be 15 or 23?) Good

LI (LII)

1–5 Of the malicious/evil-speakers
5 their reward
   concerning heretics/schimatics (*dissentoribus*)
6–7 the scoffing by/laughter of the righteous at the evil-speakers (*opprobrio*)

LV (LVI)

10–11 the difference between the written and the spoken word (Vulg: *In Deo laudabo verbum; In Domino laudabo sermonem*)

LVII (LVIII)

3 of sinners
11 of rewards

LXI (LXII)

10 sound teaching
12 of works

LXII (LXIII) concerning the King

LXIII (LXIV)

3 of/concerning workers of iniquity (*malignātibus*/malignantibus)

LXIV (LXV)

1 concerning prayers
8–13 N.B. of the benefits granted to us (*beneficiis*)

LXV (LXVI)   N.B. of the praises to be given to God (*dandis*)

13 on prayers

LXVII (LXVIII)

3 of the righteous

26 of the places appointed (*de assignatis locis*)
30 of (the) war-mongers/of the people that delight in war

LXXI (LXXII)

4 The duty of a/the King (*regis*)

LXXIII (LXXIV)

8–17 Good

LXXVII (LXXVIII)

5 The mandate/command given to our fathers
8–10 Events related in the Old Testament
11 the wonders of God (*mirabilia* – as in Vulg. or *miracula*)
22 the reason

LXXVIII (LXXIX)

10–11 N.B. of those unwilling to hear/listen to the Lord

(Gap: LXXVIII–LXXXVIII: is this right?)

LXXXVIII (LXXXIX)

19–37 God's promise to David

XCI (XCII)

10 of the gift of the Lord (*domini*)

XCIII (XCIV)

20 of/concerning confession
12 who is blessed

XCVI (XCVII)

7 of carved/graven images (*sculptilibus*)
11 a worthy comment

204

XCVII (XCVIII)

5 of worship

XCVIII (XCIX)

5–7 good

CI (CII)

9–10 He will not be angry for ever (irascetur)
    with a complaint about the Lord's anger (*domini*)
14–22 Good/Mark well

CIII (CIV)

35 Mark well

CV (CVI)

31 Mark well
42 Mark well

CVIII (CIX)

4–28 what he says about the sinner (peccatore)
8–9 of the sinner

The Catesbys 1485–1568: The Restoration of a Family to Fortune, Grace and Favour

DANIEL WILLIAMS

The historical debate concerning the rise of the gentry, begun by Tawney in 1941,[1] is still very much in the vogue. The history of this quintessentially English social group has been traced from the thirteenth to the seventeenth century and various periods within this considerable time span have been ascribed to its emergence.

Whereas the debate about origins is still essentially inconclusive, it has given rise to certain generally accepted conclusions upon the social and political role of the gentry up to the great institutional changes of the nineteenth century. Alan MacFarlane and others have highlighted the central importance of that role. They see the pervasive and consistent local influence of this 'governing' social group as a key factor in any explanation of why English Society was so different and distinct from those of its continental neighbours. Establishing, it is argued, a bedrock of administrative and class continuity, conducive to political stability.[2]

The continuity of gentry influence in the provinces and as a stepping stone to Westminster springs from its control of the onerous and ubiquitous offices of Justice of the Peace, and Member of Parliament. Offices that nevertheless had an intrinsic value within the shire community and were seen as stepping stones to higher, lucrative office and patronage. The wealth of the gentry was based on land, its acquisition and exploitation but also upon patronage and the rewards of office. These two factors were the mechanisms of class survival, though not the driving force. That essential dynamic was not class solidarity or mutual self-interest but rather cut-throat competition, infra-class rivalry and the need for protection against avaricious neighbours.

The importance of this perennial competition for the more tangible elements of social and political hegemony – wealth, the status of judicial

---

1 R. H. Tawney, 'The Rise of the Gentry', *Economic History Review*, xi (1941), 1–38. His observation that the sixteenth century was 'surmounted with greater difficulty by the heirs of ancient wealth ... than by men of humble position or more recent eminence', is certainly borne out by the evidence cited in this paper, *ibid.*, p. 8.

2 A. Everitt, *Change in the Provinces* (1972), p. 13; particularly A. Macfarlane, *The Justice and the Mare's Ale* (1981), pp. 196–9; E. P. Thompson, *Whigs and Hunters* (1975).

participation, the acquisition of land and above all access to crown and noble patronage – calls into question earlier, more comfortable theories of shire communities predicted upon the class solidarity and mutual interest of a landed oligarchy. It is certainly at odds with Lapsley's superficially attractive vision of Merry England:

> We can see a group of men obscure enough if measured by national consequence but of weight in local affairs: rich men, or moderately so, for the most part dwelling peaceably in their habitations and accustomed to work together in the administration of local affairs. They are men qualified by their lands and their knighthood to discharge these functions, and chosen it would seem, rather than others equally qualified by reason of their taste and aptitude for such business.[3]

Evidence of the violent and competitive world of the Catesbys and their class between the thirteenth and the seventeenth centuries does not bear out this rosy picture. The county community or rather the landed class which formed that community, was not simply mutually antagonistic but set against itself by other stronger loyalties and interests.

Dr Virgoe describing East Anglian society in the fifteenth century concludes that the horizontal relationships of the gentry as a local class were much less important or significant than the vertical ones of Bastard Feudalism between the gentry retainers and their noble patrons.[4] This had been the case in the fourteenth century and was to remain the case for the greater part of the fifteenth century. However, from the 1470s onwards, even these vertical ties between the retained shire gentry and the aristocracy based, for the lucky ones, upon the mutually benefiting practice of Good Lordship, were giving way to the much more one sided relationship between the gentry and the growing power and pervading influence of the Crown in the provinces. The same period also witnessed the discernible transition from an atavistic to a capitalist gentry bringing with it new competitive elements into the age-old struggle for dominance. The advent of the cash nexus was also deeply exploited by 'new monarchy'.

The growth of royal power and the extension of direct crown influence – particularly under the early Tudors – into the mechanisms of provincial life changed the basic ground rules for the survival and prosperity of the landed classes in a way that intensified infra-class rivalry and competition. In the fifteenth century there existed within the

3 G. Lapsley, *Crown, Community and Parliament* (1951), p. 82.
4 R. Virgoe, 'Crown, Magnates and Local Government in Fifteenth-Century East Anglia', in J. Highfield and R. Jeffs (eds.), *The Crown and Local Communities* (Gloucester, 1982), pp. 82–4.

world of Overmighty Subjects and the practice of Bastard Feudalism, a precarious balance of interest in the exercise of crown patronage that enabled office, land and advancement to be channelled to the gentry class through the intermediary of the magnates. By the early sixteenth century this process was breaking down, bringing the gentry, cap in hand, into direct contact with the powerful and capricious will of autocratic and perhaps paranoid monarchs like Henry VII and Henry VIII.

To fall foul of such kings with long and vindictive memories could result in very hard circumstances indeed, against which there was no longer the prospect of the benign intercession of a 'Good Lord' and from which the only possible path was that of submission and long and costly service with no ultimate guarantee of the restoration of grace or favour. In the capitalist world of Enclosures and land exploitation, even landownership itself was not enough. What was needed was the capital to work it.

At this point the irony of the title of this paper will become apparent. Without royal favour and access to royal patronage, ancient lineage and social status could not be enhanced or even sustained. This was particularly true of the Catesby dynasty whose introduction to Tudor monarchy was particularly inauspicious in 1485. The history of that family spans many centuries, but its rise and fall neatly covers the period of the rise of the gentry from 1300 to 1605. Conventional wisdom sees the Catesbys of the Tudor period as 'decaying gentry' leading inexorably to their dramatic and shameful fall in 1605 when Robert Catesby – the last of the line – was exposed and killed as the principal conspirator in the Gunpowder plot. Their Tudor fate therefore presents important evidence in the 'gentry debate'. It highlights the traditional political hazards of involvement in fifteenth and sixteenth century dynastic politics. There was also the perennial hazard of physiological failure, the extinction of the male line or of long minorities. The latter problem was particularly serious for tenants-in-chief under the Tudors for such minorities were institutionally exploited by the crown through the Court of Wards. It was common practice for the wardship and the marriage of the heir to be negotiated by the Court. Thus taking the administration and the revenues of the entailed estate out of the hands of the family for long and often crucial periods. Underpinning these dynastic perils, was the ubiquitous and all pervading hazard of royal disfavour. Under such circumstances, Edward Gwynne's compliment to Sir Simon Archer in 1626 that his family had 'bin so tenacious of theyre nobility'[5] rings true for other surviving ancient and genteel dynasties over the previous century. As he read the letter, Sir Simon might well have reflected upon the recent and spectacular demise of one of his most influential and

5 Quoted by K. B. McFarlane, *The Nobility of Later Medieval England* (Oxford, 1973), p. 6.

longstanding neighbours of previous centuries, the Catesbys. Indeed the Archers had benefited directly from their fall through purchase of the Catesby manor of Tanworth.[6]

The sale of such important tracts of family property, symptomatic of genteel decay, emphasises the essential 'Social Darwinism' of that process. The main branch of the Catesbys sold out and lost out not only to their landed neighbours of ancient lineage but also to the new rising gentry of the Tudor period bringing with them the wealth and the aptitudes of the professions, of commerce or of efficient sixteenth century husbandry. Such was the relationship between the emerging Spencers and their declining Catesby kinsmen by marriage in West Northamptonshire.

This is not the place to explore the origins of that illustrious family which in our own time has made the quantum leap to royalty. Nevertheless Spencer origins lie somewhere in between the bogus and contrived connection with the Despenser earls of Winchester and their so-called humble origins as successful sheep farmers and graziers. The evidence reveals strong connections with the Catesbys from early in the fifteenth century:[7] initially through service, later as prosperous financial backers, and finally through marriage, as kinsmen and equals in wealth and influence if not ancestry, of their Catesby patrons. Eventually, by the early years of the seventeenth century, they overtook and supplanted the Catesbys establishing their *caput honoris* in the manor of Althorp, purchased from the Catesbys in 1508.[8]

It was an accident of history that Sir Robert Spencer was created Baron Spencer of Wormleigh in 1603[9] and two years later the head of Robert Catesby was impaled upon a traitor's spike. Yet such accidents of history are symptomatic of that intimate and primeval struggle for survival, wealth and patronage that underlies the surface tranquillity of kinship and mutual interest amongst the governing elites of the shire.

The decline and fall of the Catesbys can be superficially explained as a consequence of dynastic misfortune, economic failure, overt Catholicism and subsequent treason between 1568 and 1605. Such an explanation, however, begs the question of why this happened. How did such an ancient and respected family arrive at such a precarious and desperate predicament? The circumstances of the family's history between 1485

---

6 Public Record Office (hereafter PRO) E.40/4326, 12374, 13491, 13495, though the purchase was not at first hand.

7 *Ibid.*, particularly E.40/6433, 8416 and the Will of William Catesby, (25 August 1485), PRO, Prob. 11/7 Reg. Logg fol. 15.

8 George Baker, *The History and Antiquities of the County of Northampton* (London, 1822–30), 2 vols., 1, 106, 538.

9 G. E. Cokayne, *The Complete Peerage of England, Scotland and Ireland, Great Britain and the United Kingdom*, ed. and revd. by V. Gibbs *et al.* (1910–59), vol. 12, pt. 1, p. 159.

and 1568 offer a complex and tragic explanation. That of a loyal, dynamic and patient Midland dynasty not permitted by fortune and the Tudor monarchy to live down the technical treason of their ancestor William Catesby on Bosworth Field. William, for reasons involving the Stanleys[10], that now can only be hinted at but were probably notorious at the time, became the scapegoat for the Yorkist Dynasty. He was the only man of note to be executed after the battle. Others like the Howards or the Percys were to be forgiven but not William and his progeny. The writer of the historical portions of the Crowland Chronicle, who most probably knew the victim, expressed the tragedy and the hypocrisy of the situation with his usual candour and insight:

> There was also taken prisoner [at Bosworth] William Catesby who occupied a distinguished place amongst all the advisers of the late king (Richard III) and whose head was cut off at Leicester as a last reward for his excellent offices.[11]

In the event, this execution was to be the first and not the last act in this Tudor tragedy. The family with all its atavistic energy, intelligence and ingenuity struggled manfully to live down the stigma and the consequences of the subsequent Act of Attainder. (One rather touching, minor contribution to this process is to be seen upon William Catesby's memorial brass in Ashby St Leger's church. It reads with a pardonable slip of the truth that he died on 20 August 1485, that is before the battle rather than after it.[12] One wonders how many other hitherto undetected examples exist of this retrospective attempt to disguise those who fell on the wrong side at Bosworth.) The family's lack of ultimate success in this very human endeavour was due in part to a close sequence of extended minorities, but above all to the malice, exploitation or indifference of succeeding Tudor monarchs, compounded by their advisors and favourites. It was *not* that the Catesbys failed to adapt to the new circumstances and ground rules of the sixteenth century, rather that they were never given the chance. Herein lay the tragedy.

In the final hours before his execution at Leicester on 25 August 1485, William Catesby, a friendless and deserted victim of the vicissitudes of fifteenth-century politics drew up his last will and testament. As he did so his fears were not for his own fate but that of his children and their

---

10 See my article, 'The Hastily drawn up Will of William Catesby, esquire, 25 August 1485', *Transactions of the Leicestershire Archaeological and Historical Society*, LI (1975–6), pp. 43–51.

11 H T. Riley, Ingulph's *Chronicle of the Abbey of Crowland with the Continuation by Peter of Blois and Anonymous Writers* (Bohn's Antiquarian Library, 1854), p. 505.

12 Ashby St Leger Church, transcribed in J. Evans and J. Britton, *A Description of the County of Northampton* (1813), pp. 47–8.

children. How right he was. In desperation he expressed the pious, though futile, hope that the new king and his successors 'will be good and gracious lord to them, for he is called a full gracious prince'.[13]

This was not to be. His heirs and successors struggled to restore family fortunes in the teeth of Tudor disfavour and exploitation. The reasons for this were financial as well as political and personal. The Tudor policy, already discernible under the Yorkists, of demanding cash payments for favour, patronage or office. Again a new situation that helps to explain the failure of the Catesbys and the success of the Spencers. At the beginning of the Tudor period, the Spencers had no real need for royal patronage. They had the capital and the expertise to build up their fortune as graziers.[14] When they reached the point of serious social advancement they had money enough to pay for royal patronage and favour. With the Catesbys the reverse was true. Following the seizure after Bosworth of William's considerable plate and tangible wealth by the new king, his counsellors and favourites, the family desperately needed the restoration of royal favour but lacked the cash to pay for it. A predicament exploited by many, including the Spencers themselves.

The modest, though at times, dramatic rise of the Catesbys between c. 1330 and 1485 was predicated upon qualities and conditions that were mutually interrelated. These were: their professional participation in and knowledge of the processes of the Common Law which dates back to the thirteenth century;[15] their ancient ancestry as a cadet branch of the Essebys, a dynasty tracing its origins back to the Conquest; their personal qualities of intelligence, opportunism and ruthlessness that survived surprisingly intact from generation to generation; but above all, early and continuously maintained traditions of service to the crown and the benefits that accrued from such service under the Plantagenet, Lancastrian and Yorkist kings. The mutual benefits of such direct contacts and service are best expressed in the words of one of their Northamptonshire neighbours, Sir Thomas Tresham, looking back from the complexities of the early Tudor environment to the period of his family's greatest prosperity and standing under the Lancastrian kings:

> under whom they were dignified with many noble offices and
> advancements and lived in high prosperity, and at whose feet

13 PRO Prob. 11/17 Reg. Logg fol. 15.
14 Mary E. Finch, 'The Wealth of Five Northamptonshire Families', *Northamptonshire Record Society*, xix (1955), chapter III, pp. 38ff.
15 PRO, E.47/67; *Placia de Quo Warranto* (Record Commission, 1818), pp. 401, 402.

and in whose service sundry of them ... have faithfully ended their lives with honour in the field.[16]

What had been true of the Treshams was true also of the Catesbys. Sir William Catesby, who lived through the middle years of the fifteenth century, served in the household of Henry VI. His importance within the shire community of Northampton facilitated his transition from Lancastrian to Yorkist service after 1461; he was retained by both Edward IV and his *de facto* vice-regent in the Midlands, William, Lord Hastings.[17] Under their patronage he reaped the generous rewards for such service that had advanced his dynasty in the past. It is clear from the history of the Catesbys that a crucial element in this benign patronage was marriage to a series of wealthy, landed heiresses which marks the rise of Catesby prestige and landed fortune. Such alliances are a clear indicator of social advancement. Through Yorkist influence his heir, also William, married Margaret, the daughter of Lord Zouch.[18]

This William of the next generation, a man of extraordinary legal and administrative talents and powerful Yorkist connections, took the family fortunes to their highest point.[19] The usurpation of Richard III offered even greater opportunities for this astute lawyer, who was soon to become a royal Squire for the Body, Speaker of the House of Commons and an influential member of Richard's council.[20] From this position of national importance William Catesby used all his considerable legal, social and political talents towards the acquisition of what can only be described as an extensive patrimony of landed estates forming a near contiguous bloc reminiscent of a feudal honour, at the confluence of the Leicestershire, Northamptonshire and Warwickshire borders and centred upon the Family Seat at Ashby St Leger.[21]

Through his extraordinary efforts, which also resulted in the acquisition of a proportionate amount of money, plate and other moveable assets,[22] William and his family stood in the summer of 1485 with all the necessary attributes of political influence – land, status and ancestry – poised on the brink of enoblement. In the event, everything

16 Historic Manuscript Commission, *Report on MSS in Various Collections*, iii (Tresham Papers), p. 27.
17 See Daniel Williams, 'From Towton to Bosworth: the Leicestershire Community and the Wars of the Roses', *Trans. Leics. Archaeol. & Hist. Soc.*, LIX (1984–5), p. 34.
18 *The Hastily drawn up Will of William Catesby, op. cit.*, p. 44.
19 *Ibid.*, pp. 46–7.
20 *Ibid.*, pp. 45–6.
21 *Ibid.*
22 PRO, E.154/2/4; *Calendar of Patent Rolls, Henry VII* (HMSO, 1956), i. 99 (henceforth, *CPR*.

was to be lost through the capricious God of Battles on Bosworth Field. Royal patronage gave way to deep royal hostility and exploitation under the new Tudor king, Henry VII. This turn of events was to endure throughout the Tudor period. Of course the Catesbys only gradually became aware of the intrinsic hopelessness of their new fate. In their ancient family traditions they fought to revive their fortunes.

William was attainted by Parliament in November 1485[23] and his lands and possessions seized and confiscated. As an astute lawyer he had tried to make provision for the seeming unlikely, though obviously not impossible, contingency that was soon to befall him. He established a series of Trusts and Feoffments to Uses involving his uncle Sir John Catesby, Justice of Common Pleas, whose possessions were to be specifically exempt from the consequences of his nephew's attainder.[24] These provisions fell through as a consequence of Sir John's unexpected death early in 1486 followed by a thorough inquiry in the following year, initiated by the crown into William Catesby's pre-Bosworth possessions.[25]

The consequence of all this was that the entire Catesby patrimony was divided up between Henry VII and some of his closest supporters at the time, Sir James Blount, Sir John Risley and Sir David Owen and others. These grants were made by Letter Patent in Male Tail.[26] On the face of it the Catesby lands were lost to the family for ever. The complete absence of grace and favour at this early point in the new reign is illustrated by a legal judgement related to the claims of one of William's younger sons, John Catesby, to the manor of Althorp. This had been previously promised to John by his bachelor uncle the judge, Sir John Catesby. Despite the strength of the Catesby claim made by William's widow Margaret, the uncompromising judgement was that John Catesby, son of William and Margaret Catesby, shall be for ever excluded from all title to the premises (of Althorp).[27]

The case itself illustrates Margaret's immediate problem – isolated and disgraced even from cadet branches of the family – of providing for her three sons and two daughters. Fortunately there were those willing to speculate upon the acquisition of a Catesby connection bringing with it the remote (at this point) possibility of the annulment of the Act of Attainder. There were at least two people who, for reasons of self interest, were willing to take such a gamble. One of these was John Spencer, already a man of substance who had played a role as

23 *Rotuli Parliamentorum* (Record Commission, 1767–1832), 7 vols., vi, 275–8.
24 *Ibid.*, p. 278.
25 W. Campbell, *Materials for a History of ... Henry VII* (Kraus, 1965), i, 536.
26 *CPR.*, Henry VII, i, 209, 231, 275 *et passim.*
27 *Materials for a History of ... Henry VII*, op. cit., ii, 328.

financial backer in the late William Catesby's landed acquisitions.[28] He also, at the time, was the lessee for grazing purposes of considerable portions of the confiscated Catesby estates. John (soon to become Sir John) Spencer was, significantly, the founder of the Spencer landed fortune in Northamptonshire and Warwickshire who purchased the former Catesby manors of Wormleighton (Warwickshire) and Althorp (Northamptonshire).[29]

Of equal importance to what was to follow, John's father, William Spencer, had married the sister of an astute but obscure Northampton-shire lawyer, soon to become Henry VIII's ruthless and notorious financial · agent and counsellor, Sir Richard Empson. The attractions of the Catesby name and the expectations of these new and aspiring members of the Northampton shire community can only be imagined. What is certain from the evidence is that George Catesby, the heir, married Sir Richard's daughter Elizabeth. Not a good match but indicative of the loss of status the family had suffered. At all events John Spencer, as part no doubt of a pre-arranged plan, loaned Richard Empson and his new son-in-law 200 marks 'for the restitution of the said George'.[30]

By such means – the influence of Empson and the payment of a substantial fee to the crown, loaned by Spencer – the attainder against William Catesby's heirs was to be revoked, shortly after Margaret's death, in October 1495. The Act specified that George Catesby was to enter into his father's inheritance without the payment of livery of seisin to the crown. This must have been some kind of grim Tudor joke. There was to be no seisin. In fact so constraining were the conditions specified in the Act of Restitution that what the heir actually received were uncertain prospects of reversions to his father's and indeed his mother's former properties. All grants of forfeit lands made by royal Letters Patent were to stand. They were of course grants made in Male Tail. John Alcock, Bishop of Ely (Henry VII's former Chancellor), Richard Empson and John Spencer were to hold the remainder of the lands (chiefly Margaret Catesby's own inheritance) for seven years. Finally the heir was to pay (presumably from his own resources) an annual rent to the crown of £100 'during pleasure'.[31]

Little grace and even less favour: it is difficult to find any tangible benefit to the heir in the entire transaction. Those who brought the restitution about seem to have done well for themselves one way or another. George Catesby spent the rest of his life, no doubt with loans

28 PRO Prob. 11/7 Reg. Logg. fol. 15.
29 *The Wealth of Five Northamptonshire Families, op. cit.,* p. 38.
30 PRO, E.40/8333.
31 *CPR*, Henry VII, ii, 40–1; *Rot. Parliamentorum*, vi, 490–2.

supplied by Sir John Spencer and legal advice from Sir Richard Empson, buying out the entailed possessors of his father's forfeited estates.[32] There was little family money at hand, his father's chattels valued by the crown at over 1000 marks had already been divided up between the king and John Alcock,[33] to whom William had somewhat unwisely committed his entire moveable property. Consequently George was forced, amongst other financial expedients, to mortgage his mother's property and even to sell the marriage of his daughter Audrey to another 'rising' family, the Newhams of Newham near Daventry, for 200 marks.[34]

The laborious and costly process of buying out those with a title to his family estates was to be the solid achievement of George Catesby. The restoration of his position at the head of his family, and of his local status, persuaded other cadet branches to return lands they had steadfastly refused to give to his mother.[35] The *Inquisition Post Mortem* following his death in May 1507 reveals the restitution of a considerable portion of the pre-Bosworth Catesby estates in Leicestershire and Oxfordshire as well as the Northamptonshire manors of Gretton, Sillisworth and Ashby St Leger along with the Warwickshire properties at Lapworth and Wellesbourne and others.[36] What the *Inquisition* does not reveal is the extent of mortgage and leasing at disadvantageous terms upon these estates incurred in the buying out process. Indeed by its very nature such a survey indicates a liability to the crown rather than a description of tangible family assets. The possessions described in George's will were modest enough. His assets did not even stretch to the erection of an elaborate marble monument over his parents' tomb[37] in Ashby St Leger church; his executors could only afford the brass that still survives today. The profits from his restored lands went to those with the capital to exploit them. Added to this was the unfortunate fact that George died before his heir William came of age, resulting in the first of a series of costly minorities for the family at crucial times in its fortunes.

George's father-in-law was to suffer the same fate as his father, William Catesby. He was sacrificed as a scapegoat for Henry Tudor's unpopularity and executed as an act of appeasement by the new king, Henry VIII.[38] Once again the family fortunes were to be rescued by the

---

32 PRO, E.40/9162, 7390, 5060, 10, 255.
33 *CPR*, Henry VII, i, p. 99.
34 PRO, E.40/5075.
35 *Ibid*, E.40/7390.
36 *Calendar of Inquisitions Post Mortem, Henry VII*, vol. iii (1504–9). HMSO, 1955), nos. 99 to 104.
37 William Dugdale, *The Antiquities of Warwickshire*, (Coventry, 1765), pp. 789 (henceforth Dugdale).
38 S. B. Chrimes, *Henry VII* (1972), pp. 316–17.

efforts of an able and astute widow. Elizabeth Catesby, née Empson, married Thomas (later Sir Thomas) Lucy, a Warwickshire squire who had served in court as one of the king's Sewers.[39] Through his own and his wife's connections at court, Thomas Lucy secured the wardship of the Catesby heir, William,[40] thus preventing a further depletion of the family fortunes.

In 1512 a stroke of much needed luck came the way of the Catesbys. Sir John Risley, still in possession of the major Catesby estates in Warwick shire, Ladbrooke, Rodburn and Bishopeston, died without issue and so the estates reverted to the Catesby heir.[41] The crown of course took the first fruits. A new IPM was taken to assess the heirs liability to the crown upon possession. The grant of wardship was reissued in November 1512 no doubt on payment of a further and larger fine.[42]

Even so, under the protection of Sir Thomas Lucy and with the restoration of most of the pre-1485 Catesby inheritance, the rehabilitation of the family in the Midlands seemed at last secure.

Unfortunately, the physiological hazard once again manifested itself at an inopportune moment. William died in 1517, still a minor. The estate devolved upon his brother Richard, at that time only twelve years of age.[43] Thus a further long period of minority ensued, with its opportunities for further alienation of family assets. This time competition for the lucrative wardship of the next heir was to be more intense. Sir Thomas Lucy paid an obligation to the crown[44] for the wardship of Richard but so too did another less benign interested party, Sir John Spencer, who had a significant financial interest in the manor of Radbourn, previously leased to him by Sir John Risley.[45] The Spencer wealth won the day and Richard's wardship went to Sir John. In this way he not only secured the lucrative exploitation of the Catesby estates for the next eleven years but also, on payment to the crown, Richard's marriage to his daughter Dorothy.[46] For the Spencers this marriage was a sign of social advancement; for the Catesbys, it was to mark a further downward turn in both their fortunes and status.

39 *Letters and Papers ... Henry VIII*, Domestic, (HMSO, 1920 etc.), i, no. 190, doc. 1; Dugdale, p. 505.
40 *Ibid.*
41 *Inquisition Post Mortem*, George Catesby, (Warwick 8 June, 1512), PRO Chancery, Series ii/27/35.
42 *Letters and Papers ... Henry VIII* op cit., no. 190, doc. 1.
43 *IPM*, William Catesby, Southam, (8 March 1518), Chancery Series ii/32/21.
44 *Letters and Papers ... Henry VIII*, 2, pt. 11, p. 1489.
45 *Ibid., The Wealth of Five Northamptonshire Families, op. cit.*, p. 39, quoting Spencer MSS Althorp, no. 1518 and further material in the Spencer archives.
46 *Letters and Papers ... Henry VIII*, 2, pt. ii no. 4272; John Bridges *History and Antiquities of Northamptonshire* (Oxford, 1791), 2 vols., 1, 18.

Richard Catesby came of age in about 1528 and eventually took seisin of the greater part of the family estates, painstakingly restored by his long dead father, George. Even here there were legal complications, the manor of Bishopton (Warwickshire) granted to Sir John Risley in 1487 was not to be restored until 1543.[47] His mother, Elizabeth, lived on with tenacious vigour, marrying again and living with her new husband, according to the terms of her generous dower, in the family home at Ashby St Leger.[48] Richard experienced difficulties in meeting her dower income charged upon rents from the manors of Lapworth, Bushwood, Henley, Tanworth and other Warwickshire lands.[49]

Nevertheless, on the face of it, times looked propitious. Sir Richard Catesby was now, on parchment, an extensive landowner within the Midland shires who held in chief of the crown. In previous centuries such a status would have marked him out for service with its certainties of lucrative patronage. In 1528, under Henry VIII and the institutionalised cash nexus, for the Catesbys it meant extensive service and obligations but little reward beyond a knighthood. Even that accolade opened up new obligations rather than opportunities.

Sir Richard fulfilled his part of the contract of 'Good Lordship' to his Tudor sovereign Henry VIII. He carried out his expected but nevertheless onerous duties of Justice of the Peace, Justice of Gaol Delivery and at times Sheriff of Northamptonshire and Leicestershire/Warwickshire.[50] He served as Member of Parliament and served with distinction as Surveyor of Sewers, Surveyor of Chantries and presided over the Royal Commission upon Enclosures for the Midlands.[51] His services to his sovereign were to be more direct. He was one of the Esquires detailed to welcome Anne of Cleves. He arrayed his tenants under his personal command to serve in the rear guard of Henry's French campaign of 1544.[52]

For all this service and loyalty nothing was returned, apart from a perilous captaincy of artillery in Ireland for his son, Edward Catesby, in 1531.[53] At a time when others benefited mightily from royal favour and office, when dynastic, landed fortunes were laid by the purchase of the

47 PRO, E.40/13335.
48 *Letters and Papers, Henry VIII*, vol. 8, no. 1119; PRO, E.40/A.5075, 4417, see also E.40/3206, 3207 by which Elizabeth's forty years lease of the Manor of Epwell in 1531 involved its sale by Sir Richard in 1546.
49 *Ibid.*, 4417.
50 *Letters and Papers, Henry VIII*, 14, vol. 2, nos. 38, 435, 17, 19, 21, 302 p. 147 *et passim*; see also I. S. Leadham, *The Domesday of Enclosures* (1897), pp. 485 ff., 403–4.
51 *Ibid.*
52 *Letters and Papers, Henry VIII*, no. 14 vol. 2, no. 572; no. 19, vol. 1, no. 273, p. 155, no. 276.
53 *Ibid.*, vol. 4, pt. III, no. 5, p. 325.

lands of the dissolved religious houses and chantries, for Sir Richard Catesby there were to be no rewards. Grace and favour went to the 'new men' of the Tudor establishment not to a tainted family associated with the notorious last Yorkist king. There was a further problem, lack of capital. Those who benefited from the sales of monastic lands were those with the ready cash to buy them. This, the Catesbys had sorely lacked since the confiscation by the crown and council of William Catesbys plate and assets after Bosworth. The expensive process of buying out the holders of the forfeited Catesby estates along with the outflow of revenue from periods of wardship, meant that the opportunity to build·up capital just was not there. Those who profited from the Catesby lands were not the owners but the lessees, like the Spencers with their capital and their expertise in pasture husbandry – the same people who on payment to the crown were granted the wardships.

It could be argued that Sir Richard added to his family's problems with three marriages and twelve children. Certainly the terms of his will reveal the almost complete dispersal of his modest share of plate to his numerous daughters and daughters-in-law.[54] Here again there was to be no help at court. He had to find placements for his sons in trade or amongst the households of his richer and more influential neighbours, like Sir Thomas Vaux, Lord Harrowden.[55] The marriage of his heir had to become a saleable commodity. It was sold to William Wyllington of Barcheston, Warwickshire for 630 marks: a marriage that brought status to the bride rather than the groom.[56]

The same pattern of unreciprocated service was to continue during the reign of Edward VI. Indeed, throughout Sir Richard's majority the Catesby archives reveal the tell-tale signs of the financial difficulties of 'decaying gentility': the sale of ancestral lands; the granting of long leases on disadvantageous terms; the re-mortgaging of property; the sale of standing timber; the marriage of daughters into families of inferior rank.

Concurrently, their new Spencer kinsmen prospered mightily and were rich enough to take on the burdens of the *buzones* of the shire. In 1545 the Spencer estate held in chief from the crown (only a portion of their other assets in plate, money, livestock and leased pastures) was valued at £454 13s 4d per annum[57] – almost certainly a considerable undervaluation.[58] As wealthy graziers they prospered under the

54 Bridges, *op. cit.*, 1, 18, PRO Prob. 11/19 Tashe.
55 *Letters and Papers, Henry VIII*, vol. 9, no. 697, p. 234; PRO, E.40/6609, 3205.
56 *IPM* Sir Richard Catesby, Northampton, 22 October 1553, PRO Chancery Series ii/101/85.
57 *The Wealth of Five Northamptonshire Families, op. cit.*, pp. 39–40 and footnotes.
58 *Ibid.*

inflatory conditions of the period, and at this stage in their family history had little need for royal patronage – though the wherewithal to acquire it was there in abundance.

The Catesby predicament was the opposite, there was no escape from the spiral of decline. Sir Richard Catesby died in 1553, tragically for the dynasty preceded by his eldest son and heir. The estate devolved upon his grandson William,[59] necessitating a further prolonged and debilitating minority. The Catesby lands once again passed into the crown's hands via the Court of Wards. In return for loyalty and services rendered to secure Queen Mary's succession in 1554 Sir Robert Throckmorton was granted the marriage of the heir William and an annuity of 40 marks from the revenues of the manor at Ashby St Leger.[60]

This marriage, in the event, sealed the doom of the Catesbys by introducing the heir into a Catholic household. In the short term, William's minority under the Elizabethan court of Wards and Liveries, was again financially ruinous. William, the last of the Catesbys to receive knighthood, came of age in 1568. He was given seisin on the payment of the considerable fine of £159 17s 8`d[61] – a further serious drain to the crown from their already depleted finances. The total annual value of the Catesby lands in 1568 were £319,[62] considerably less than that of their former retainers the Spencers, standing as we have seen at over £454 per annum.[63] In fact the gap was even greater, for the total of £319 consisted of £109 in possession and £210 in reversion.[64] It was the recurring Catesby predicament: the Tudor fine for livery greatly exceeded its disposable annual income from land. As William Catesby Esquire for the King's Body had feared in 1485, the Tudor dynasty had not given Good Lordship to his progeny. Without it the family, for all its efforts, could not thrive in the new capitalist conditions of the sixteenth century.

The marriage of the Catesby heir, William, into a Catholic family, an event no doubt approved of, if not actually arranged by, Mary Tudor, was, seen retrospectively, to be the final fatal act of crown interference in the misfortune of the dynasty. As events turned out, Sir William's conversion to Catholicism ended the family's conventional orthodoxy and with it all prospect of any future reconciliation between him and Elizabeth I. Indeed the systematic state pillage through recusancy and

59 Baker, *op. cit.*, 1, 245; Dugdale, *op. cit.*, p. 790.
60 *CPR, Philip and Mary*, (HMSO, 1937) vol. 1, 1553–4, p. 84, see R. Davey, *The Nine Days' Queen* (1909), pp. 249–50.
61 PRO, E.40/13270.
62 *Ibid.*, 12, 375.
63 *The Wealth of Five Northampton Families, op. cit.*, p. 39.
64 PRO, E.40/12, 375.

other penal fines accelerated the decline of the already depleted reserves of family assets leading to the final symptom of genteel decay: the sale of major ancestral estates. The ultimate pillage came with the Attainder following the Gunpowder Plot of 1605.

Little wonder the patience of the last of the line, the wild and desperate Robert Catesby, snapped with almost, but not quite, devastating consequences for the new Stuart king, James I. The Gunpowder Plot can never be condoned, but in the circumstances described in this paper, it can certainly, in part, be explained.

The Sermons of Roger Edgeworth: Reformation Preaching in Bristol

JANET WILSON

During the years of uncertainty from 1535 to 1560 the Reformation took root unevenly throughout England, spreading more rapidly in London, the traditional 'Protestant underworld', the south-east and port towns like Hull and Bristol, but making less progress in outlying areas like Lancashire, Cornwall, Devon and parts of Yorkshire.[1] Although it is now a commonplace that at the grass roots level the movement was sporadic in its progress, often winning only local acceptance and just as often encountering pockets of resistance, this description fits the situation in Bristol during the 1530s better than any other. In this town, traditionally a centre of religious dissent, the new religion made some headway among the groups of craftsmen and artisans formerly associated with Lollard heresy and won new recruits from among the merchant class and members of the local corporation.[2] But the strong opposition it met from the local conservative clergy meant that throughout the 1530s Bristol became a theatre of conflict between Catholic and Protestant clergy in which the laity was also involved, often tangentially, since religious differences became compounded with social and economic issues.

Informed comment on the confusion of these troubled times comes from the Catholic preacher Roger Edgeworth: the vicissitudes he suffered during twenty years of preaching in the West Country from 1536 to 1553 are some indication of the uphill struggle that the conservative clergy had to maintain its traditional status within the community. In the preface to his *Sermons* (published in 1557) he comments:

> Against such errours with their appendeceis I haue enuehied ernestlie and oft in my sermons in disputations and reasoninge with the protestauntes, vntill I haue be put to silence, either by

1 See D.M.Palliser, 'Popular Reactions to the Reformation during the years of Uncertainty 1530–1570' in *Church and Society in England; Henry VIII to James I*, eds. F.Heal and R.O'Day (London, 1977), pp. 36–7.
2 On Lollardy in Bristol see J.A.F.Thomson, *The Later Lollards 1414–1520* (Oxford, 1965), pp. 20–51; K.G.Powell, 'The Social Background to the Reformation in Gloucestershire', *Transactions of the Bristol and Gloucestershire Archaeological Society*, 92 (1973), 98–100 (cited hereafter as *TBGAS*).

general prohibitions to preache, or by name, or by captiuitie, and imprisonment, of all whiche (I thanke God) I haue had my parte.[3]

A prebendary of the second stall of Bristol Cathedral from the time of its foundation in 1542, Edgeworth had also been since around 1536 a canon residentiary of Wells Cathedral. In the reign of Edward VI he was persecuted and probably imprisoned for his beliefs by the arch-Protestant William Barlow who was bishop there from 1548 to September 1554.[4] The preface concludes:

> ... I preached also in manye sermons at the cathedrall Churche there, (in Bristol) where I am one of the Canons, ... I was manie times and longe discontinued by the odious scisme that was nowe lately, and by the doers of the same. And in like maner in the Cathedrall Churche of welles, ... I lacked no trouble by bishop Barlowe and his officers.[5]

From a comment in one of the last three sermons in the collection, preached in early 1553, 'nowe that it hath pleased them more fauourably to loke vpon me, and to lycence me, I shalbe glad to retourne to that my old exercise', it would seem that his preaching in both dioceses during the Edwardian reformation was warranted controversial enough to be muzzled for some five or six years.[6] On Queen Mary's accession, however, he was promoted to the chancellorship of Wells Cathedral.

Sermons very fruitfull, godly and learned was published in response to the fourth decree of the legatine court of 1555 that a uniform Catholic doctrine be made available to assist in the Marian restoration.[7] They are mainly Henrician (some are Edwardian) and contain exaltations of the Royal Supremacy; a single pro-papal reference and a reference to the 'catholike churche' are probably later interpolations.[8] That these sermons were considered to conform to the Marian prescriptions on religion is proof that in homiletic writing, as in other aspects of the restoration, conservative survival was often a substitute for the full

---

3 *Sermons very fruitfull, godly and learned* (Caly, 1557), sig. +3 (STC 7482); (cited hereafter as *Sermons*); abbreviations have been silently expanded and literals corrected. References are also given to 'An edition of Roger Edgeworth's *Sermons very fruitfull, godly and learned*', 2 vols., ed. J. M. Wilson, unpublished D. Phil. thesis (Oxford University, 1985), II, p. v. (cited hereafter as 'Edgeworth's *Sermons*'). Forthcoming as *The Sermons of Roger Edgeworth*, D. S. Brewer.

4 'Edgeworth's *Sermons*', I, pp. 71–92.

5 *Sermons*, sig. +3ᵛ; 'Edgeworth's *Sermons*', II, pp. v–vi.

6 *Ibid.*, sig. 4A3; II, p. 325.

7 The synod's twelve draft decrees were published under the title *Reformatio Angliae ex decretis Reginaldi Poli Cardinalis, sedes Apostolical Legati Anno MDLVI* (Rome, 1562; facs. repr., London, 1962). They are printed in *Concilia Magnae Britanniae et Hiberniae a Synodo Verolamiensi, AD CCCXLVI ad Londoniensem AD MDCCXVII*, ed. D. Wilkins, 4 vols. (London, 1737), IV, pp. 121–6.

8 *Sermons*, sigs. 2B4ᵛ, 2C2ᵛ, 3L2ᵛ; 'Edgeworth's *Sermons*', II, pp. 116, 118, 263.

Catholic scheme of belief.[9] Their purpose – which was to instruct the laity confused by twenty years of religious change in the essentials of the faith – was probably achieved by their anti-Protestant propaganda as much as by their doctrinal content. Edgeworth's frequent complaints at the reformation changes and his attacks on Protestant practices would have constituted reminders in 1557 of what had disappeared and what was once considered heretical. By being neither too dogmatically anti-papal like the Henrician sermons of such contemporaries as Stephen Gardiner and Cuthbert Tunstal, nor purely prescriptive like the Marian homilies of Thomas Watson, Edmund Bonner or Leonard Pollard, they offer a · unique picture of the resources of orthodox belief being marshalled to withstand the enormous pressures of change.

Edgeworth belonged to the party known as the 'conservative Henricians' which included Bishops Gardiner, Tunstal and Bonner, who acknowledged the Royal Supremacy under Henry but reverted to Catholicism with the Pope under Mary. Born in the Marches of Wales around 1486–7 and educated at Banbury Grammar School and Oriel College, Oxford (graduating with a D.Th), he first arrived in Bristol in 1525 as Prior of the Guild of Kalendars.[10] The guild was traditionally a lay and clerical fraternity of some distinction: it had once housed the town's muniments and it had a theological library. Among the duties incumbent upon the prior (who had to be of MA status) were giving a weekly lecture and explaining disputed points of scripture. Edgeworth was the last prior with a degree in theology, in fact the only one of any distinction in the last forty years of the guild's existence, and the decline of its fortunes and activities date from his departure in 1528.[11] Of his subsequent whereabouts little is known other than that he attended the Blackfriars legatine court of 1529 which debated the King's divorce, as a legal advisor, in the employment of either Cardinal Wolsey or John Longland, Bishop of Lincoln. He next appears in the records of Wells Cathedral in April 1536 as a canon residentiary.[12]

During the 1530s, when he was preaching in Bristol, the town was in the grip of a prolonged religious crisis. Hostilities between Catholic and Protestant clergy focussed around Hugh Latimer, rector of West Kingston in Wiltshire in 1533 and Bishop of Worcester from 1535–9. Latimer's challenge to the *status quo* sparked off conflict between the

9 D. Loades, *Politics and the Nation, 1450–1660* (3rd edn., London, 1986), p. 246, attributes Mary's failure to her inability to distinguish between religious conservatism and full Catholicism.

10 'Edgeworth's *Sermons*', I, pp. 39–57.

11 Ibid., pp. 60 2; N. Orme, 'The Guild of Kalendars, Bristol', *TBGAS*, 96 (1978), 35–52.

12 'Edgeworth's *Sermons*', I, pp. 62–7.

town corporation and the clergy for control of the pulpit which accelerated the decline of the church in the medieval civic community. This is further evidence of the gradual secularisation of religion in the West Country which was due principally to the Crown's encroachment on the town through the church. But civic and economic factors also contributed to the church's decline. The situation was somewhat stabilised in 1542 in response to Henry's more conservative religious policies after 1539 and the founding of the new diocese of Bristol; this led to the division of the clergy into a clerical élite (who had stronger associations with the lay élite who controlled them than with the parish clergy whom they regulated) and a greatly impoverished group of parish clergy (dependent on the parish laity). The long term outcome, however, was a dramatic decline in the educational standards and wealth of the clergy, a fragmentation of its autonomy and a corresponding strengthening of the secular forces in the town.[13]

An explosive dispute with far-reaching consequences broke out in Lent 1533 when Latimer, at the invitation of the local clergy, preached against purgatory, images and the Blessed Virgin. This was met with disfavour by the clergy who had originally invited him and they took steps to prevent him from returning at Easter.[14] But Latimer's preaching converted an influential member of the local clergy, John Hilsey, Prior of the Dominican friary, who then advised Dr Thomas Bagard, the Chancellor of the diocese, to allow him to preach once more. At this the clergy again reacted angrily and sent in their own preachers to counter-attack.

In the course of the dispute, however, conservative preaching became associated with treason: two of the invited preachers, Dr Nicholas Wilson and Dr Edward Powell, were later imprisoned for denying the Royal Supremacy (Powell was executed for treason in 1540 while Wilson was pardoned on 29 May 1537).[15] Latimer's most vociferous opponent, Nicholas Hubberdyne, greatly offended the townspeople by claiming that twenty or thirty men were heretics and 'that Rome cannot be destroyed, nor can it err'. These and other conservative doctrinal statements against the authority of the church created even greater discord:

13 M. C. Skeeters, 'The Clergy of Bristol, c. 1530–c. 1570', unpublished Ph.D thesis (University of Austin, Texas, 1984), pp. viii–ix, 219 ff.; I have been indebted to Dr Skeeters' suggestions in revising this paper.
14 The affair is discussed by Skeeters, 'Bristol Clergy', pp. 51–88; and G. Elton, *Policy and Police: The Enforcement of the Reformation in the Age of Thomas Cromwell* (Cambridge, 1972), pp. 112–17; 'Edgeworth's *Sermons*', I, pp. 67–71.
15 On Powell and Wilson see Elton, *Policy and Police*, pp. 113, 388, 401.

for many that favoryed Latomer and hys new maner of prechynge and other many that favoryd Huberdyne yn hys old maner of prechynge, both the sayde partes hath ben more ardente now sens Ester then they wer before.[16]

A set of articles against the 'synastrall preching' of Powell and Hubberdyne was forwarded to the King's council and depositions were taken against both parties. But although the commissioners supported Hubberdyne and criticised Latimer, it was the former who was sent to the Tower while the latter, who strongly supported the royal divorce, returned to London to work for the Reformation.

The conservative party never really recovered its strength after this crisis which was the only occasion during the Reformation in which the full resources of the clerical body – monks, friars, chantry priests, parish incumbents, stipendiary priests, ecclesiastical officials – drew on lay support and made a concerted stand against reform and thus the corporation which had come to support Latimer because he enjoyed royal favour.[17] The institutional changes of 1538 to 1540, the decline in the number and wealth of the clergy and in its educational standards, meant that the conservative reaction to the spread of Protestant ideas in the diocese was vitiated; it either took the form of individual disagreement such as that of John Kene, the conservative rector of Christ Church, or of conservative policies such as those of John Bell, Bishop of Worcester from 1539 to 1543, or Thomas Bell, the sheriff of Gloucester, whose hatred of Protestants was well known; it was seldom a matter of large scale resistance.[18] The corporation's victory, on the other hand, was tenuous and unable to rely on Cromwell's support it became increasingly vulnerable to external influences: the local clergy, diocesan authorities, different factions of the townspeople.[19] When George Wishardt, the Scottish Protestant radical, was imprisoned for his preaching in 1539, for example, the corporation, which had been under conservative influence, fearing widespread disorder, bowed to local pressure and released him holding sureties for his return.[20]

Although it is unlikely that Edgeworth participated in the crisis of

16 Documents relating to the affair are found in the appendix to J.Foxe, *Acts and Monuments*, ed. G.Townsend, 8 vols. (London, 1841), VII which is unpaginated.
17 Skeeters, 'Bristol Clergy', pp. 36–43.
18 On clerical education and income see Skeeters, op. cit., pp. 147–167; on the conservative reaction after 1533 see Elton, *Policy and Police*, pp. 118–19; Powell, 'Social Background', 107, 110, 114–17; 'The Beginnings of Protestantism in Gloucestershire', *TBGAS*, 90 (1971), 146, 149–51.
19 Skeeters, 'Bristol Clergy', pp. 71, 88–9; cf. Elton, loc. cit.
20 Elton, *Policy and Police*, pp. 119–20; Skeeters, 'Bristol Clergy', pp. 81–8.

1533, he was strongly associated with the conservative clergy and a sermon he preached in defence of purgatory, tentatively dated at early 1537, may have been provoked by the troubles of that year when Latimer once more came under violent personal attack.[21] He was certainly an opponent of the reformer, and his comment in the preface that his preaching at Redcliffe Cross 'was interrupted many yeares by the confederacie of Hugh Lathamer, then aspiringe to a bisshopriche, and after beinge bishop of worcester, and ordinary of the greatest part of the sayd Bristow, and infecting the whole' confirms that seditious preaching after 1533 continued in an unsystematic fashion throughout the diocese.[22] Latimer's 'confederacy' in the 1530s consisted of disciples whom he licensed to evangelise the reformed doctrines such as his chaplain Thomas Bennett and the martyrs-to-be Thomas Garrett and Robert Barnes; they had both been involved in reforming activities in Bristol in the 1520s.[23] These 'light preachers' incurred the hostility of the conservative secular and ecclesiastical forces during the 1530s and there is little indication that the local clergy followed up their proselytising activities.

Edgeworth's sermons may have been constituted evidence of Catholic survival in 1557 but this consisted, as I have indicated, mainly of reaction to the sweeping religious changes which encouraged a popular Protestantism to emerge in Bristol; even basic expositions receive polemical treatment. He upholds the doctrines reasserted in the six Articles of 1539 such as auricular confession, transubstantiation, clerical celibacy; and he rails against the neglect of practices which had become a matter for the individual conscience, such as the Lenten fast. But the collection reveals how much ground had been lost as early as 1537 on issues such as image worship, saints and purgatory, which were disputed in the years following the break with Rome. His fiercest denunciations remain in the realm of complaint; the anticlericalism of the laity in Bristol who make their own interpretations of scripture; the monopoly of trade at the incorporation of the Merchant Venturers Association in 1552; the assaults of Protestant priests on the traditional church services and practices – from which can be discerned the increasingly diminished

21 Ibid., pp. 117–19; pp. 81–8.
22 *Sermons*, sig., +3ᵛ; 'Edgeworth's *Sermons*', II, p. v.
23 On Protestant preaching see Powell, 'Beginnings', pp. 148–9; Elton, *Policy and Police*, pp. 36–7, 121; on Garret and Barnes's early association with Bristol see Skeeters, 'Bristol Clergy', pp. 280–1; on Barnes's moves in 1537 see Lusardi's introduction to Thomas More, *Confutation of Tyndale's Answer*, eds. J. P. Lusardi, R. L. Marius, R. J. Schoeck, L. A. Schuster, *The Yale Edition of the Complete Works of St Thomas More* (New Haven, 1963–), VIII (1973), pp. 1403–4 (cited hereafter as *Confutation*).

role of the conservative clergy in organising and regulating the religious life of the city:[24]

> Here among you in this citie som wil heare masse, some will heare none by theyr good wils, some wil be shriuen, som wil not, but for feare, or els for shame, some wyll pay tithes & offeringes, som wil not, in that wors then the Iewes which paid them truly, and fyrst frutes & many other duties beside. Som wil prai for the dead, som wil not, I heare of muche suche discension among you.[25]

In the last group of three sermons his objections to the liturgical reforms of Edward's reign – the Anglican ordinal and the communion services outlined in the Books of Common Prayer – are more outspoken and these laments effectively constitute a résumé of the devastation of the past twenty years.[26]

Edgeworth's preaching on disputed topics indicates the inherent weakness of the conservative position in Bristol after the 1533 crisis. In his apology for purgatory, preached sometime in 1537, the famous preacher he alludes to who 'did laboure sore to impugne the sayde meane place, saiyinge, that if there were anye such place at all, it is a place of ease, quietnesse, and rest' is probably Latimer.[27] The reformer had renewed his assault on the doctrine in 1536 in an attempt to make the King change his mind on the matter and in his famous sermon to convocation of that year. In the outbreak of seditious preaching in the Worcester diocese in early 1537 he once more became a target for the conservative clergy. But Edgeworth does little to reinforce this attack; the first Henrician formulary of the faith, the Ten Articles, had been passed in July 1536 and the hedging uncertainty of his apology reveals that he was shackled by the ambiguous wording of the tenth article which recommends prayers for the dead with the qualification 'forasmuch as the place where they be, the name thereof and the kinds of pains there, be uncertain to us by scripture'.[28] Describing purgatory as 'the middle or meane place betwixt heaven or hell' and admitting the impossibility of providing scriptural proof for its existence, Edgeworth renames it 'A'. The traditional purgatory, a place of fire, torments and

---

24 See below, pp.00–00, 00–00; on the 'brotherhood of merchants' see *Sermons*, sigs. 3G3–3v; 'Edgeworth's *Sermons*', II, pp. 244–5.

25 Ibid., sig. 3G1ᵛ; II, p. 243.

26 Ibid., sigs. 4H1ᵛ–2; 4I1ᵛ; 4I4ᵛ–K1; II, pp. 355, 359–60, 363–4; see below, pp. 17–18.

27 *Sermons*, sig. F1ᵛ; 'Edgeworth's *Sermons*', II, p. 24.

28 *Formularies of the Faith put forward by Authority in the Reign of Henry VIII*, ed. C. Lloyd (London, 1856), p. 17. See pp xv–xxxii for another slightly different version of the Ten Articles printed by Berthelet in 1536 entitled *Articles devised by the Kynges highness maiestie to stablyshe christen quietnes*.

pains, is now abandoned and instead he merely stresses the danger to the Catholic scheme of salvation of accepting the Protestant purgatory: prayers, good works and penance would be neglected:

> To denye the sayde A. and to say yat there is no such thing, bringeth a man to a carnall libertye, and geueth man occasion boldly to continue in sinne to hys liues ende, trusting then to crye God mercye for his misliuinge, and then to go through (as they speake) I trow they meane to go by and by to heauen, as well as he or she that hath liued in vertue & prayers, paine, and penance all the dayes of their liues.[29]

Paradoxically he seems to concede ground to the Protestants by describing their 'new purgatory'. Within a year of this apology the doctrine had lost its remaining official status. By 1540 the word 'purgatory' had been dropped from the official teaching of the church and in the third Henrician formulary, the *King's Book*, the relevant article is entitled 'Of Prayers for the Souls Departed'.[30]

That the new belief had found some acceptance in Bristol is evident from the use of Protestant terminology in a number of wills of merchants dating from the mid 1530s: references to Mary and the saints as intercessors are replaced by phrases such as 'trusting in the merits of Christ's passion to rest in heaven'.[31] In the 1540s infrequent prosecutions of preachers in the dioceses of Worcester and Gloucester (into which Bristol was absorbed in 1541) who denied the existence of purgatory suggests that the debate continued, but in the *Sermons* purgatory is only referred to subsequently as 'the skyrte of hell'.[32]

Edgeworth's cautious treatment of other topics which were deemed indifferent to salvation by the Ten Articles further suggests that he modified some of his views according to the pressure of public opinion: in Bristol this was probably shaped by Lollard beliefs. Pilgrimages are dismissed:

> An old vse hath peruerted the name of a Pilgryme, because folke were wont to go from place to place to honour saintes in places dedicate for theyr honour, and to kysse theyr images, and they onelye in times past were called Pilgrimes, therefore nowe men

29 *Sermons*, sig. F1; 'Edgeworth's *Sermons*', II, p. 24.
30 *Formularies*, p. 375; on purgatory see further A. Kreider, *English Chantries: the road to Dissolution* (New Haven, 1979), pp. 104–16.
31 See Powell, 'Social background', 117–19; 'Beginnings', 143–4; cf. Palliser's proviso on interpreting material from wills in 'Popular Reactions', pp. 39–40.
32 *Sermons*, sigs. X1, 3K4; 'Edgeworth's *Sermons*', II, pp. 94, 260. Powell, 'Social Background', 110, 115; 'Beginnings', 149–51.

thinke the proper signification of this worde Pilgrime to be none other but such as goeth about such deuocions, but his significacion is more generall, it signifieth a wayfaringe man or woman ...[33]

The saints are referred to once as 'the gloryous companye of heauen', but the habit of relying on them and on the Blessed Virgin as intercessors is criticised as 'a certayne vehemencie in desiring as it wer for Gods sake, or for the loue of our Lady, or of al the sayntes of heauen, or for their faithes sake, by which thei trusted to be saued'.[34] The popular confusion over image veneration which prevailed at the time of the monastic dissolutions in Bristol from 1538 to 1540 is criticised in another sermon; his target is those townspeople who gave their children the images cast out of monasteries and friaries, wrongly calling them idols. Insistent that Protestant lay preachers have perpetrated this misconception, Edgeworth attempts to correct it merely by differentiating an image (representing a true god) from an idol (representing a false god).[35]

The rest of this paper will examine the contents of the *Sermons*, specifically Edgeworth's preaching techniques, his attitude to lay reading of the scriptures and the Protestant bibles and his defence of doctrines which remained unchanged under Henry. The two sermons dealing with purgatory and images occur in a series of six on the seven gifts of the Holy Ghost preached at Redcliffe Cross in Bristol between 1535 and 1542. The bulk of the collection, however, consists of a sequence of twenty sermons on the First Epistle of St Peter which was preached in Bristol Cathedral from c. 1542–c. 1553. Two sermons on the creed and ceremonies which also exist in MS Bodl. Rawl. D. 831 may have circulated separately as expositions of the faith during Mary's reign.[36]

In most aspects of structure, treatment of theme and scriptural exegesis the collection reveals the influence of the humanism which Edgeworth would have encountered at Oxford and which paradoxically brings him closer to his Protestant opponents than to his Catholic allies.[37] Like Latimer he follows the 'old' method of preaching: he presents a theme or topic under simple headings such as the seven gifts

33 Ibid., sig. 2V4ᵛ; II, p. 200.
34 Ibid., sig. 2V3ᵛ; II, p. 199.
35 Ibid., sigs. K4ᵛ–L2; II, p. 46–8.
36 'De Ceremoniis Traditionibus', fos. 1–6; 'De Articulo Fidei', fos. 7–16ᵛ. Both are signed by Edgeworth; the second is holograph. They are tentatively dated between 1550–60. See 'Edgeworth's *Sermons*', I, pp. 9–13 for a discussion; II, pp. 82–113 for the texts which are printed facing the 1557 versions.
37 J. W. Blench, *Preaching in England in the Late Fifteenth and Sixteenth Centuries* (Oxford, 1964), pp. 73–8, 87–94 finds evidence of the 'ancient' style in Catholic and Protestant sermons after 1535.

of the Holy Ghost and he expounds the First Epistle of St Peter *secundum ordinem textus*.[38] In the first sermon of this series he follows Colet's historico-critical method of exposition by introducing geographical and historical material relevant to the epistle.[39] This humanist bias is also apparent in his use of Erasmus's *Novum Instrumentum* and *Annotationes*, in his preference for the literal rather than the four-fold method of scriptural interpretation and in his avoidance of the *distinctio*. The fashion for this kind of preaching is attributable to Colet's influential lectures on the Pauline Epistles at Oxford in 1498 and to his followers like Grocyn, who lectured on the supposed works of Dionysius the Areopagite at St Paul's and Oxford, or the Protestant George Stafford from Pembroke College, Cambridge who in 1525 adopted the literal approach in his New Testament lectures in preference to using the *Sentences* of Peter Lombard. There is reason to believe that continuous exposition of a book of the New Testament was unofficially offered as an alternative to the *Sentences* as part of the requirement for the D.Th at Oxford when Edgeworth was there.[40]

The application of humanist methods, however, does not mean that Edgeworth embraced in a thorough-going manner humanist principles with respect to biblical translation. When encountering the laity reading the newly available vernacular bibles, he maintains the orthodox ecclesiastical policy propagated by Thomas More in the 1520s. As a port town, Bristol was a traditional centre for receiving and disseminating heretical literature, and in the 1520s, it has been suggested, Lollard and Lutheran groups may have become part of a reform movement based round the activities of a Bristol bookseller, Richard Webb.[41] On examining Webb when he was Chancellor, More commented that heretical books were so freely available in Bristol that they were 'throwen in the strete & lefte at mennys dores by nyght, that where they durste not offer theyr poysen to sell, they wolde of theyr cheryte poysen men for nought'.[42]

---

38 He describes his method in the preface: '...when I shoulde preache oftentimes in one place, I vsed not to take euery day a distinct epistle or gospell, or other text, but to take some proces of scripture, and to prosecute the same, part one day, and parte another daye, ...' *Sermons*, sig. +3ᵛ; 'Edgeworth's *Sermons*', II, p. v.

39 Ibid., sigs. 2D1–E3; II, pp. 121–8.

40 See Blench, *Preaching in England*, pp. 29–31; 'Edgeworth's *Sermons*', I, pp. 50, 55–6 on the humanists' influence; S. L. Greenslade, 'The Faculty of Theology' in *The History of the University of Oxford*, Vol. III: *The Collegiate University*, ed. J. McConica (Oxford, 1986), pp. 297, 308 on the statutes of 1564–5.

41 Skeeters, 'Bristol Clergy', pp. 279–82; Powell, 'Social Background', 109.

42 More, *Confutation*, p. 812; cited by Skeeters, op. cit., p. 282; Powell, 'Beginnings', 142–3. This incident probably occurred early during More's tenure as Chancellor (26 October 1529 – 16 May 1532).

In the fourth sermon on the gift of science of c. 1538–9 Edgeworth complains of 'those that so arrogantly glorieth in their learnynge had by study in the englysh bible, and in these sedicious Englisshe bokes that haue bene sent ouer from our englyssh runagates nowe abidynge wyth Luther in Saxonie.'[43] A recurrent theme is the dangers of unsupervised reading of the scriptures. This, he claims, causes:

> enuie, & disdainyng at others, mockynge and despisynge all goodnes, raylynge at fastynge and at abstinence from certaine meats one daie afore an other, by custome or commaundemente of the churche, at Masse and mattens, and at all blessed ceremonies of Christes church…[44]

The practice also contributes to the decline of trade: 'I haue knowen manye in this towne, that studienge diuinitie, hath kylled a marchaunt, and some of other occupations by theyr busy labours in the scriptures, hath shut vp the shoppe windowes, faine to take Sainctuary'.[45] His strongest objection, however, is to the anticlericalism of the 'pseudapostles' or 'leude gospellars' who usurp the authority of the priest:

> Of all suche greene Diuines…it appeareth full wel what learnynge they haue, by thys, that when they teache anye of their Disciples, and when they gyue anye of theyr bookes to other menne to reade the fyrste suggestion why he shoulde laboure suche bookes, is because by this (say they) thou shalt be able to oppose the best priest in the parish, and to tel him he lieth.[46]

Like More he believed that independent reading of difficult passages, made without the guidance of a theologically trained clergy, leads to heresy:

> The wordes of God in scripture which afore were hard, by the exercise and labour of catholike clerkes be made very softe, yea more softe, easye, and soople then oile, and be made harnes and dartes, or weapons for the preachers. Of the hardnes of scriptures (in which our new diuines finde no hardnesse) riseth al heresies.[47]

It was because of his disagreement on this very point – that the church

---

43 *Sermons*, sig. H3ᵛ; 'Edgeworth's *Sermons*, II, p. 36.

44 Ibid.; see the proclamation of April 1539 restricting reading of the bible in *Tudor Royal Proclamations*, ed. P. L. Hughes and J. F. Larkin, 3 vols. (New Haven, 1964), I, *The Early Tudors* (1485–1553); II, *The Later Tudors* (1553–1587), I, 191 (cited hereafter as Hughes and Larkin).

45 *Sermons*, sig. L3ᵛ; 'Edgeworth's *Sermons*', II, pp. 49–50.

46 Ibid., sigs. I4–4ᵛ; II, p. 41.

47 Ibid., sigs. K1ᵛ–2; II, p. 43.

has an intermediary role for the laity – that the Protestant translator of Matthews Bible, John Rogers, was sent to the stake in 1555.[48]

The phenomenon of women preachers who undertake to teach and reform their menfolk may have originated in Lollard practice.[49] Edgeworth's stand is based on the appeal to the traditional theory of female subjection for which he finds precedent in the New Testament (ignoring the examples of prophetesses in both Testaments which the Lollards used to justify the existence of women preachers).[50] Principally he objects to the challenge to the social hierarchy of authority and hence his educated, priestly authority which they represent. He says:

> S. Paule ... woulde that a woman if she wold learne anye thing for her soule health, she should aske of her husbande at home, that he may teach her if he be so well learned, or that he maye aske of them that be learned, and so teache his wyfe, least peraduenture if women shoulde haue resorte vnto learned men, to reason matters, or to aske questions for their learnynge, by ouermuche familyarity some further inconuenience might mischaunce to bothe parties .... For I will not suffer a woman to be a teacher, least peraduenture taking vpon her to be a maistres she may wexe proude and malaperte. She must consider her creation, that a woman was last made, and first in faulte and in sinne. Wherfore it besemeth women to knowe their condicion & to be subiect, and not to refourme and teache menne.[51]

Although Edgeworth implicitly criticises Erasmus's belief in the self-instruction of the laity expounded in his famous treatise *Paraclesis* (the English translation of which he almost certainly knew), nevertheless he shares the view held by Thomas More and contemporaries such as William Barlow (in his anti-Lutheran phase) in his 1531 treatise *A dialogue describing the original ground of these Lutheran factions and many of their abuses*, and John Standish in his Marian treatise, *A Discourse wherein is debated whether it be expedient that the scriptures shold be in English for all men to read that will,*

48 A. G. Dickens, *The English Reformation* (London, 1964), p. 132.
49 See M. Aston, 'Lollard Woman Priests?' in *Lollards and Reformers* (London, 1984), pp. 49–70; John Yonge, a Bristol man examined for heresy in 1448, held that preaching was allowed except by women; see Thomson, *Later Lollards*, p. 37; *Register of Thomas Beckynton, Bishop of Bath and Wells*, i, ed. H. C. Maxwell-Lyte and M. C. B. Dawes, *Somerset Record Society*, 49 (1934), p. 122. Women were listed as unsuitable to read the scriptures in the proclamation of 1543; see *Statutes of the Realm* (1817), III, p. 896.
50 Aston, 'Lollard Women Priests?', pp. 55–6; this view was also held by the humanist Juan Luis Vives; see *Vives and the Renascence Education of Women*, ed. Foster Watson (London, 1912), pp. 55–6.
51 *Sermons*, sigs. I2–2ᵛ; 'Edgeworth's *Sermons*', II, p. 39.

that the scriptures should, in theory, be made available in the vernacular.[52] He says:

> I haue euer bene of this minde, that I haue thought it no harme, but rather good and profitable that holie Scripture shoulde be hadde in the mother tong, and with holden from no manne that were apte and mete to take it in hande, specially if we coulde get it well and truely translated, whyche wyll be verye harde to be hadde. But who be meete and able to take it in hande, there is the doubte.[53]

The official sanction given to the Protestant bibles by the Henrician church – the Great Bible was ordered to be placed into every church of the realm in 1538 – was the most far reaching victory enjoyed by the new faith. Like most of his party Edgeworth at first refused to concede defeat in this area; he made his own translations of the scriptures and criticised the inaccuracy of the vernacular bibles. The translation of *imago* as 'idol', for example, provoked what became a standard Catholic complaint, that by this means the Protestants have bought the people into heresy.

> They would haue that this latine worde *Imago* signifieth an Idole, and so these new translations of the english bibles hath it in all places, where the translatours would bring men to beleue that to set vp Images, or to haue Images is idolatrye.[54]

As in his defence of purgatory, however, Edgeworth's challenge to the Protestant 'mistranslations' remains in the realm of debate and would hardly have discredited the newly acquired authority of the disputed words. In discussing the Reformers' translation of *pietas* by 'godliness', for example, he ranges over the meanings of the vernacular 'piety': 'mercy, pity, compassion' (for the terms 'piety' and 'pity' were not differentiated until the end of the sixteenth century). Then, turning to *latria* and its alternative *religio*, he arrives at a definition which is close to the modern sense of 'piety': 'the true worshippynge of GOD, or the inwarde habite, ... by which, a manne or a woman hauing it, is inclined to goodnesse, and made well disposed, ... to serue GOD, and to do hym worshippe'.[55] Yet there is no indication that this was ever accepted. In dealing with the disputed text I Pet. 5:1: 'Seniores ergo qui in vobis sunt

---

52 See T. More, *The Apology*, ed. J. B. Trapp, *The Complete Works* (New Haven, 1979), IX, p. 13; Barlow's treatise was reprinted in 1553 by Caly after the bishop had abjured his Protestantism (STC 1462); Standish subtitled his discourse as 'A question to be moved to the hyghe courte of Parliament' but there is no indication that this was ever done. (STC 23207–8).

53 *Sermons*, sig. H4; 'Edgeworth's *Sermons*', II, p. 37.

54 Ibid., sig. K4ᵛ; II, p. 46.

55 Ibid., sig. M2; II, p. 53; the following discussion is largely drawn from 'Edgeworth's *Sermons*', I, pp. 147–50.

obsecro senior' (AV: 'The elders who are among you, I exhort who am also an elder') he draws on the same argument that Thomas More had used to refute Tyndale's translation of the Greek *presbyteros* by 'senior' or 'elder'. Tyndale had intended to subvert the visible church and the priesthood by claiming that the priest is nothing but an officer to teach and not to be a mediator between God and man. Edgeworth points out that 'elder' implying merely age lacks the connotation of authority conveyed by *presbyteros* and he stresses the principle of election which is at the heart of the Catholic doctrine of orders. 'Albeit euery olde man, or auncient man is not a Prieste, but onely suche as by prophecye, or election or imposition of a prelates hande is piked out & chosen'. But this position is undermined by his use of Tyndale's translation, 'these seignours or elders that we call priests', which had appeared in all the Protestant bibles except Taverner's Bible of 1539.[56] These debatable words – *episcopus, religio, idolum, pietas, presbyteros, senior* – appear on the list of ninety words which Stephen Gardiner hoped to retain in their original or have englished with as little change as possible. They were presented to convocation in 1542 when errors of translation in the Great Bible came to be corrected and Edgeworth's discussions in sermons dating around this time indicate the essential agreement which existed among members of his party on this issue.[57]

It is therefore at first surprising that Edgeworth apparently accepts other translations which More had deemed controversial: for example he nowhere makes reference to the famous Tyndale/More dispute over the translation of *caritas* by 'love' instead of 'charity': he settles for the phrase 'love and charity'.[58] Tyndale's translation of *ecclesia* by 'congregation' instead of 'church', to which More had also objected, appears in the doublet 'congregation or church' confirming that acceptance of this word had been virtually guaranteed by its appearance in the Great Bible.[59] And he seems to have silently adopted the Lutheran translation of 'overseers' for *episcopi* instead of 'bishops' because the Henrician formularies had used 'overseers and superattendants'.[60]

56 *Sermons*, sig. 4B2; 'Edgeworth's *Sermons*', II, p. 328; see Tyndale, *An Answer unto Sir Thomas More's Dialogue called The Supper of the Lord*, ed. H. Walter, Parker Society (Cambridge, 1850), pp. 16–17; More, *A Dialogue Concerning Heresies*, eds. T. M. Lawlor, G. Marc'hadour, R. C. Marius, *The Complete Works of St Thomas More* (New Haven, 1981), VI, pp. 286, 289–90 (cited hereafter as *Dialogue*); *Confutation*, pp. 182–9.

57 The full list is printed in Wilkins, *Concilia*, IV, p. 861.

58 More, *Dialogue*, pp. 286–9; *Confutation*, pp. 199–203; N. Davis, *William Tyndale's English of Controversy*, Chambers Memorial Lecture (London, 1971), pp. 6–8.

59 'Congregation' appears seventeen times in the *Sermons* of which thirteen occurrences are alternatives to 'church'.

60 W. Tyndale, *Obedience of a Christian Man* in *Doctrinal Treatises*, ed. H. Walter,

These choices reinforce the impression that, despite the conservative reaction, the use of authorised Protestant bibles effectively undercut the Catholic defence of a decade earlier.

Yet in dealing with doctrines upheld in the Six Articles, Edgeworth remains steadfast: he strongly defends clerical celibacy, transubstantiation, the Catholic teaching on confession and baptism and other threatened beliefs such as the incarnation. Denial of transubstantiation was a tenet of the Bristol Lollards in 1510–11 and the Protestant assault on the doctrine gathered momentum in 1547.[61] In the *Sermons* it appears in the form of a challenge to the clergy's traditional powers as a consecrating and sacrificing ministry: but he retaliates with simple exposition rather than theological argument.

> ... so manye miscreauntes and misbeleuers so little regarde the blessed and mooste reuerende Sacramente of the Aultare, and also the Sacramentall confession of synnes vnto a Prieste, as thoughe Christe were not able by his Godlye power to make of breade and wine, his owne fleshe and bloude, and to geue power to a priest by his wordes to dooe the same likewise, Or as thoughe GOD were not able by his officer to deliuer men from the prison and bondage of their synnes.[62]

The anticlericalism of the late 1530s is replaced by an antisacramental feeling as the Protestant challenge to conservative authority degenerates from debate to acrimonious abuse of Catholic priests and heckling of those devout who attend Catholic services and follow the traditional observances. They are derisively nicknamed 'hipocrites, and folish phariseis', or 'Pope holye horeson' by Protestants who with 'their babling in the church, and mocking of diuine seruice letteth and

---

Parker Society (Cambridge, 1848), pp. 279–80; More, *Confutation*, p. 187. See *Formularies*, pp. 109, 287; *episcopi* is also translated as 'overseers' in the Anglican ordinal of 1550; see *The Two Books of Common Prayer set forth by the authority of Parliament in the reign of Edward VI*, ed. E. Cardwell (2nd edn, Oxford, 1841), pp. 408–9.

61 Thomson, *Later Lollards*, pp. 46–7; measures were taken to enforce uniformity before the *Order of Communion* was issued in Lent 1548: a 'Proclamation concerning Irreverent Talkers of the Sacrament' (27 December 1547); an 'Act against revilers of the Sacrament and for Communion in Both Kinds' (16 January 1548). See *Documentary Annals of the Reformed Church in England 1546–1716*, ed. E. Cardwell, 2 vols. (Oxford, 1844), I, no. V; Hughes and Larkin, I, 296; F. J. Clark, *Eucharistic Sacrifice and the Reformation* (2nd edn., London, 1963), pp. 100, 536–7; C. W. Dugmore, *The Mass and the English Reformers* (London, 1958), p. 116.

62 *Sermons*, sig. 2RI'; 'Edgeworth's *Sermons*', II, p. 183.

hindreth other men from theyr praiers, and from attending and hearing gods seruice'.[63]

> If a man abstaine from whitemeate this holye time of Lente, you will call him hypocrite, and dawe fole, and so rap at him, and strike him with youre venemous tongues, and vse him as an abiecte, excludynge him out of your companie.[64]

Two sermons on disputed texts in the series on St Peter's First Epistle provide Catholic teaching on the sacrament of orders in refutation of Tyndale's doctrine of a 'priesthood of all believers'. In the seventh sermon Edgeworth distinguishes a spiritual priesthood won by baptism and self sacrifice, a 'generall laye presthoode', from 'the order of presthode, farre aboue the foresayd lay priesthoode in dignitie and in authoritie'.[65] But in the eighteenth sermon, preached after the Anglican ordinal of 1550, exposition of the traditional role and duties of the priesthood is interwoven with a description of the new clergy, largely recruited from the artisan classes, which challenges the conservative hierarchy: 'these leude ministers be made nowe a dayes of shoemakers, smithes, coblers, and clouters, as well maryed as single'.[66] He implies that the status of the calling has degenerated by this influx of married priests with 'theyr shameful and incestious bawdry, which they would couer wyth the name of matrimony, so by them sclaundring that holy sacrament'.[67] Their swift conversion from their secular vocations has meant a reluctance to abandon their former materialistic pursuits, in particular for what he terms *vere turpe lucrum*, 'filthy or vnhonest gaines'.

> So a priest that hath refused worldly trouble & toyling, and giuen him selfe onelye to the seruice of God, may not with his honesty (yea but with his shame) giue him selfe to worldly cheuesance, marchandise, chopping and changing, byeng good chepe, selling deare.[68]

Moral decline is matched by the financial impoverishment of the Edwardian clergy (many of whom lacked benefices) as is apparent, for example, in the competition to preach endowed sermons.

> And some there be that maketh a marchaundise of the worde of God, vsinge their preaching & teaching all for lucre & aduauntage, *Turpiter affectantes lucrum*, vnhonestly, gredy & hongrie for money & lucre, thinking all that lost that goeth beside their berdes, or that

63 Ibid., sigs. 3Z1ᵛ; 3N4ᵛ; 2V1; II, pp. 318, 275, 196.
64 Ibid., sig. 3I2ᵛ; II, p. 254.
65 Ibid., sig. 2V1–1ᵛ; II, pp. 195–6.
66 Ibid., sig. 4A4; II, p. 326.
67 Ibid., sig. 4E3; II, p. 343.
68 Ibid., sig. 4D1; II, p. 336.

they cannot get, it greeueth them that any men should open theyr mouthes in a pulpet but them selues, that so they might gather in their sermon nobles.[69]

Edgeworth's views on the sacraments and on the powers of bishops and priests are known from the answers he gave in 1540 to Cranmer's questionnaire, when he served on a commission to discuss doctrine preparatory to the third Henrician formulary, the *King's Book*.[70] But although he draws from the formulary for his teaching on orders and the ministry, the image of an ideal Catholic priesthood is outmoded by the social reality of an ill educated but vociferous and highly active clergy, drawn from the lay professions, whose energies are unleashed to attack and ridicule the old order:

> ... if a preist saye his mattens and euensonge, with other diuine seruice dayly, according to his bounden dutye, he shall be mocked and iested at, yea and not onelye of lighte braynes of the layfe, but also of men of oure owne cote and profession, leude and folyshe preistes, that nother serue God deuoutly, nor the world iustely nor diligently, but geue them selues to walkinge the stretes, and beatinge the bulkes with theyr heeles, clatteringe lighte and leude matters, full vnseminge for theyr profession, and some of them more geuen to reading these folishe englishe bokes full of heresies, then anye true expositours of holy scriptures.[71]

This picture of the deteriorating status and the functions of the clergy emerging from the sermons preached in the final years of Edward's reign is supported by the figures: by the late 1550s Bristol parish livings fell vacant for periods spanning six to twenty six years; the parishes were served instead by untenured stipendiary curates who were paid by the parishioners and who, unlike the clergy they replaced, were poorly educated.[72] Is Edgeworth then to be seen as a lone voice declaiming

---

69 Ibid., sigs. 4D1ᵛ–2; II, p. 337; on endowed sermons see Skeeters, 'Bristol Clergy', pp. 134–6, Powell, 'Social Background', 109.

70 The questions and the commissioners' answers exist in MS Lambeth Stillingfleet 16, fos. 69–143; they are printed in G. Burnet's *History of the Reformation in England*, ed. N. Pocock, 7 vols. (London, 1865), IV, Collection III, no. 21, pp. 443–96; Edgeworth's answers are analysed by E. C. Messenger, *The Reformation, the Mass and the Priesthood*, 2 vols. (London, 1936–7), I, pp. 278–91; F. van le Baumer, *The early Tudor Theory of Kingship* (1940, repr., New York, 1966), pp. 79–83; 'Edgeworth's *Sermons*', pp. 118–123.

71 *Sermons*, sig. 3Z1ᵛ; 'Edgeworth's *Sermons*', II, p. 318.

72 Skeeters, 'Bristol Clergy', pp. 147–51; that clerical poverty became widespread is pointed out by R. H. Pogson in 'Revival and Reform in Mary's Tudor Church: A Question of Money', *Journal of Ecclesiastical History*, XXV, 3 (1974), 251–2; see also F. Heal, 'The Economic Problems of the Clergy' in *Church and Society*, especially pp. 108–13.

against the abuses of the old religion which he witnesses and interprets as a policy of attrition on the part of the Protestant preachers?

As the *Sermons* reveal many of his views were susceptible to local and national pressure and it is undoubtedly this capacity to modify them, even to conform, that ensured his survival through to Mary's reign. As a member of the clerical élite in Bristol he further protected his position by fostering links with other members of the professional cathedral clergy who became powerful in the diocese under Edward and Mary.[73] Catholic survival in these cases was due to political prudence rather than tenacious committment to a system of belief. In his defensive preaching, therefore, there is continuity but predictably little development of the arguments in favour of the church that More had used, and to this extent the *Sermons* make little contribution to the literature of Reformation debate.

Yet an unexpected legacy of Edgeworth's essentially embattled position is the vitality of much of his preaching particularly when lamenting the religious changes and in appealing to his Bristol audience to ignore them. In this respect he has been ranked as a kind of Catholic counterpart to Latimer: his lively colloquial style using vivid images, epithets and idioms of popular speech and a wide variety of proverbial sayings drawn from both literary and colloquial sources, is distinctive.[74] It is perhaps not surprising that common features of style as well as structure should be discernible in both Catholic and Protestant sermons dating from this period because, as Professor Norman Davis has demonstrated, both sides preached 'a language of controversy'.[75] But it is finally striking that homilies demonstrating Catholic survival, which are *a priori* limited in the defence they can provide, should be memorable mainly for their literary qualities: their innovative language and varieties of style. This suggests that in Bristol as elsewhere, Reformation conflict, while symptomatic of profound social change, succeeded in bringing the spoken language to a new level of literary expressiveness.

---

73 Skeeters, 'Bristol Clergy', pp. 234–7, 242–9; 'Edgeworth's *Sermons*', I, pp. 98–9.
74 Blench, *Preaching in England*, pp. 121–6; 'Edgeworth's *Sermons*', I, pp. 170–7.
75 *William Tyndale's English of Controversy*, pp. 3, 19–21.

Plate 1 Miniature portrait of Pierre Sala attributed to Jean Perréal, with inscription in mirror writing. British Library, Stowe MS 955, fos. 16b–17

Plate 2 Emblematic portrait of Louis de Chandio. Paris, Bibliothéque nationale, MS fr 1194, fos. 6b–7

Plate 4 Medallion portrait of Charles V added to the
Hours of Bona Sforza by the Horenbout workshop in 1520.
British Library, Add. MS 34294, fol. 213

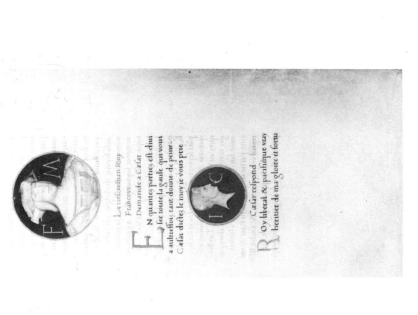

Plate 3 Circular portraits of Francis I and Julius Caesar,
in vol. I of *Les Commentaires de la guerre gallique*, 1519.
British Library, Harley MS 6205, fol. 3

Plate 5 Henry VIII,
by Lucas Horenbout.
By courtesy of the Syndics of the
Fitzwilliam Museum, Cambridge

Plate 6 Margaret of Austria in the character of St Elizabeth. Enlarged detail
from the Hours of Bona Sforza. British Library, Add. MS 34294, fol. 61

Plate 8 Border decoration by the Milanese artist of the Hours of Bona Sforza. British Library, Add. MS 34294, fol. 76

Plate 7 Border decoration by the Milanese artist of the Hours of Bona Sforza. British Library, Add. MS 34294, fol. 109b

Plate 10 Unknown man, 1572,
by Nicholas Hilliard. *By courtesy
of the Syndics of the Fitzwilliam Museum, Cambridge*

Plate 9 Circular portrait of Henry VIII incorporated into the
decoration of a charter dated 1524. *By courtesy of Messrs Sotheby's*

Plate 12 Unknown lady, aged 32. San Marino, the
Henry Huntington Library, HM 1727, fol. 1

Plate 11 Katharine of Aragon
with her pet marmoset,
by Lucas Horenbout.
*By courtesy of the Duke of Buccleuch
and Queensberry, KT*

Plate 13 The lost prayerbook of Elizabeth I, showing miniature portraits of the Queen and the Duke of Anjou by Nicholas Hilliard, about 1581. British Library, MS Facs. 218

Plate 14 Portrait of Henry VIII in the Croke girdle book. British Library, Stowe MS 956, fol. 1b

Plate 1 Beverley Minster. Putting the cart before the horse

Plate 2 Beverley Minster – Woman beating man

Plate 3 Bristol Cathedral – Woman beating man

Plate 4 Master bxg – Woman carted off in three-wheeled barrow

Plate 5 Durham Castle Chapel – Woman carted off in wheelbarrow

Plate 6 Westminster Abbey – Woman beating man with distaff

Plate 7 Westminster Abbey – Woman beating man's bare bottom

Plate 8 Israhel van Meckenem – Woman beating man with distaff

Plate 9 Erhard Schön – Woman beating man's bare bottom

Plate 10 Bristol Cathedral – Man on sow and woman on goose charging
against each other

Plate 11 Westminster Abbey – Mercenary love

Plate 12 Albrecht Dürer – Mercenary love

Plate 13 Westminster Abbey – A family of apes

Plate 14 Israhel van Meckenem – A family of apes

Plate 15 Beverley Minster – Fools dancing

Plate 16 Israhel van Meckenem – Men and fool dancing round a woman

Plate 17 Beverley Minster – Fool making faces

Plate 18 Arnt van Tricht – Towel-rail; Woman embraced by fool

Plate 19 Beverley Minster – Monkey playing the bagpies on a dog

Plate 1 The Ashwellthorpe Triptych, general view, open

Plate 2 The Ashwellthorpe Triptych, central panel. The Seven Sorrows
of the Virgin

Plate 3 The Ashwellthorpe
Triptych, left panel. Christopher
Knyvett with St Christopher

Plate 4 The Ashwellthorpe
Triptych, right panel. Catherine (?)
van Assche with St Catherine

Plate 5 The Ashwellthorpe Triptych, general view, closed. St John the
Evangelist and St Barbara

Plate 6 The Ashwellthorpe
Triptych, left wing. The arms of
Christopher Knyvett

Plate 7 The Ashwellthorpe
Triptych, right wing. The arms of
Catherine (?) van Assche

Plate 8 New Buckenham Church. Arms above west door (left side)

Plate 9 New Buckenham Church. Arms above west door (right side)

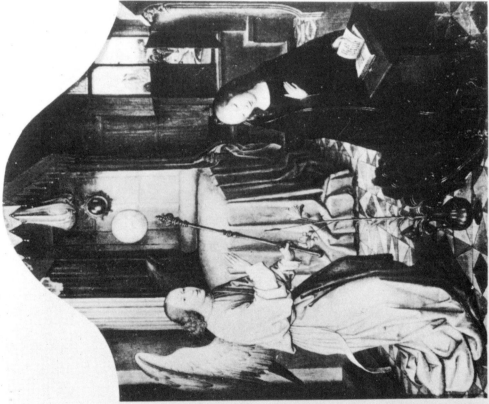

Plate 10 The Magdalen Master. Triptych of the Annunciation. Brussels, Musées Royaux

Plate 11 The Ashwellthorpe Triptych, left wing. Detail of Christchild

Plate 12 The Ashwellthorpe Triptych, right wing. Head of Catherine (?)
van Assche

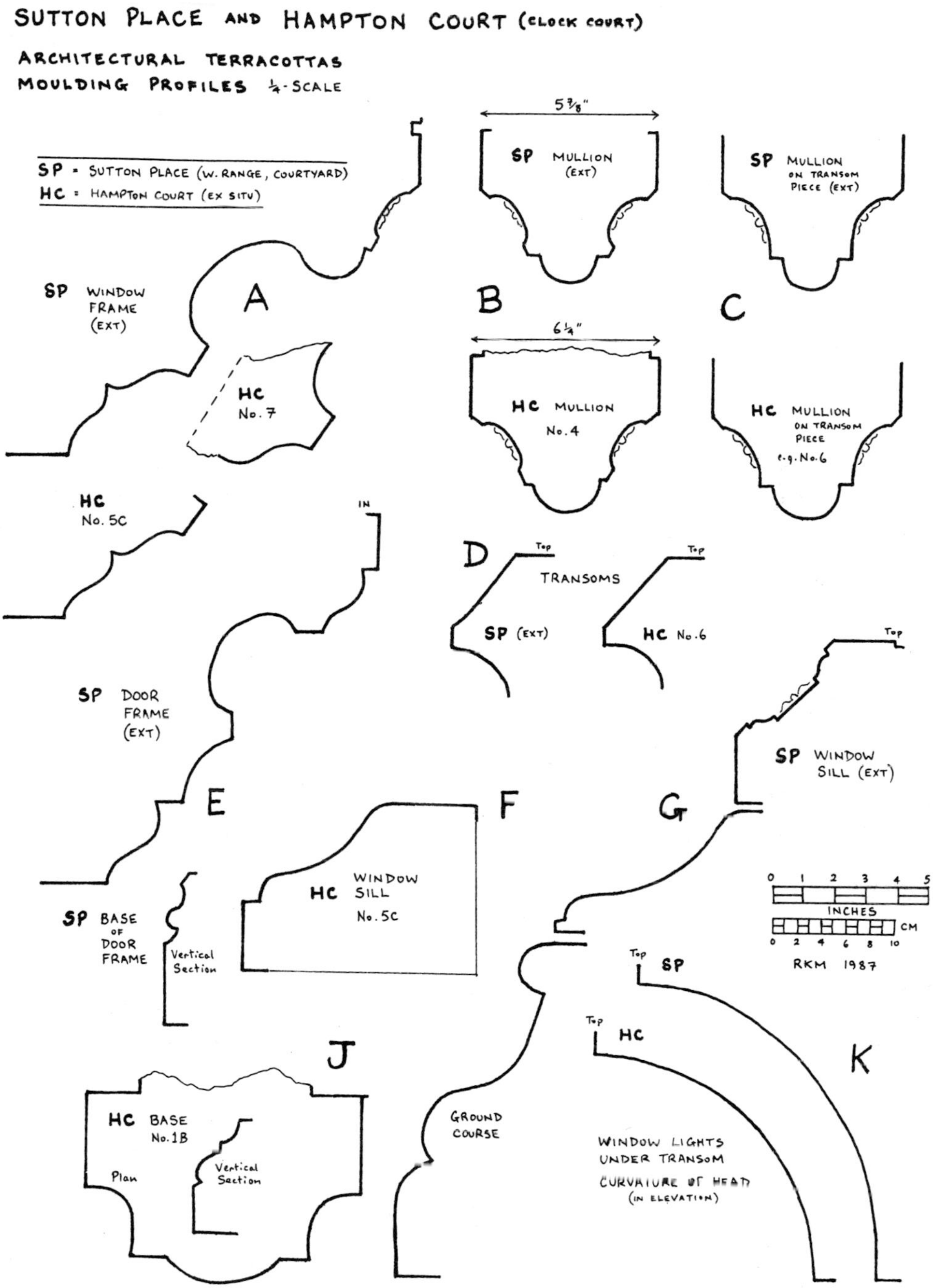

SUTTON PLACE AND HAMPTON COURT (CLOCK COURT)

ARCHITECTURAL TERRACOTTAS
MOULDING PROFILES ¼-SCALE

SP = SUTTON PLACE (W. RANGE, COURTYARD)
HC = HAMPTON COURT (EX SITU)

SP WINDOW FRAME (EXT)

A

5⅜"

SP MULLION (EXT)

B

SP MULLION ON TRANSOM PIECE (EXT)

C

HC No. 7

6¼"

HC MULLION No. 4

HC MULLION ON TRANSOM PIECE e.g. No. 6

HC No. 5C

IN

D

TRANSOMS

Top   Top

SP (EXT)   HC No. 6

Top

SP DOOR FRAME (EXT)

E

F

G

SP WINDOW SILL (EXT)

SP BASE OF DOOR FRAME

Vertical Section

WINDOW SILL No. 5C

HC

0 1 2 3 4 5
INCHES
0 2 4 6 8 10 CM

Top SP

RKM 1987

J

HC BASE No. 1B

Plan   Vertical Section

GROUND COURSE

Top HC

K

WINDOW LIGHTS UNDER TRANSOM
CURVATURE OF HEAD (IN ELEVATION)

Plate 1 Sutton Place and Hampton Court: moulding profiles (terracotta)

Plate 2 Sutton Place: terracotta
window mullion (courtyard, east side)

Plate 3 Hampton Court: terracotta
pieces from Clock Court excavations,
1976 (mullion no. 4 reconstructed
on base no. 1 B

Plate 4 Sutton Place: terracotta window sill (courtyard, east side)

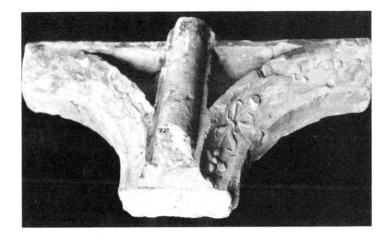

Plate 5 Hampton Court: terracotta window head from Clock Court
excavations, 1976

Plate 6 Sutton Place: terracotta window frame and window head beneath
transom (courtyard, east side)

Plate 7 Broughton Castle: Queen Anne Bedroom, north window, sill (detail)

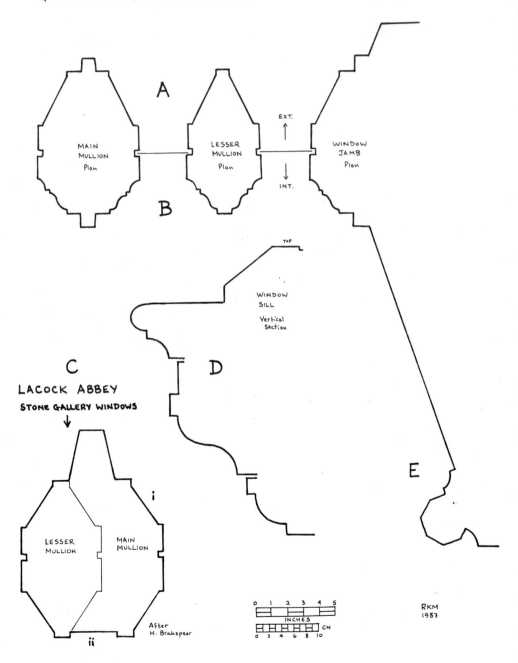

BROUGHTON CASTLE (OXFORDSHIRE)
QUEEN ANNE'S BEDROOM : N. WINDOW

A

EXT.
INT.

MAIN
MULLION
Plan

LESSER
MULLION
Plan

WINDOW
JAMB
Plan

B

TOP

WINDOW
SILL
Vertical
Section

C

D

LACOCK ABBEY

STONE GALLERY WINDOWS

E

LESSER
MULLION

MAIN
MULLION

i

ii

After
H. Brakspear

0 1 2 3 4 5
INCHES
0 2 4 6 8 10 CM

RKM
1987

Plate 8 Broughton Castle and Lacock Abbey: moulding profiles (stone)

Plate 9 Lacock Abbey: the Brown Gallery, window (south side)

Plate 10 Blois, the Château: the Francis I wing, first floor window (courtyard elevation)

Plate 11 Longleat House: bay window, ground floor level (south front)

Portrait of Denzill Holles. National Portrait Gallery

Plate 1 The Virgin and Female Martyrs, English, late fifteenth or early
sixteenth century. Alabaster relief, set in wood frame, 20½in. h. 14½in. w.
Mead Art Museum, Amherst College, gift of George B. Perry in memory of
his son, Gordon B. Perry, 1955. 1960.8

Plate 2 St John the Baptist and Prophets, English fifteenth century.
Alabaster relief, 16½in. h. 10in. w. Fogg Art Museum, Cambridge, Mass.
Courtesy of the Harvard University Art Museums (Fogg Art Museum), gift of
Mr and Mrs George Sarton. 1943.3

Plate 3 Christ in Majesty, English, early twelfth century. Wall painting on
ceiling of chancel, Church of St Mary, Kempley, Glos. Courtesy of the
Royal Commission on the Historical Monuments of England

Plate 4 Sacrament of the Holy Mass, German, fifteenth century.
Biblia Pauperum, fol. 94v, MS lat.8201, Munich,
Bayerische Staatsbibliothek. Courtesy of the Bayerische Staatsbibliothek

Plate 1 Hans Holbein: The Ambassadors, 1533, National Gallery, London

Plate 2 Hans Holbein: The Ambassadors, 1533, National Gallery, London.
Detail showing the Star of David on the floor behind the skull

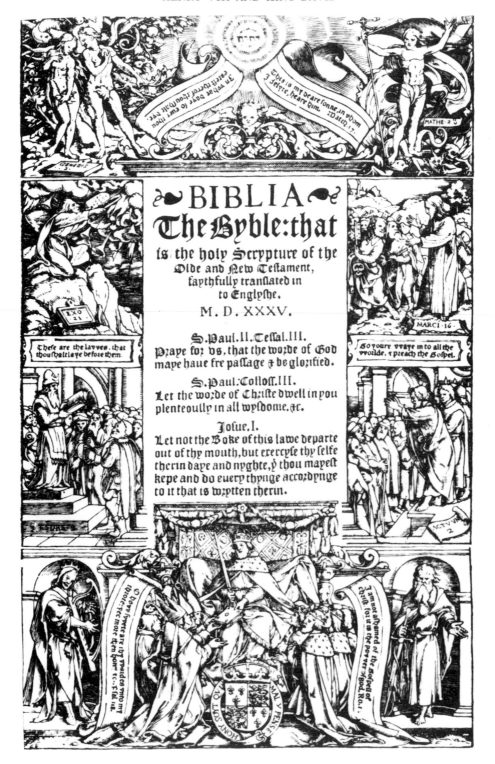

Plate 3 Title page of Coverdale's Bible, 1535

Plate 4 Title page of Thomas Cranmer's Bible, 1539

Plate 5 Psalter of Henry VIII, 1540, BM Royal 2A XVI, fol. 3. Henry VIII as
'Beatus Vir'

Plate 6 Psalter of Henry VIII, 1540, BM Royal 2A XVI, fol. 30. Henry VIII
as King David killing Goliath

Plate 7 Henry VIII's reading desk, Victoria & Albert Museum. Detail of lid

Plate 8 Psalter of Henry VIII, 1540, BM Royal 2A XVI, fol. 79. Henry VIII
as King David in Penitence, with overtones of the Agony in the Garden